Higher Education Policy Series 38

Higher Education in a Post-Binary Era
National Reforms
and Institutional Responses
Edited by David C.B. Teather

Jessica Kingsley Publishers
London and Philadelphia

The right of the contributors to be identified as authors of this work has been asserted by them in accordance with the Copyright, Designs and Patents Act 1988.

First published in the United Kingdom in 1999 by
Jessica Kingsley Publishers Ltd
116 Pentonville Road,
London N1 9JB, England
and
325 Chestnut Street,
Philadelphia, PA19106, USA

Copyright © 1999 Jessica Kingsley Publishers

Library of Congress Cataloging in Publication Data

Higher education in a post-binary era: national reforms and institutional responses. – (Higher education policy; 38)
1. Education, Higher 2. Universities and colleges 3. Educational change 4. Education and state
I. Teather, David C.B.
378.1'012'09049

British Library Cataloguing in Publication Data

A CIP catalogue record for this book is available from the British Library

ISBN 1 85302 627 1

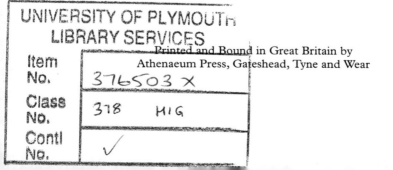

Printed and Bound in Great Britain by
Athenaeum Press, Gateshead, Tyne and Wear

Contents

Part V Conclusions

List of Tables

List of Figures

This book is to be returned on
or before the date stamped below

Higher Education Policy Series
Edited by Maurice Kogan

Higher education is now the subject of far reaching and rapid policy change. This series will be of value to those who have to manage that change, as well as to consumers and evaluators of higher education in the UK and elsewhere. It offers information and analysis of new developments in a concise and usable form. It also provides reflective accounts of the impacts of higher education policy. Higher education administrators, governors and policy makers will use it, as well as students and specialists in education policy.

Maurice Kogan is Professor of Government and Social Administration at Brunel University and Joint Director of the Centre for the Evaluation of Public Policy and Practice.

Changing Relationship between Higher Education and the State
Mary Henkel and Brenda Little
ISBN 1 85302 645 X pb
ISBN 1 85302 644 1 hb
Higher Education Policy 45

Part-Time Higher Education
Policy, Practice and Experience
Tom Schuller, David Raffe, Brenda Morgan-Klein and Ian Clark
ISBN 1 85302 669 7 pb
ISBN 1 85302 668 9 hb
Higher Education Policy 47

Innovation and Adaptation in European Higher Education
The Changing Conditions of Advanced Teaching and Learning in Europe
Edited by Claudius Gellert
ISBN 1 85302 628 X pb
ISBN 1 85302 535 6 hb
Higher Education Policy 22

Structure and Financing of Higher Education
in Russia, Ukraine and the EU
Edited by Paul G. Hare
ISBN 1 85302 442 2 pb
Higher Education Policy 41

Preface

There is a Chinese saying: 'May you live in interesting times!' This decade has indeed been interesting – one might even say turbulent – for higher education in the three jurisdictions which are the focus of this book. In Australia, Britain and Hong Kong, binary systems of higher education established a generation ago have been swept aside and unprecedented numbers of existing institutions have acquired the title 'University'. This book explores, through the eyes of senior members of these new universities, how they perceived these changes and how their institutions are responding to the opportunities and challenges of the new order.

The book had its origins in a research project on 'the missions and roles of newly-designated universities' which I initiated in 1994 soon after my arrival at Hong Kong Baptist University. I am grateful to HKBU for funding which enabled me to revisit universities in Australia, Britain and New Zealand at that time, and also to colleagues in the universities I visited for their unfailing helpfulness and courtesy.

I had, after graduating in the 1960s from London, embarked upon an academic career which, by good fortune, has enabled me to work for extended periods of time in each of these countries. Each of the universities and colleges at which I worked was recognisably a member of the same 'family' of institutions, sharing a heritage that links higher education throughout the British Commonwealth. But in each institution I observed features which reflected particular characteristics of the sociocultural context, or which I could best interpret as idiosyncrasies reflecting the particular circumstances of the foundation and development of the institution itself and the particular characteristics of individuals who contributed to the shaping of institutional life.

The universities considered in this volume are not so dissimilar as to render accounts of their development unfamiliar terrain to those with some experience of similar systems. But these case studies are set in contexts that are sufficiently different to heighten the reader's awareness of the existence of important assumptions which could easily go unnoticed had all the cases been from within a single system. This is one of the great benefits of comparative studies.

However, there is a tendency for those who guide higher education systems from outside, notably politicians and bureaucrats, to rely on solutions invented elsewhere. This is especially the case in colonial situations, such as Hong Kong, but is also evident in many OECD countries. Cross-jurisdictional comparisons can indeed illuminate and, if used with care, their results can contribute to policy development. But all too often imported solutions are solutions to other people's problems. They fail to yield the expected improvements in local practice because they fail adequately to take account of local social, cultural and economic contexts.

In this book there are both case studies of individual institutions and chapters that have been written to provide overviews of the higher education systems of which the case study institutions are a part. The authors of the three overview chapters have taken different, but complementary, approaches to their brief. As in the case studies of the individual institutions, each serves to illuminate the others.

I should like to thank the writers of the case studies and the writers of the systems overviews. They are all busy people, most of them responsible for the ongoing development of their institutions, and taking time out to write is never easy. I should like to thank my wife, Dr Elizabeth Teather, who is also an academic, for many discussions of higher education matters. Mitra Li and Sally-Anne Jackson typed my own chapters and other materials for the book.

To whom will this collection of essays be of value? The accounts are contemporary, referring, in the main, to events of this last decade. They have not, therefore, been winnowed by the passage of time. But, being contemporary, they will be of immediate use to all who wish to make sense of the recent reforms of our higher education systems and to all who have an interest in the development of universities – and their teaching, research and service functions – into the twenty-first century.

David C.B. Teather
Hong Kong, July 1997

Part I

Introduction

Chapter 1

The Global Context and the Higher Education Reforms

David C.B. Teather

The global context – global change

In the closing decade of the twentieth century we are living in a world of great change. Peter Drucker (1993), perhaps the best known of all writers on management in the English language, calls it a period of transformation. He states:

> Every few hundred years in Western history there occurs a sharp transformation. We cross what in an earlier book I called a 'divide'. Within a few short decades, society rearranges itself – its world-view; its basic values; its social and political structure; its arts; its key institutions. Fifty years later, there is a new world. And the people born then cannot even imagine the world in which their grandparents lived and into which their own parents were born. (p.1)

Drucker describes three previous transformations of western society: in the thirteenth century the European world became centred in the new city; in the fifteenth century was the Renaissance; in the forty years from 1775 to 1815 was the industrial revolution. Drucker claims that our period, two hundred years later, is such a period of transformation.

If Drucker is right, if we are – in the closing years of the twentieth century – mid-way through a period of fundamental transformation, we need to reflect upon and interpret these changes. We need to ask: what will life be like in the future? What needs to be done to prepare for the future? What are the implications for the educational opportunities we offer to young, and older, people in our societies?

There is, of course, an alternative perspective. The *significance* of the changes that Drucker describes are open to question. Surely there are some enduring human qualities, values, aspirations, norms of behavior, that transcend even the all-encompassing transformations about which Drucker writes. We can all observe that the application of science and technology has transformed, is transforming, our physical world – bringing both great benefits and opportunities and the potential for great catastrophes also. The greater the power we command, the greater the potential for using that power wisely or foolishly. But we might well ask whether the forces that motivate men and women to act wisely or foolishly have changed overmuch. It is two millennia since the dramatists of Ancient Greece wrote their plays, four centuries since Shakespeare set kings and queens, nobles and commoners on the stage of the Globe Theatre. What playwrights wrote then resonates powerfully with our experience today.

One of my colleagues at Hong Kong Baptist University, who has a major preoccupation with the future of China, is currently studying the writings of the Warring States period (403–221 BC). He is doing this in order to understand more fully the wellsprings of Chinese approaches to diplomacy and international relations. He sees these as highly relevant to the future development of this part of the world.

So there are differing interpretations of our contemporary situation. One is of radical transformation. An alternative interpretation stresses the endurance of fundamental attributes, values and norms of behavior.

Another important claim that Drucker makes is that the transformation of our own period, unlike the transformations which occurred in the thirteenth, fifteenth, and late eighteenth centuries, is not '...confined to western society and western history. Indeed it is one of the fundamental changes that there no longer is a "western" history or, in fact, a "western" civilisation. There is only world history and world civilisation – but both are "westernised"' (1993, pp.2–3).

Others, concerned with business and economics (such as Ohmae (1991)), also write of a 'borderless world'. But social scientists viewing the world from different perspectives stress the continuing endurance of fundamental differences between peoples. Thus Huntington (1993) identifies eight 'major civilisations' in the world today – Western, Confucian, Japanese, Islamic, Hindu, Slavic-Orthodox, Latin American, African – and states:

> ... differences among civilisations are not only real; they are basic.
> Civilisations are differentiated from each other by history, lan-

guage, culture, tradition and, most important, religion. The people of different civilisations have different views on the relations between God and man, the individual and the group, the citizen and the state, parents and children, husband and wife, as well as differing views of the relative importance of rights and responsibilities, liberty and authority, equality and hierarchy. These differences are the product of centuries. They will not soon disappear. (p.25)

Furthermore, Huntington hypothesises that the fundamental source of conflict in the twenty-first century will not be primarily political or economic but cultural. With the ending of the Cold War:

...international politics moves out of its Western phase, as its centerpiece becomes the interaction between the West and non-Western civilisations and among non-Western civilisations. In the politics of civilisations, the peoples and governments of non-Western civilisations no longer remain the objects of history as targets of Western colonialism, but join the West as movers and shapers of history. (p.23)

Such considerations may seem tangential to the ostensible focus of this book, namely the responses of universities in three jurisdictions[1] to the challenges and opportunities presented by the recent reforms of higher education systems in these jurisdictions. But the injunction to 'think globally and act locally' has become widely adopted as a sensible strategy, not only by members of environmental movements but by people from business, politics and many other walks of life. It is crucial for universities.

Senior members of traditional universities in the British Commonwealth have long laid claim to a heritage which positions their universities globally, in the service of humankind as a whole. Thus a former Vice-Chancellor of the University of Melbourne, speaking at a meeting of the Association of Commonwealth Universities, said:

The primary commitment [of a university] with respect to the pursuit and dissemination of knowledge must be to the world, and not just to the community which gave it birth and which supports it ... a university must be committed to the acquisition and dissemination of knowledge beyond mere reference to the needs of particular times and places. (Derham 1979)

1 These jurisdictions are Australia (a 'Commonwealth'), Britain (a 'United Kingdom') and Hong Kong (formerly a British colony, now a 'Special Administrative Region' of China). 'Jurisdiction' is the term used in this text to cover all these situations.

Stephens (1977) discusses what he describes as the 'very powerful late 19th century and early 20th Century priority of establishing universities as international centres of excellence,' (p.181) and comments that the appeal of the international dimension is immense. Some, particularly in England, saw this international dimension in opposition to the work of the university in the service of its local region (Truscot 1945; Edwards 1979) and, as will be discussed below, the polytechnic sector of higher education was formally established in England in 1967 to give, *inter alia*, greater emphasis to the local and regional responsibilities of higher education institutions.

Current trends to further internationalisation of higher education (de Wit 1995; Knight and de Wit 1997) flow from more general trends towards globalisation. They reflect the need for university graduates to be able to work effectively, not only in their country and culture of origin but also in other countries and in productive interaction with other cultures. They reflect the fact that developments in technology (in the broadest sense) are international and that university research has often to take account not only of work being done next door but also of work being done on the other side of the world. The consequent trends in internationalisation impact on all the major dimensions of university activities, from the design of courses and the recruitment of students to the conceptualisation of the work of the academic enterprise itself. In this, the idea of the university as a facilitator of links and bridges between the community in which it is situated and communities elsewhere, and as an interpreter and sometimes a mediator, assumes increasing importance and relevance.

The three jurisdictions – Australia, Britain and Hong Kong

The three jurisdictions whose higher education systems and institutions are considered in this book – Australia, Britain and Hong Kong – have some striking differences as well as similarities, as Table 1.1 shows. Britain was, in the late eighteenth and early nineteenth centuries, the cradle of the industrial revolution and became the major maritime power of the nineteenth and early twentieth centuries. At its zenith the British Empire encircled the globe. The last 50 years, from the independence of India and Pakistan in 1947 to the return of Hong

Kong to China in 1997, have seen the transformation of that empire to a Commonwealth, a loose association of independent states.

Table 1.1 Selected Characteristics of Australia, Britain and Hong Kong

	Australia	*Britain*	*Hong Kong*
Area ('000 sq km)	7682	245	1
Population (millions)	18	58	7
Predominant Language	English	English	Cantonese
Governance	Federation of 8 states/ territories	Union of 4 countries	Special Administra- tive Region of China
Date of Universal Suffrage	1894–1902	1928	1991
Date of Universal Education	1872–1893	1870	1971
GDP per capita (US$): 1995 1980 1965	18720 11290 2090	18700 8580 1830	22990 5790 670

Source: Australian Encyclopaedia, Encyclopaedia Britannica, Hong Kong Yearbook, International Encyclopaedia of Education, World Bank.

By the end of the Second World War, which left much of Europe in ruins, the USA had emerged as the undisputed leader of the Western world. Since then, Britain, like Portugal, Spain, Holland, France and other former colonial powers, has had to adapt to changing circumstances and a markedly different role in the world. Britain's dilemma for much of this time has been epitomised by its geographical position – a group of Atlantic islands off the coast of the European mainland. Politically, Britain is positioned somewhat uneasily between Continental Europe on the one hand, with which it shares many centuries of cultural evolution, and its former colonies in North America on the other, with whom it is linked by a common language.

In 1789, 23 years after the American colonies gained independence from Britain, the first British colony was established in Australia – a land mass which turned out to be almost identical in size to Continental USA. Its climate, in particular its aridity and propensity for prolonged droughts, was beyond the experience of the British settlers and caused great hardship; yet the indigenous Australian peoples had lived in equilibrium with the land for more than 40,000 years.

Australia remains a sparsely populated country, with a language and predominant culture drawn from Britain. While the mythology of the Australian outback plays an important part in the Australian self-image, over half of all Australians live in five coastal cities – the capitals of the five mainland states. Since the 1950s new settlers have come from Southern Europe, the Middle East and Asia. Today the Australian economy is oriented towards Asia, but cultural ties with Europe remain strong and, as elsewhere in the West, the latter half of the twentieth century has seen considerable cultural influence from the USA.

In 1842 Britain took possession of Hong Kong Island and by the end of the nineteenth century had gained control, through treaties with the government of Imperial China, of all the 1000 sq km of land which was returned to China in mid-1997. This now forms the Hong Kong Special Administrative Region of the People's Republic of China. In the nineteenth century Hong Kong grew as a free port and safe haven for ships of the China trade. The communist victory on the mainland in 1949 was accompanied by the migration to Hong Kong of people, capital and manufacturing expertise and Hong Kong became Britain's only industrialised colony. After 1978, when mainland China embarked upon its 'open door' economic policy, most of Hong Kong's manufacturing industry was relocated to the mainland, lured by cheaper labour and cheaper land. Today Hong Kong firms employ over five million people on the mainland, while Hong Kong has transformed itself into a metropolitan, service economy analogous to that of London, New York and Tokyo.

At the time of writing (mid-1997) Hong Kong is the most modern of the cities of the Chinese world. Indeed, in recent decades Hong Kong has rapidly gained status as a first-world city. With a population of 6.5 million, GDP per capita was US $24,500 in 1996 – exceeding that of Australia, Canada, Germany and the UK and next only to Japan and Singapore in Asia (Howlett 1997). Resources, both public and private, have flowed into higher education,[2] creating a system of universities that has come of age in this decade.

2 Each undergraduate student at universities in Hong Kong paid a fee of HK $43,100 (US $5500) per annum in the academic year 1996–97 and this contributed approximately 18 per cent of the operating costs of these universities. Most of the balance came from the Hong Kong government.

As was noted above, and as Table 1.1 well illustrates, the three jurisdictions that are the focus of this book differ in a number of important respects. Yet, through an accident of history, they share a higher education heritage that has much in common.

Universities in post-industrial society

The major trends that have affected higher education institutions in these three jurisdictions in the last decade can conveniently be considered under three headings. First, there are trends which are affecting higher education in all post-industrial countries. Second, there are trends which are affecting higher education in these three jurisdictions, and also in some others which share common structural features arising from their common origins in the British Commonwealth. Third, there are trends that impact uniquely the institutions in one jurisdiction because of circumstances unique to that jurisdiction.

A major factor affecting higher education in post-industrial countries is the growth of what has become known as the 'knowledge society'. Increasing proportions of the working populations find work in occupations that require higher education qualifications, often in the service sector of the economy. Such qualifications are obtained in the higher education institutions, so increasing numbers of potential students apply for admission. Not only is entry to higher education important for school leavers but demand increases for continuing professional education also. So the activities of the higher education institutions directly affect the life chances of a very much higher proportion of the population than was formerly the case.

Far from being 'small, poor and for the most part treated with indifference', as Roger Scott in Chapter 2 describes Australian universities in the 1940s, universities today in all three jurisdictions are seen by governments and society as large, reasonably well resourced institutions which form an important component in a larger framework of education and training provision which articulates with the world of employment. Because the number of students to be taught has increased markedly over the years (a matter to which we shall return in more detail in Chapter 11), the size and cost of the higher education system has become a significant item of government expenditure. For this reason also, higher education institutions have come under increased government, and public, scrutiny.

The idea of the knowledge society conjures up not only the need for more, and more effective, education and training but also the potential economic and social benefits of research. In the short term, applied research has the most obvious appeal to many, but a complementary approach for the longer term is to lay the foundations for future prosperity and well-being by researching and developing expertise in broader fields identified as having potential for economic and social benefits. In addition to teaching and research, however, the knowledge society provides opportunities for universities to extend the provision of services to their communities via consultancy and other mechanisms (Teather 1982).

The advent of the knowledge society thus creates an increase in demand for all three areas of university work: teaching, research and service. In all three areas, however, there is likely to be the potential for both public and private benefit arising from increase in supply. So the question that has been asked with increasing insistence, especially in those jurisdictions that have difficulty in raising sufficient public funds or with governments ideologically opposed to doing so, is what proportion of the cost of increasing supply should be borne by the public purse and what proportion should come from other sources.

This issue, of the apportionment of costs for the supply of services which inextricably yield both public and private benefits, has been complicated by a shift in the frame of reference[3] in which one views the transaction between provider and beneficiary. There are, for example, a number of analogies that can be used to describe the relationship between teacher and student or between university and student. Adopting a collegial model of the university, the student is viewed as a junior member of a community – of which the academic is also a member. In the context of this model, a master/apprentice analogy could be appropriate and, indeed, is often used in thinking about the training of research students. Another common analogy, which stresses the role of academics as professionals, is that of professional/client. In recent years, however, governments in Britain (as Barnett and

---

3 In 1989 Bourke listed several major changes which the then current reforms of Australian higher education sought to bring about, including the development of an alternative language, derived mainly from the business world and implying a changed set of values for the discussion of university matters and the definition of a new relationship between the university and the state, which is having the effect of bringing publicly-funded universities into the corporate organisation of the state (quoted in Teather (1990)).

Bjarnason indicate in Chapter 5) and, more recently, in Australia, have stressed the supplier/consumer analogy.

Each of these analogies emphasises some aspects of the teacher/student relationship at the expense of others. The analogy of student with consumer is particularly problematic. In most transactions in which a person is a consumer, the consumer can be expected to have, or to have access to, a sufficiently complete understanding of the product he or she is purchasing to make an informed and responsible choice. In the case of education, however, the purchase is of a service, the purpose of which is to change, or to develop in the consumer the capacity to change, his or her understanding. This change in understanding is effected over time, in the case of a degree program over several years. Because, under such circumstances, it may not be fully appropriate for the student to choose, others choose on the student's behalf. These others may be the state, through the funding of places in universities, or, in private systems of education and with more junior students, it is often parents who foot the bill and make the choice.

At the same time as governments have been increasing the proportion of the total cost of higher education to be paid by students – and thus implicitly encouraging students to act like consumers in a market environment – increasing emphasis has also been placed on the vocational purposes of higher education. A Treasury brief to the incoming New Zealand government of 1987 identified four major functions of education, of which three are relevant to higher education – namely *fulfilment* (of an individual's interest or latent abilities and aspirations), *integration* (of the individual into the community, the wider society, and the roles and responsibilities the individual may assume as an adult) and *economic* functions (to prepare the individual for his or her economic role). The Treasury brief makes the interesting point that the balance between these functions of education in post-industrial societies of the English-speaking world has changed over recent times. In the 1960s most emphasis was placed on the fulfilment function. But in the harsher economic climates of the 1970s and 1980s the loss of social consensus and perceptions of social breakdown led to renewed emphasis on the integration and economic functions (New Zealand Treasury 1987).

Most universities in Australia, Britain and Hong Kong are public institutions but the proportions of their budgets funded by the state vary considerably, both between and within these jurisdictions. Furthermore, the public institutions established in each of these three jurisdictions are not the only organisations providing higher education services. Much continuing professional education is offered by companies in-house, and many other organisations offer research and consultancy services. Increasingly, both universities and other higher education providers operate across national boundaries – in Hong Kong, for example, the number of local institutions offering MBA degrees is dwarfed by the number of overseas institutions offering similar qualifications either independently or in co-operation with local public or private higher education providers.

Several factors, including those discussed above, have resulted in universities in the three jurisdictions becoming much larger and having to respond more quickly and in a more co-ordinated manner to changes in their external environment. There has been a marked shift in many institutions to different styles and structures of management, which, together with the reconceptualisation of students as consumers, has led to a reduction in the power of academics as a class. Barnett and Bjarnason, in Chapter 5, suggest that in the British situation this is a direct result of government policies, a change that Halsey (1992) encapsulated in the title of his book on the academic profession in Britain, *Decline of Donnish Dominion*.

To summarise, major trends which have affected higher education in post-industrial countries in recent years have included growth in size and scale[4]; increasing demand for teaching, research and service functions; increasing competition from other organisations, including competition from organisations which are based in other countries; and (a matter to which we shall return in Chapter 11) increasing use of information and communications technology. When we consider changes in conceptualisation of the relations between teachers and students, or changes in management of universities, we begin to deal with trends which may be more specific to the three jurisdictions which are the focus of this book and of some others which share common structural features arising out of their common origins. What are these common features and how did they arise? To answer such questions we shall now turn to the evolution of higher education in the three jurisdictions – Australia, Britain and Hong Kong – over the last 30 years.

---

4   This growth, to mass higher education, occurred first in North America and, more recently, elsewhere.

Binary policies and unified systems

In the early 1960s, in Australia, Britain and Hong Kong, 'higher education' in the public mind meant the universities. In each of these jurisdictions the use of the term 'university' had been restricted to a particular kind of institution. Universities had evolved over many centuries in Europe and the particular versions of these institutions established in the capital cities of the Australian states from 1850 onwards and in Hong Kong in 1911 were deliberately modelled on the universities of England, Scotland and Ireland.[5] In addition to the universities, a variety of other institutions provided education and training which extended to post-school level. These included technical institutes and business colleges, teachers' colleges and agricultural institutes.

In 1965 in Australia, in 1967 in Britain and in 1971 in Hong Kong, governments in each of these jurisdictions adopted binary policies of higher education. Such policies assume separate roles and responsibilities for universities on the one hand and for non-university or 'public sector' institutions of higher education on the other. Such public sector institutions were designated as Colleges of Advanced Education (CAEs) in Australia, Polytechnics in England and Hong Kong, and Central Institutions in Scotland.

Binary policies were adopted in Australia and Britain at a time of considerable expansion of demand for higher education. By designating a distinct group of non-university institutions as providing genuinely 'higher' education, the governments of the day were able to channel a significant proportion of the expansion into these institutions. This had the dual effect of permitting the universities to retain their former élite characteristics to a greater extent than would otherwise have been possible and of providing places for students in the non-university sector at a lower cost than would have been incurred had all the expansion taken place in the universities. Eric Robinson (1968), in England, called the polytechnics 'the people's universities'; Trevyaud

---

5   This close modelling is neatly encapsulated in the Latin motto of the University of Sydney, the first university to be established in Australia. Under the stars of the Southern Cross in the university crest, the motto proclaims: *Sidere Mens Eadem Mutato*. The idea behind this motto is that although the university exists under a different sky, the values it upholds are those of the universities of Britain. Sixty years later, in Hong Kong, the University of Hong Kong was established as 'a secular, technological, English-language university, sited in Hong Kong but intended chiefly for students from the mainland ... [funded] to promote the use of English in China and enlarge British influence and trade in the Far East' (Mellor 1992, p.xiii).

and McLaren (1976), in Australia, referred to the CAEs as 'equal but cheaper'!

During the next quarter-century, these public-sector institutions thrived and expanded access to higher education for a new generation of upwardly-mobile young people and for older people already in the workforce. In each jurisdiction these institutions raised awareness of alternatives to the traditional universities, stressed the vocational relevance of higher education and developed distinctive styles of management.

This period also witnessed convergent evolution between the institutions of higher education separated by the binary line. Thus institutions in the public sector began teaching at higher levels, progressing from the teaching of diplomas to first degrees, then postgraduate coursework degrees and, in some cases, research doctorates. Applied research, often attracting funds from private sources, became part of their activities. Many universities also moved into the newer professional areas that had been pioneered by the non-university institutions, developed consultancy activities and adopted less collegial management practices.

Beginning in 1987 in Australia, 1991 in Britain and 1994 in Hong Kong, the binary lines were repositioned. In England and Wales all the former polytechnics adopted the university title, as did a number of former Central Institutions in Scotland.[6] In Australia, where the CAE sector contained a greater diversity of institutions and the Commonwealth government encouraged the formation of fewer, larger institutions, mergers between existing universities and CAEs, and between CAEs themselves, led to the designation by State governments of almost all the resulting institutions as universities. In Hong Kong two former Polytechnics and a former College were designated universities.[7] In short, in Australia, Britain and Hong Kong the number of universities approximately doubled.

It is fascinating to see how, in a quarter of a century, binary policies were adopted, flourished and then outgrown in each of these three jurisdictions. Davies (1989) traces the roots of the binary policy in

6 In Northern Ireland the only polytechnic had already merged with the New University of Ulster to form the University of Ulster in 1984.
7 More recently, in May 1997, the Open Learning Institute of Hong Kong became the Open University of Hong Kong. Lingnan College and the Hong Kong Institute of Education are likely to be future contenders for university titles.

Australia to attitudes and values that were current in Britain between the two world wars and argues 'if economic considerations play a powerful role in the determination of policy, so too does educational ideology' (p.3). Higher education in Hong Kong, as a British colony, was influenced even more directly by developments in Britain.

If educational ideology did, as Davies argues, play such an important role in the establishment of these binary systems, it is tempting to expect that their demise in the closing decades of the twentieth century might represent a greater acceptance of the need for more inclusive higher education systems. Such inclusive systems should be capable of developing the talents not only of the élite minority selected by family background and school accomplishment but should also be capable of offering to many that which, for Edwards (1982), is the characteristic feature of higher education: preparation 'to cope with the rapid changes in work and life, especially those changes arising from the continual impact of new knowledge and new techniques' (p.20). These are matters to which we will return in the final chapter.

Summary

This chapter began by identifying some key issues of our times in a global context. It then provided some historical and contemporary background on each of the three jurisdictions – Australia, Britain and Hong Kong – that are the focus of this book. Attention then focused on higher education systems, initially in post-industrial societies in general and then on the changes of recent decades that have been shared in common by the higher education systems of these three jurisdictions.

Now to the chapters which follow. Chapters 2, 5 and 8 provide, in different ways, overviews of higher education in Australia, Britain and Hong Kong respectively. They describe and analyse significant changes that have taken place in these higher education systems, referring in particular to the period during which the binary lines were repositioned – in 1987–88 in Australia, 1991–92 in Britain and 1994 in Hong Kong – and to the subsequent evolution of the resulting 'unified' systems.

These overviews are complemented by six chapters which provide case studies of individual institutions that acquired university title and status in the context of these system-wide reforms. The authors of these case studies provide the perspectives of leaders of the new generation of universities on the opportunities and challenges of institution building in these turbulent times. In the final chapter we return to themes which address, in general terms, prospects for the future of the higher education enterprise in each of these jurisdictions.

Part II

Australia

Chapter 2

The Reform of Higher Education in Australia

Roger Scott

Jane Nichols (1995) writing in *Campus Review*, suggests that:

> Nostalgia is a tricky if pleasantly self-indulgent emotion. It should be tempered by rigorous efforts at objectivity and some attempt at self-criticism.

> Sometimes those with nostalgia for the old days in universities can exhibit misty-eyed romanticism and longing for an imperfectly remembered past. And those who idealise the past often paint the present in stark, negative terms....

> Academics individually and collectively should grasp the realities of both the past and the present, and show a willingness to work as a part of a wider community for a better educated, fairer and wider future. (p.8)

To set the context for the discussion of Australian tertiary education, I want to accept this implied challenge and reflect on the past as a guide to the future. I will do this through the device of identifying decennial milestones of change that I experienced in my own association with several Australian tertiary institutions, including the two chosen as case studies for this collection. The milestones stretch from 1957 (the date of the Murray Report) to 1997.

Before 1957: genteel poverty

Sir Robert Menzies, the prime minister who commissioned the Murray Report on universities, can rightly claim a pre-eminent role in the history of tertiary education. Pre-war universities had been under-resourced pale imitations of British undergraduate institutions, heavily dependent on the outcome of negotiations with State governments for limited funds to supplement their fee income. The Second World War had stimulated awareness of the absence of a scientific and research culture in these institutions and the need for greater injection of funds from the Australian Commonwealth government.

The most significant changes for the future of tertiary institutions had occurred in 1942 and 1946 with respect to the broad powers of the Commonwealth government. Uniform taxation introduced as a wartime emergency measure was entrenched as a regular feature of the federation, unbalancing it forever. This allowed for support for expanding the quantity and quality of secondary education, and included everything from war memorial libraries to swimming pools.

For universities, there were direct grants and also provision of scholarships for school-leavers and others with appropriate levels of attainment. There were specific funds to encourage enrolments of returned servicemen and, as part of the same impetus to national reconstruction, the founding of the Australian National University (ANU) as a specifically research-oriented institution, the first new university since before the First World War. Nevertheless, in Allan Martin's (1990) words, in the 1940s the Australian university could still be described as 'small, poor and for the most part treated with indifference by a society hardly renowned for its concern about things of the mind' (p.95).

1957: penetrating the élite

1957 was a national milestone with the publication of the Murray Report, which led a systematic approach to Commonwealth funding support for universities and a stronger policy presence through a national commission.

Sol Encel (1989) has suggested that:

> The Murray Report was based on the principle that, in exchange
> for a high degree of autonomy and self-determination, the universi-

ties were required to provide certain services to the community. It described the provision of trained manpower as the most urgent of these tasks, in order to satisfy the demands of the community at large, and industry, commerce and government in particular. (p.15)

The authors of the report noted that the demand for all university graduates was bound to rise, although they seriously under-estimated the rate of this rise. The growth in federal funding for university places marked the beginning of a process of opening up universities to a wider range of students. The report recommended the establishment of triennial funding, administered by a central grants committee and predominantly funded by the federal government. Prime Minister Menzies moved to ensure that the recommendations were adopted in full and that the necessary funding support was forthcoming.

It is important to remember just how parlous was the state of universities at the time of the Murray Report. Pre-Murray universities did not exist in a golden age of thriving intellectual fervour despite the strong sense of collegiality which underpinned the policy-making bodies within universities at this time, when there were few specialist administrators such as full-time Vice-Chancellors. Universities were isolated organisations not much connected to political processes or any wider social movements.

Jane Nichols (1995) suggests that:

> Universities of the past catered for a social elite who had privileged access to both financial and cultural capital which enabled them to qualify to enter higher education, on the one hand, and to support themselves while they were there on the other. Scholarships were handed out on the basis of 'academic merit' which apparently was also largely the property of people who owned the other kinds of capital. The few working-class kids who made it to, and through, university in the 1950s are remembered precisely because they were exceptional. (p.8)

1957 was a personal milestone, as I matriculated from a Church of England boarding school, where I had been 'a scholarship boy'. I was only exceptional because of the lack of competition for access to university. Only five of my classmates aspired to going on to university; the bulk did not even proceed to the final year of schooling. Most went back to the family farm or to family businesses, unchallenged by even the hint of unemployment.

Most of my new classmates at university 'bonded' themselves to a State education department desperate to recruit teachers to meet a commitment to expanding secondary education beyond a handful of high schools concentrated in the main towns. I was unusual in settling for the lower financial rewards but the greater curriculum flexibility of the Commonwealth scholarship.

In 1957, the University of Tasmania was a geographically divided campus, with all but the arts and law faculties situated in the present location at Sandy Bay. I commuted from the central campus on 'The Domain' for geography classes and for all sporting facilities; my accommodation was at Christ College, a combination of student residence and theological training institution characteristic of university facilities of that period.

At the start of my five years there, the university drew its staff overwhelmingly from British universities, few of whom had much interest in research and none of whom held doctorates. By the time I left, there was a sprinkling of Americans, usually eccentric fringe-dwellers, and an occasional Australian returning from overseas study.

The positive side of this environment was that there was a strong commitment to teaching demonstrated by most staff, especially if students showed much enthusiasm for their subjects. Classes were small by current standards – less than 100 in the first year, divided into eight or nine tutorials which met weekly, often taught by honours students or part-time casuals. Upper level classes had no tutorials but, with a couple of devastating exceptions, staff were usually accessible. My somewhat eccentric combination of majors included public administration, which had an otherwise entirely mature age student enrolment taught in the evening mainly by practitioners. It was evening study which offered that access to the talents because of the economic constraints perceived to rule out full-time study for all but the independently wealthy.

The student body became aware over time of the very low standing of the institution, which was in turmoil after the scathing criticism of a local Royal Commission – opinion which was later reinforced when the Murray Committee reported.

1967: the beginning of mass higher education

By 1967 the fruits of the Murray Report were obvious. Funding was flowing from the federal government to assist universities to cope with a rising demand for tertiary study. There was also the start of a trend towards recruitment of Australian staff, although most were expected to have acquired overseas qualifications.

The expansion of demand associated with greater numbers progressing through high school had been met, in part, by the upgrading of the old Sydney Technical College sequentially via a technology title to the University of New South Wales. Plans were afoot to build Macquarie, which was determined to be a 'proper' university.

But the University of Sydney, when I was teaching there in 1967, was still the magnet for the cream of students, the social as well as the intellectual élite, with the richer ones cramming into prestigious halls of residence located on a campus mimicking the Oxbridge college system and poorer ones commuting from the city after work for evening study. Students now have legitimate complaints about the size of classes, but Sydney in this period was in danger of having its quality compromised by the demand for access.

My first-year class consisted of 850 students, taught in two sessions on the same day. Tutorials were larger and less frequent than in Tasmania a decade previously but still a massive logistics nightmare. In addition, the perceived tyranny of end-of-year examinations had been diminished by semesterisation and increased use of continuous assessment. The university was a powerful and self-contained social microcosm, diverse and vital, although (as in Tasmania) evening students tended to have a more instrumental view of their purpose in attending.

A change of time and place meant that the staff mix was entirely different from that of Tasmania in the 1950s. The sheer size of the university and enrolments in the department meant a large and diverse group of academics. The older ones were British who were emigrating or seeking a career advancement and a brief respite from austerity, or European refugee intellectuals, of whom Professor Henry Mayer was the most distinguished and influential. The younger were Americans and Australians with American doctorates. There was a significant body of graduate students who received excellent training and motivation as some compensation for the dismal experience of those early undergraduate years. Research was clearly identified as an expectation of all staff and this, ultimately, fed back into the quality of teaching.

The problems of mass demand on existing university institutions had already sown the seeds for a division of labour which was intended to allow universities to concentrate on their own self-proclaimed higher mission. The Chair of the Universities Commission had produced the 1964 Martin Report, which laid the basis for the establishment of Colleges of Advanced Education (CAE), a new style of teaching-only institution, cheaper and more subordinate to the needs of State employing authorities. This was to build upon existing structures in the technical education area and was administered by its own slightly more modest structure, not a commission but the Commonwealth Advisory Committee on Colleges of Advanced Education (CACAE).

In 1968 the CAE sector was effectively extended by including provision for Commonwealth funding to teachers' colleges, which had previously been the absolute preserve of State governments. Additional multi-purpose CAEs were created which incorporated teacher education, business studies and engineering courses. These recruited new staff, inevitably from universities, rather than being burdened by the inheritance of longer-established institutions. One such institution was the Canberra College of Advanced Education (CCAE), founded in 1969, which I joined in 1972 as foundation principal lecturer in politics.

My first period at CCAE encompassed the era of the Whitlam administration,[1] which provided a dramatic fillip to participation in higher education through the abolition of fees. The main beneficiaries were mature age students, especially women, who could study locally at no cost beyond their time and forgone income. The CAE sector also brought access to degree study to many in lower socio-economic groups who had never regarded orthodox universities as appropriate to their needs. The strong vocational focus of CAE courses, derived, in part, from a technical heritage, changed the perception of what constituted a legitimate range of activities for tertiary study.

Many of the staff moved across from teacher-training colleges with a strong focus on pedagogy. Even staff recruited from universities with a strong research tradition tended to focus on the content and methodology of teaching. First-year classes remained relatively large but timetables were geared to students with additional responsibilities, whether child-rearing or employment, and efforts were made to incorporate a strongly practical and applied component.

from a technical heritage, changed the perception of what constituted a legitimate range of activities for tertiary study.

Many of the staff moved across from teacher-training colleges with a strong focus on pedagogy. Even staff recruited from universities with a strong research tradition tended to focus on the content and methodology of teaching. First-year classes remained relatively large but timetables were geared to students with additional responsibilities, whether child-rearing or employment, and efforts were made to incorporate a strongly practical and applied component.

Many practices now commonplace in all universities represented major innovations first developed in the CAE sector as part of its defining characteristic. Yet, as these organisations grew in confidence and flourished with the increase of resources which followed their success in recruiting students, their staff felt the need to identify with other members of the academic community in the university sector and to compete for funding and recognition of the applied research appropriate to their own institutions. Ironically, just when this parity of esteem was becoming widely recognised, the government acted to eliminate the basis of differentiation of the whole sector.

1977: the battle for parity of esteem

1977 was another milestone of change before that metamorphosis which occurred a decade later. At the national policy-making level, a series of reports on the future of the Technical and Further Education (TAFE) sector – starting off with the Kangan Report – led to the decision to integrate three previously separate commissions for universities, CAEs and TAFE colleges into a single Commonwealth Tertiary Education Commission (CTEC). This body still had a statutory distance from ministerial direction and there were powerful independent councils for each of the three components, but this decision clearly signalled the presence of a new competitor for the federal dollars available to support tertiary students.

The year was also a personal milestone which reflected the continuing tension and cultural divide between the existing components of the binary system. The attenuated processes associated with my unprecedented appointment from a CAE principal lectureship to a professorship in an established university underlined the extent of the gulf between the CAE and the older university ethos and, particularly the impact of collegial processes in decision making.

Where CAEs were built on a strongly authoritarian pattern of internal management with powerful community representation on governing bodies, university staff felt more empowered to contest decisions taken by central management. In this case, a majority of the departmental staff were unconvinced about my merit relative to that of an internal candidate. Every available mechanism for dissent was mobilised to upset the decision of the selection panel, including a hearing by the State Ombudsman and personal threats to 'send me to Coventry' if I had the temerity to persist in exercising my right to accept the university's offer. (I did and they didn't.)

The wider significance of the milestone might be that it pointed to shifting ground, at least among policy makers, about the reality of differences enshrined in the notion of a binary system. CAEs were attracting high-quality undergraduate students, moving to award a full range of post-graduate coursework degrees and to make inroads into the research activities once sacrosanct to universities. The rationale for giving universities separate and privileged treatment was starting to look thin.

1981 became a small signpost to the future, when the federal Liberal/National government lead by Malcolm Fraser started to examine the rationality of supporting separate small institutions in close proximity to each other with broadly similar functions. Treasurer Phillip Lynch headed a 'razor gang' which conducted the first skirmishes aimed at amalgamation through combination of universities and CAEs. In Queensland this meant the take-over by James Cook University of its immediately adjacent neighbour, the Townsville College of Advanced Education, and the combination of all the Brisbane CAEs into a single institution, Brisbane College of Advanced Education (BCAE). I have written elsewhere of the Amalgamation of James Cook University with the Townsville CAE (Scott 1988).

Generally, the pattern was similar – either a university devouring its smaller teacher-training neighbour or several CAEs being banded together like pioneer caravans facing the rigours of the Wild West. In retrospect, this was a mere pipe-opener, a straw in the wind indicative of bureaucratic aspirations which were modified in 1981 by political resistance. The main event was delayed until 1987, with John Dawkins as the ringmaster.

1987: the Dawkins era of reconstruction

A number of milestones were reached in 1987, almost all of them connected directly or indirectly with John Dawkins. The first of these was the creation by the Commonwealth government of the mega-department of Education, Employment and Training (DEET) with Dawkins as its first minister. McCollow and Knight (1993) suggest that this 'signalled that the Hawke government intended to treat education as a direct instrument of economic policy. This involved not only the directing of its efforts towards the provision of the needed 'human capital' but its subjection to further efficiency measures and its pursuit of educational marketing opportunities' (p.15).

The issuing of epoch-making Green and White Papers followed closely. These were not the outcome of deliberations by an independent expert committee like the major policy documents which preceded them but the outpourings from within the new department and from the minister's own staff – and directly attributable to the individual preferences of the new minister.

In summary, the Green Paper established a set of new ground rules by which the binary system of universities and CAEs was effectively swept away. This was accomplished by creating an arbitrary minimum size below which existing institutions would not be able to survive as independent publicly-funded entities, resulting in pressure on many CAEs and a few smaller universities to become part of a larger organisation. In addition, funding formulae and public rhetoric encouraged existing relatively large universities to become even larger. Finally, a mechanism was created for the absorption of all CAEs into the university sector by processes of amalgamation and/or sponsorship.

After a perfunctory period of discussion, the Green Paper turned White – that is moved from a discussion paper to an action plan. The process then began of implementing this plan by the reconstruction of existing institutions forced upon State authorities.

These new institutions, many fewer in number but most much larger, were then subjected to a considerably more stringent set of conditions if they wished to have access to maximum Commonwealth funding as part of the newly introduced Unified National System (UNS). Profiles of the range and enrolment levels in courses were to be negotiated with a joint planning committee representing the interests of States as well as the Commonwealth. There was also increasing specification of the internal management arrangements of universities, which were examined during site visits to discuss profiles.

In particular, greater emphasis was placed upon universities becoming increasingly self-reliant in terms of additional funding earned by consultancies and the charging of fees for a range of postgraduate awards. There was also heavy pressure to engage in marketing courses to overseas students.

The Commonwealth Tertiary Education Commission (CTEC) was presumed to be dominated by the self-interest of universities, whose spokespeople had dominated the policy debate about the future of the sector, and was replaced by a National Board for Employment, Education and Training (NBEET). This body was more directly accountable to the minister and, in turn, controlled a series of subordinate councils, including one more directly related to the employment components of the new department. In addition, membership of all these boards and councils provided for a wider range of interests, especially those of employers and trade unions.

Implementation was necessarily left to State authorities since State governments had direct control over the CAE sector through separate Boards of Advanced Education which exercised influence over governance and curriculum despite the predominance of Commonwealth funding. In some cases, CAEs which were proximately located were absorbed by universities; in others a metropolitan university acted as a sponsor for the transition of a collection of CAEs into a single new university. For example, the metropolitan University of New South Wales sponsored a new institution called Charles Sturt University, which consisted of two CAEs each with multiple campuses.

In the case of the Queensland University of Technology (QUT), a metropolitan institute of technology first achieved university status in its own right after a quality assessment process at State level then absorbed the majority of CAE teacher training campuses in Brisbane which could not pass a similar assessment. My own connection with these events was through serving on the external committee which undertook the assessment of Queensland Institute of Technology (QIT). My invitation to serve followed a decade of service on various accreditation and course advisory boards. (For further details on the establishment of Queensland University of Technology see Chapter 4.)

Canberra was a special case since the major university operated under direct federal control and the existing CAE was linked somewhat ambiguously to the government of the Australian Capital Territory (ACT) which was in the process of creation in the same time-frame.

Minister Dawkins made it clear that this was a test case which needed to demonstrate the feasibility of his general model.

As newly-appointed Principal of the Canberra CAE, my first task in late 1987 was to assist in the preparation of the College's response to the Green Paper. This involved developing strategies for remaining independent while meeting the growth targets required to meet the minimum size requirement for entry to the Unified National System. CCAE also sought to align itself with the DOCIT group, the Directors of Central Institutes of Technology, and earlier had flirted with the idea of changing its name to the Canberra Institute of Technology. More significantly for the future, I also worked closely with the ACT territorial administration which was preparing the way for the creation of State-like powers under an elected ACT government.

In a general overview chapter it is superfluous to trace the Byzantine processes which led to an outcome in which:

1.   The Senate of the Australian National University (ANU) rejected amalgamation with the CCAE but embraced the Institute of the Arts.

2.   The CCAE was privately (and accurately) blamed by Minister Dawkins for not being compliant enough in the latter stages of negotiations and threatened with a permanent veto on university status under any conditions other than subordination to the 'sponsorship' of the ANU.

3.   The federal legislation introduced to create the amalgamated institution was withdrawn when it was clear that it would be opposed by the minor parties who held the balance of power in the upper house.

4.   The University of Canberra was created shortly afterwards under the sponsorship of Monash University, a solution which surprised but was ultimately approved by the new ACT government and also surprised and was tolerated by DEET.

Chapter 3 – written by Don Aitken, who succeeded me as Vice-Chancellor when family concerns led me away from Canberra and, ultimately, to QUT – provides a wider perspective on these events.

Underlying the failure of the proposed amalgamation in Canberra was the same set of forces and attitudes which bedevilled similar proposals at State level where universities were being brought into an uneasy affiliation with elements of the CAE sector. The root cause of the problem was the incompatibility between the academic cultures and aspirations of the two institutions and, in particular, the same unbending superiority complex which had characterised a generation of university teachers in their dealings with CAEs.

1997: vocationalism, managerialism, resurgence of differentiation

Keating in retrospect

Writing in the middle of 1995, I suggested that 'it would be tempting to continue the classical theme and suggest that the CAE sector can be likened to Horace's captive Greece, rendered subservient to the Roman legions of the traditional universities but capturing the organisational culture and the policy agenda of the whole sector' (Scott 1995d, p.12).

It seemed then that the experience of students in all universities had been shaped dramatically by the values of vocationalism and managerialism which were the distinctive features of the old CAE sector. In particular, the adoption of performance indicators and the quality measurement mechanisms recognised the key role of teaching. Led by institutions like QUT with a proud heritage drawn from the CAE sector, there appeared to have been an increasing appreciation that teaching matters. Students were to be put in a position to choose their courses with harder information than in the past and they were expected to become increasingly discriminating as they were required to bear, directly or indirectly, an increased percentage of the costs of their own education.

As the federal Labor government led by Prime Minister Paul Keating entered its later years, the management of universities experienced a similar change of focus, with government intervention to ensure that traditional notions of autonomy were modified in the interests of ensuring more direct accountability for the public funds which continued to be pumped into universities, albeit in declining amounts. Funding had been made conditional upon meeting public policy objectives, in terms of the range of students, courses, campuses and delivery mechanisms, as well as the entrenching of various performance indicators aimed at reassuring the paymasters that universities were delivering social benefits in sufficient quantities to justify their continued levels of support.

A series of reports in the early 1990s examined basic propositions about the utility of tertiary education in meeting economic needs in particular. The surge of enthusiasm for competency-based training pointed to a focus on narrowing the purposes of education to preparation for employment.

The final years of the Keating administration, which ended with the federal election of 1996, also saw the establishment of another wave of claimants on the federal public purse, based, like CAEs two decades before, upon the triple attractions of subservience to external control, immediate vocationally-applied curriculum outcomes and low cost. It was almost as if the spiritual heirs of Dawkins had given up on universities, despite the indigestion created by devouring the CAEs, and had turned instead to the Technical and Further Education (TAFE) sector. The resurgence of interest in TAFE had its historical roots in the report of the Kangan Committee back in 1973–1974 and the recognition given to the sector in the tripartite CTEC structure and increased federal funding a few years later. This policy surge was unprecedented in the lack of critical analysis of differentiation between TAFE and universities on the one hand and between TAFE and the secondary schools on the other.

Under the enthusiastic sponsorship of both union officials and business leaders, TAFE seemed to be the preferred alternative among the funding options and great efforts were made to persuade the public in general, and parents in particular, of the benefits of TAFE courses as an alternative to university entrance. For the moment, there is some evidence to suggest that many students (and many TAFE staff) measure their success in terms of using generous articulation provisions to progress into universities.

It would not be beyond the realms of possibility to find in the future that TAFE institutions are offering a full range of degree awards and that staff will be expected to undertake research in these fields in the interest of creating parity of esteem for their institutions with the expanded university sector. Already there are a few straws in the wind, with the Canberra Institute of Technology, a renamed TAFE college, circumventing regulations preventing the offering of Australian degrees by acting as a surrogate for the award of a North American institution in the burgeoning field of hospitality management.

Dr Don Anderson, founding Chair of the Committee for the Advancement of University Teaching, has predicted that 'The most likely model to occur in Australia, either by design or default, is something like the Californian three-level structure of community or regional colleges, State universities and research universities...'. Addressing the Queensland symposium *Preparing University Teachers in*

Australia and New Zealand, he observed that TAFE already aspired to university status and, he argued, vocational education and training was not less worthy than higher education. 'Is a course in golf management at the Gold Coast (Campus of Griffith University) any more intellectually demanding...than a course for electronics technicians at a TAFE?' he asked. (cited in Juddery 1996b, p.3).

McCollow and Knight (1993) argue that:

> The preference for TAFE is underwritten by three related matters. First, there is the federal policy intention, articulated in the Carmichael report, that by the end of the decade more than 90% of all 20 year olds should be undertaking some form of post-compulsory education. Second, the per capita costs of TAFE is around half that of universities. Third, TAFE training is seen as more directly linked to industry needs. (p.15)

They then note that:

> Concerns have been expressed about the narrow instrumentalism of this approach and about whether it can actually achieve the goals that the Commonwealth has set for itself. However, the Commonwealth government has to date been remarkably successful in using its funding-based muscle to drive reform in education in the direction it wants (p.15).

Where does this leave universities, especially facing the 'funding-based muscle' of the hard-nosed economic rationalists installed in Canberra by the 1996 federal election? This event had led to the rejection of the outgoing Labor administration and the installation of a Liberal/ National Coalition government.

In 1996 universities were already less financially dependent on governments than at any time in the past. The growth of commercial income, fee-paying revenues from overseas students and postgraduate coursework linked to real costs meant that some universities and certainly some faculties in most universities obtained more than half their income from entrepreneurial activities. Even the undergraduate charges via the Higher Education Contribution Scheme (HECS) represented 22 per cent of real costs, considerably higher than the tuition fees abolished by Whitlam in 1972. This shift towards private funding was a deliberate policy of the Keating government, justified in terms of easing the burden on general taxation but also exerting increasing pressure on universities to respond to market forces and consumer preferences.

All this should not be welcomed uncritically, either by students or taxpayers. There is a potential for unpopular research to remain unfunded, and for a detrimental impact on standards if student customers exert market pressure without the countervailing influence of professional associations and peer review. Any return to full-fee funding and free markets associated with vouchers and open competition (as envisaged in the manifesto of the then opposition Coalition at the time of the 1993 general election) would reinstitute the levels of social inequality of the 1950s, when the rich exercised pressure on the university system to produce an exclusive and self-perpetuating élite.[2]

It may well be, as Jane Nichols (1995) suggests, that the level of government funding under Keating, and its associated policy, ensured an appropriate level of public accountability. This accountability was justified by the proposition that universities do not exist solely to serve the interests of their staff but to meet wider social objectives – so that devices such as profile negotiations and broader budget controls relate to the government's recognition of the need to fund these wider purposes.

These developments were seen by many universities, especially the older ones, as a process of bureaucratisation and control which had within it the seed of danger that universities would be reduced to an arm of the public service. Vocationalism and managerialism were seen to discount the traditional role of universities which can only be

---

2   The Whitlam abolition of fees did not create the social revolution in terms of access to tertiary study which was anticipated. Working class aspirations tended to rise no higher than TAFE. A 1995 study by Birrell and Khoo reveals an interesting sidelight on this question of class and access. In 1991 one in seven university students spoke a language other than English at home. Rather than being an underclass, offspring of migrants are higher achievers – perhaps because of the commitment of parents and the absence of distraction of mainstream youth culture and wider anti-intellectualism.

This represents an unprecedented degree of social mobility within a single generation to overcome the handicap of social class, an achievement which is more marked among recent migrants than groups here long enough to be socialised into dominant culture. Birrell and Khoo (1995) suggest that this outcome renders anachronistic support for current policies designed to overcome the disadvantage presumed to be suffered by students from non-English speaking backgrounds. 'Australia's sometimes maligned educational institutions have provided a ladder of opportunity for significant numbers of migrant youths from lower socio-economic backgrounds' (Birrell and Khoo p.54).

It has also been suggested that the same is increasingly true of women, who are generally doing better rather than worse than the average. The problem for females and for students from a non-English speaking background arises when they seek to break into the higher ranks of the professions for which they are currently educating themselves, especially including the management of tertiary institutions.

performed at arms-length from direct social control. (See Scott 1995a; 1995b;1995c).

Higher Education Review Committee (The Hoare Committee)

It is important to recognise that the growing significance of the managerialist ethos was already well entrenched before the federal election of 1996. A Higher Education Review Committee had been appointed in June 1995 by Simon Crean, a former national union official before his entry to parliament, a minister whose main interest and expertise lay in the employment dimensions of his diverse portfolio.

The committee was appointed as a result of discussions on the 1995 Budget, during which the Expenditure Review Committee's agenda had linked higher education spending to wider issues of public sector reform. The responsibility of central agencies such as Treasury and the Industry Commission made it necessary to look beyond advice from the Higher Education Council and to seek the opinions of experts from the corporate sector.

The committee was headed by David Hoare, a prominent businessman, who was Chairperson of Telstra (a leading telecommunications provider), and included Peter Coaldrake, a contributor to this book. The terms of reference required the team to address the following specific matters:

- accountability arrangements and reporting requirements for public funds
- the effectiveness of organisational structures in universities
- the effectiveness of governance structures
- employment and personnel practices
- financial management arrangements and practices
- the effectiveness of the use of institutional asset stock
- the appropriateness of the current division of responsibilities for higher education between Commonwealth and State governments

In its report tabled in December 1995, the Hoare Committee identified several sources of pressure on the Australian higher education sector, including:

- continued demands from government and the community for more accountability and better performance

- competition, both at home and overseas, for the patronage both of school leavers and of those seeking upgrading of skills or reaccreditation
- a policy refocus on TAFE, signalling an end to assured government-funded growth
- the impact on education of developments in information technology and communications
- mass participation and the change in the student profile, resulting in a need for economy of operations and achievement of social justice objectives
- internationalisation of higher education
- environment of the higher education sector, including their interest in maintaining autonomy, whilst responding to the above
- increasing expectation of employees for more self-determination and flexibility in the workplace. (Coaldrake 1996, pp.2–3)

Its recommendations addressed five aspects of higher education management: the need for increased financial accountability; greater involvement of governing bodies, including external representatives, in setting strategic directions; enhancement of strategic management practices, including an emphasis on reporting processes and explicit management training for senior academics involved in university governance; revision of work practices, including the formulation of tenure, as part of a process of workplace reform; and an improvement in the processes of finance and asset management.

The report received a mixed response from the media, ranging from outright opposition, to suggestions that it contained nothing new. In particular, its managerialist approach was criticised, amidst concerns that, if implemented, the recommendations would undermine the autonomy of universities and their academic staff.

Writing in *Campus Review*, Paul Jones (1996) argued that Australian universities had experienced significant democratisation since the 1970s and many had already replaced the earlier system of absolutist professordoms with one in which collegial participatory democracy had ensured that the only hierarchy would be that based on scholarly expertise. In this environment, the continuing employment of tenure was deemed a necessary requirement for the continuation of these democratic experiments. Academic autonomy, in an environment of 'reformulated tenure' would, he argued, not be protected by Hoare's presumption that merely improving managerial 'people skills' would maintain essential academic freedoms in an era of marketised universities where all disciplines become, from a budgetary perspective, potentially disposable commodities.

The Vanstone era

Higher education administrators, attempting to digest the implications of the Hoare Report, were also aware of wider pressures for change which were transforming both the business environment and the higher education sector. These were described by Doyle (1996) as an increasingly competitive environment, a greater focus on customer satisfaction, the influence of information technology on service delivery, an increased focus on economic rationalism, greater emphasis on performance management in human resource management, increased government expectations that institutions exercise flexibility and initiative, and increased government expectations of institutional accountability for performance.

Debate over the implications of the Hoare report was overtaken by interest in the impending federal election, and the attitude of a Liberal/National Coalition government to the higher education sector.

The Coalition policy document indicated approval of the trend towards a broader funding base for universities, describing it as a means of ensuring greater autonomy and flexibility for the individual institution. Higher education institutions were to be encouraged in their pursuit of non-government sources of funding, and were to enjoy greater freedom in their expenditure of government funding provided that a 'comprehensive and achievable strategic plan', complying with the overall governmental objectives and priorities for higher education, was developed and adhered to (Coalition 1996). Clearly, strategic planning, already well established in many Australian universities, would experience a renewed emphasis under a Coalition government.

The return of a Liberal-National Coalition government led by John Howard saw the 'discovery' of an eight billion dollar 'black hole' in the economy and a requirement that each minister investigate op-portunities for savings within his or her portfolio.

In a climate of innuendo, accusation and counter-accusation, the newly-appointed Minister for Employment, Education, Training and Youth Affairs, Senator Amanda Vanstone, was faced with the task of justifying her belief that the higher education sector should not be exempt from possible cuts.

Delivering the opening address, *Policy Perspectives on Higher Education Financing*, at the Centre for Economic Policy Symposium in Canberra, Senator Vanstone attempted to deflect concern over possible funding cuts to universities by questioning their efficiency and effectiveness practices. She argued that rather than already being 'cut to the bone', the higher education sector was the recipient of over five billion dollars from the Commonwealth government each year. The claim was made that funding, as a proportion of gross domestic product expenditure, had risen significantly, indicating a picture of generous and expanding public subsidy.

Yet Senator Vanstone conceded that staff/student ratios had fallen, equipment was out of date and the rapidly increasing student body was having to cope with 'overcrowded lecture theatres, inadequate libraries and dated research facilities'. As an explanation for this phenomenon she turned to the Hoare Report. Although later acknowledging that the Hoare Report had recognised 'the many improvements that have already been made in university management' (Vanstone 1996b, p.13), here she claimed that it 'identified the need for urgent implementation of improvements to university management systems'(Vanstone 1996a, p.4). In particular, she cited its requirement that all universities have proper strategic planning, effective performance management, improved work practices and budgeting, and financial management geared to the needs of increasingly commercial operations.

Following up this attack via an article in *The Age* newspaper, Senator Vanstone had a 'physician heal thyself ' message for university administrators, castigating them for their failure to recognise the role of management in achieving efficiency improvements:

> The scale of resources at issue in the current budget is trivial in comparison with the resources that could be unlocked for the sector by a concerted effort to ensure that the management of universities is at the forefront of change rather than dragging along in the rear. It's not impossible. Universities teach their business students how to do it every day. (Vanstone 1996b, p.13)

Vanstone also attacked the governing bodies of universities for their perceived poor management record, saying that they were too large and lacked managerial responsibility. Gavin Moodie (1996, p.30), in *The Australian* newspaper, quoted her as saying 'Vice-Chancellors pretty well get anything they want from them', and noted that the recently observed shift to stronger top-down management was 'still far too little – according to the minister'. Here, at least, she was supported by the Hoare Report, which had recommended that governing bodies have the ultimate responsibility for the conduct of their institutions.

The message from the new Minister for Employment, Education, Training and Youth Affairs was clear: administrative mismanagement, not an inadequate level of funding at a time of unprecedented growth, was the cause of the obvious problems in the higher education sector. Universities were seen as a well-resourced section of Senator Vanstone's portfolio (which also included the politically sensitive area of employment). A desire to maintain collegial forms of governance and an unwillingness to accommodate the requirement for strategic planning, performance and financial management, and work practices now accepted by the business and industrial sectors, was seen to be the cause of the higher education sector's inability to cope with its changing profile.

During her address to the Centre for Economic Policy Research, Senator Vanstone hinted at far more fundamental questions underpinning her government's approach to university funding. Citing a recommendation from a Commission of Audit established by the new government that Commonwealth funding take the form of contestable scholarships as a means of improving resource allocation via the market, she expressed concern that this may result in serious problems for regional universities (many of which are in Liberal-National heartland). Significantly, though, instead of rejecting the Commission's recommendation, Senator Vanstone (1996a, p.3) argued that 'any move to increase the level of contestability should be made with great care, one step at a time'.

The first of these steps was a call for universities to address the issues identified by the Hoare Report, with Senator Vanstone revealing that the question of how to structure the 'correct' balance between public and private funding for higher education was the subject of intense work prior to the delivery of the first Coalition budget. The inference must be made that the use of the Hoare Report to justify criticism of the higher education sector may have merely been a mechanism to deflect public attention from these fundamental ideologically-based questions.

The selective quotation from the Hoare Report resonated more generally with the rhetoric of the new Howard government about the virtues of small government and the need to create greater efficiency through unrestricted competition.

Universities which had accumulated a strong research infrastructure over the past century, and particularly during the good years before binarism, could now move to exploit their significant competitive advantage over recent creations whose antecedents lay in the CAE sector. There had been much posturing and manoeuvring within the Australian Vice-Chancellors' Committee (AVCC) in the build-up to the election and then subsequently as the new government developed its cost-cutting first budget. The older 'sandstone' universities and those with a strong research record formed themselves into an alliance of the 'Group of Eight', which sought to ensure that the cuts favoured the stronger in a more competitive environment.

Their preferences largely prevailed within a context in which all universities were forced to face very significant diminution of their publicly-funded income. The ground-breaking budget of August 1996 seems destined to bring about changes at least equal in magnitude to those created by the series of reforms introduced by John Dawkins between 1987 and 1990.

The most significant change related to the emphasis placed on increased student fees as a basis for either future expansion or the management of a reduction in grant-based income. The latter comprised an effective 5 per cent reduction in funding over four years, plus a further amount of at least 5 per cent relating to staff wage increases which had previously been funded centrally. An increased level of income was generated by allowing institutions to charge fees to Australian students who had not won competitive entry to high-demand courses on the same basis as non-Australian students.

This decision was related to a stronger general emphasis on tertiary study as a 'user-pays' regime rather than a publicly-funded social benefit, symbolised by alterations to HECS. This scheme had been introduced with a single level of contribution and the option that repayment be deferred until the student's income equalled, or exceeded, the national average. Changes proposed in the 1996 budget introduced a more rigorous repayment schedule for existing and future students and the expansion of the single fee structure. A three-tier schedule was introduced which at least doubled the costs of all courses and reflected (somewhat incongruously) both relative costs of course delivery and relative student demand.[3]

---

3   Medicine was on the highest band, arts on the lowest. But law, a cheaply-produced course was also on the top band because of the perceived over-supply and high earning potential of law graduates.

Many commentators have suggested that this new set of policy imperatives is wholly consistent with the broad ethos of the new government in regenerating social differentiation along the lines of the Menzies conservatism of the 1950s. Certainly, the better-off economically will now have privileged access to the most sought-after university places which will better their own life chances.

As one budget-day commentator remarked:

> The government is setting up a system where, in a competition for a university spot between two people with equivalent academic scores, a well-off person has a better chance of getting in regardless of the respective values they accord to the place. The presence of fee-paying students will not necessarily lead to a drop in standards, but it might. Already academics say they are under pressure to pass fee-paying students – from some of the students who think that buying a place entitles them to value for money, and from the university administrators who are interested in 'maximising throughput'. And despite the 25 per cent restriction on local fee places (within any one course), it will not be long before the majority of students in some courses will be fee-paying. (Armitage 1996, p.6)

This view was reinforced by comments from the respected economist and architect of the original HECS proposal, Professor Bruce Chapman. In an article entitled *A Return to Inequity*, he argued authoritatively that:

> The amendments to the higher education funding system introduced in the 1996-1997 Budget will significantly change the nature of Australian universities. It is ironic that just as a large number of countries have followed or are set to follow the HECS model, the Australian government is putting in place measures that will inevitably undermine it . (Chapman 1996, p.19)

Chapman argued that this change was misguided, from an economic as well as a social perspective:

> When the system becomes one in which enrolment is increasingly determined by the ability to pay and decreasingly determined by the capacity and motivation to learn, many able but poor students will be excluded. This wastes talent and is thus poor economics and means greater entrenchment of the nexus between an individual's socio-economic background and future life opportunities. In both economic and social terms, the policy cannot be defended. (Chapman 1996, p.19)

In addition to this re-establishment of social differentiation, there will also be a re-establishment of institutional differentiation. The effect of fee-paying students on the relative buoyancy of institutional budgets will mean that the current differential levels of student demand and financial resources concealed within the notion of a Unified National System will be rendered explicit. Over time, the strong will get relatively stronger as they exploit the benefits accrued by decades of preferment and the weak will battle to retain credibility as a legitimate alternative.

Thus the Vice-Chancellor of Melbourne University's first reaction was to demonstrate conditional enthusiasm for the changes and for the benefits which might flow from the deregulated environment they created (Gilbert 1996). By contrast, within weeks of the 1996 budget, newer institutions were announcing staff cuts and regional universities which had emerged during the Dawkins era were facing a bleak and uncompetitive future as the lowest rungs on the ladder of student aspirations.

These regional institutions had the comfort of local 'protectors', especially in dealing with Coalition governments dominant both federally and in all but one State. Other institutions in cities were more exposed but both groups were acutely aware of the threat posed by a combination of four forces :

- a commitment to a free market, with institutions able to charge fees which that market would bear

- continuing evidence of student preferences for courses offered in the established universities

- an overall cut-back in funding across the sector likely to continue for the indefinite future

- a perception held by both Liberal politicians and bureaucrats that Dawkins had allowed the creation of too many institutions in total to meet a declining demand.

Little solace was given to the 'weaker' institutions by public statements from senior political figures such as Tony Abbott, Parliamentary Secretary to Minister Vanstone, who offered comfort to the Group of Eight with remarks that 'if élite universities develop in Australia, no one should complain because education means bringing out the best in people' and further comments accepting the recognition of hierarchies based on market signals relating to quality.

Planners from these élite universities reinforced this view. An article evocatively entitled 'Dawkins's Vision Splendid Fading' reported details of a planning document *Future Arrangements for Policy Advice and Program Administration in Higher Education,* provided by ANU senior staff members Bob Arthur and Chris Burgess to Senator Tierney, Chair of the Senate Employment, Education and Training Legislation Committee:

> The demographic and participation trends over the next 5–7 years suggest that a down-sizing of the system is warranted and will be essential if quality teaching and research is to be maintained, let alone enhanced. The economy will increasingly find it difficult to absorb into professionally satisfying and community-beneficial employment the large number of such students currently graduating from universities. There is an opportunity to implement fundamental sea-change reforms which would reverse the 'levelling down' tendencies central to the Unified National System concept, and remove bureaucratic restrictions inhibiting flexibility and effectiveness. (Juddery 1996a, p.14)

Retrospective: sea change or back to 1957?

How far has Australia moved in the forty years from the Murray Report and the social environment encapsulated in the quotations from Jane Nichols which opened this chapter?

Pessimists might suggest that the only change has been the cosmetic one of allowing a wide variety of institutions to call themselves universities which were previously technical colleges and teacher-training institutions undeserving of such an ancient title. The gulf in social reality and access seems to remain undiminished.

This understates the changes within the tertiary sector and in the nature of employment. When Murray reported in 1959 there were only eight universities and an enrolment of only 45,000 students, almost all undergraduates. The great majority of my peer school-leavers in 1957 did not complete secondary education or they undertook the 'matriculation' qualification as an end in itself without any perceived need for university education in an era of full employment.

Forty years on, mass participation in some form of post-secondary education is now established. While levels of education in the general population have risen dramatically, this has not proved a passport to certainty of employment, with youth unemployment at historically high levels. The major ebb and flow in public policy has been the widening of the range of institutions incorporated in a unified university sector, expanding its total size, followed by a set of decisions aiming at disaggregation and differentiation.

Many of the newer institutions embraced in the expansionist phase are now highly competitive and providing a service valued by students and the wider community, but the social hierarchies which sustained the institutional differentiation of the 1950s are once again in the ascendancy in the 1990s.

As Bob Lingard remarked:

> There have been many achievements of the Unified National System of higher education, not the least of which is the expanded participation of young Australians and the embedding of targeted equity programs across the system. However, a number of policy dilemmas have been precipitated by the mix of regulatory and deregulatory relations between the government and the universities. (1994, p.30)

Since that was written, the Howard government has changed the mix dramatically towards deregulation without resolving the fundamental dilemma: are universities private institutions competing for individual clients or should they be regarded as part of the public fabric for sustaining wider social values?

Chapter 3

The University of Canberra

Don Aitkin

Virtually all universities, especially the oldest creations, have begun in a small way. Very many began as something else altogether, acquiring the name and contemporary purpose of a university at a time later than their foundation. What is understood by the word 'university' has, of course, varied across time and across societies; something will be said about those meanings in this chapter.

Universities are communities and, at the same time, land and buildings in a particular place and the life and endeavour that goes on in and around the buildings on that land. Thus Oxford University can be thought of as having a continuous existence since the middle of the thirteenth century on an unchanged site and in and around buildings which have been erected throughout the past seven centuries. But, of course, it did not start out as 'Oxford University', and what today occurs there, what is now considered to be 'knowledge', the sex of its students and their social origins, their preparation and later careers, the focus and organisation of its staff – these things on the whole bear small relation to what was the case in, say, the late nineteenth century, let alone in earlier centuries.

In the life of all universities of any age there are periods of transition between one shape and another. These are periods, literally, of 'reform', in which the university's structure, or purpose or social location or relationship to the state, changes in a powerful way. These are nearly always dramatic times, if only because the autonomy of the institution is invaded in some way. Whatever the formal basis of their existence, universities are usually left alone to get on with their business of learning and teaching. (Today, we would add to that business 'the advancement of knowledge', a phrase which is of our time, though past university generations would have understood something of what we have in mind). When the state intervenes in university matters there is usually a good deal of noisy debate because universities, like all relatively self-governing institutions, enjoy their autonomy.

What follows is an account of one such transition, during which the Canberra College of Advanced Education became the University of Canberra. The change of name occurred on 1 January 1990. Seven years later, the institution is still in transition but its new shape and purpose are clear enough and are unlikely to change very much over the next decade or two.

A little pre-history

Australia has been experimenting with forms of higher education since 1851, when the University of Sydney was established. By 1911 there was one university in the capital city of each of the six States; each was a colonial hybrid of higher education forms in England, Scotland and Ireland. Since interstate transport was poorly developed, and rivalries were intense, there was little communication between the universities – indeed, there was probably better and more regular communication between each of them and British universities. The first meeting of Australian Vice-Chancellors did not take place until 1920.

Each State had not only a university but at least one metropolitan technical college or institute which offered not degrees but diplomas and other awards for achievement in technical education, institutions which were to grow in importance in the twentieth century. The early years of the new century also saw the creation of agricultural and teacher-training colleges, the latter preparing their own students for teaching in primary schools and university graduates for teaching in secondary schools. After the Second World War, Australia, like other Western societies, dealt with strong and continuing demand for higher education by creating new universities – some of them, initially, 'colleges' of established universities and some completely new institutions on new sites. It also established, from the mid-1960s, a second stream of 'advanced education' institutions, many of which were based on already existing teachers' colleges and technical institutes.

The outcome was a two-tiered or 'binary' higher education system which lasted until 1988. It was inherently unstable, for a number of reasons. It was based on the assumption that there were different kinds of students, on the one hand those who were seeking an academic education and those, on the other hand, who were seeking preparation for vocations. These different needs required, so it was argued, two different types of institutions: universities and colleges of advanced education. The first would be funded to undertake research, the second would not. Unfortunately for this theory, all Australian universities had possessed large and powerful vocational streams from the beginning and there was no suggestion that medicine, law, engineering, architecture, dentistry, veterinary science or agricultural science should be transferred to the advanced education sector. The new institutions, though not funded for research, learned how to obtain funds from industry and some of them became well known for the quality of their research. The universities competed for places and began to offer courses in the areas which the colleges had pioneered, thereby further blurring any sense of real difference. Very many of the universities' newly-minted PhDs found employment in the advanced education sector and were keen to keep doing research. By the 1980s the advanced education sector had become, among other things, the principal domain which prepared people for the new professions of accounting, nursing, public relations and the like. It was larger than the university sector and increasingly irritated by funding and status differentiation that seemed to have no contemporary meaning and no good public purpose.

   In 1987 a new Minister, John Dawkins, in a new and powerful Ministry of Employment, Education and Training, made it clear that these arrangements were overdue for change. A White paper and related legislation issued in 1988 represented the most far-reaching set of changes to higher education since 1965 and brought the binary system to an end. By spelling out size criteria which encouraged institutions to amalgamate in order to be funded for research across all their teaching activities, the White Paper ushered in a hunt for partners which was to reduce a binary system of 19 universities and 44 institutions of advanced education to a 'Unified National System' of 36 universities (one or two very small tertiary institutions retained their autonomy but were not counted as universities).

Amalgamation or independence

The new Minister could only encourage amalgamation, not demand it. Since all State universities were established under State law, he needed, and obtained, the assistance of relevant State Ministers. But in the Australian Capital Territory there were two institutions, the Australian

National University (ANU, founded in 1946) and the Canberra College of Advanced Education (CCAE, founded in 1967), both of which were established under Commonwealth law. He was their Minister, since both reported to the Commonwealth parliament through him, and he soon made it clear that he wished the two universities to merge.

Such an amalgamation was not an inspired piece of public policy, however obvious it may have looked to outsiders. The ANU was originally set up to ensure that Australia had a world-class research and postgraduate university, the absence of which had seemed a great weakness during the Second World War, when Australia depended for several years largely on its own efforts for research and technical innovation. In 1960 the ANU was instructed by the federal government to merge with the adjoining Canberra University College, a small off-shoot of the University of Melbourne which had been established to provide higher education opportunities for public servants transferred progressively from Melbourne after Canberra's establishment as the national capital in 1927. The 1960 merger was not to the taste of either institution and had not been accomplished in any comprehensive way by 1988. For many practical purposes the ANU possessed its very own binary system – two higher education institutions responding to a single university council.

The CCAE was neither a former teachers' college nor a former technical institution. It was the Commonwealth's sole exercise in creating a college of advanced education from first principles. Well built, well landscaped, well provided with staff (it had the highest proportion of staff with a PhD in the advanced education system) and attractive to students, the CCAE had quite deliberately tried to do things that the ANU did not do, and possessed a wide range of degree programs preparing people for the professions; the ANU's teaching side, in contrast, was built on large faculties of Arts, Science, and Economics and Commerce, and smaller faculties of Asian Studies and Law.

While the combination of these complementary endeavours looked sensible, staff at the CCAE feared that they would disappear within the ANU and, more particularly, that their emphasis on teaching and contact with students would not survive in the research culture of the larger institution. From the ANU's perspective the CCAE was not really a university, had staff who were underqualified and offered degree programs which were outside the university's experience. Yet there would be advantages in amalgamation, especially given the government's apparent determination about size, since the merged institution would be large enough to be funded for research across all its teaching programs. (It ought to be said here that the size criterion was not made much of once the amalgamations had been accomplished and is no longer mentioned by the federal government as part of current policy.)

So, in 1989 the two institutions formed working parties and committees to explore the basis for an amalgamation of some kind. Some parts of the two institutions found the possibility of merger attractive and others did not. The process involved months of negotiation and planning, which reached the point where a formal basis for merger existed and the Principal of the college was named as the prospective Deputy Vice-Chancellor of the university. The real prospect of the merger actually occurring prompted a grass-roots revolt on the part of some ANU staff and supporters and the university's council decided by a narrow majority not to amalgamate. The CCAE council, although it had preferred independence, voted for amalgamation provided that did not become 'simple submergence' in another institution. When the ANU council rejected amalgamation the college council advised the Minister that it saw no likelihood of a merger succeeding. The Minister accepted the result and re-formed the college as the University of Canberra from 1 January 1990, under the sponsorship of Monash University (in Melbourne) for at least three years.

Independence came at a price. The negotiating process had exposed staff at the college to public scorn and derision from other academics who would not accept them as future colleagues and morale was low. Furthermore, while the college had for twenty years been allowed a good deal of freedom in building its future, there was no suggestion that it would now be funded as a university to compete with the ANU. It would plainly be one of the smaller universities in what was being called 'the Unified National System'. To cap it all, only six months into the new university's life, its Vice-Chancellor, the former principal of the college, was chosen by the new government of Queensland to be the Director-General of Education and left within a few weeks of the announcement of that appointment.

Defining the mission

A new Vice-Chancellor was appointed from the beginning of 1991 and, since he is writing this chapter, the narrative has to move, at least for a few paragraphs, into the first person. At the time of my appointment I was finishing a three-year term as Chairman of the Australian Research Council (a full-time statutory position responsible to the commonwealth parliament) and had spent 25 years in academic life as an historian and political scientist, much of it at the Australian National University (from which I was on leave). I had not been a participant in any sense in the amalgamation process and knew little of what had occurred except through the press. Nor had I had much to do with the college save through my own discipline of political science, in which the college was strong. To complete my list of apparent disqualifications, I came to the Vice-Chancellorship in a relatively unusual way; I had not been a Deputy Vice-Chancellor anywhere and my experience at the level of Dean had ended more than a decade earlier. While the University of Canberra was strong in teaching, what I knew most about was research.

I was not short of advice about what ought to be done, but spent the first few months walking, talking and listening. In February, April and May 1991 I gave three public addresses to the university about what its future might be. Most of what has happened since can be traced to the material in those speeches. It was, of course, an opportune time for the new university to be born. The Australian higher education system had been severely shaken and the settled status hierarchy implicit in the binary system had gone forever. The oldest universities now contained elements of the former advanced education system; some of the metropolitan institutes of technology were now larger than some of the old universities, and had high ambitions as well. The University of Canberra was, in 1991, one of only two colleges of advanced education (Curtin University of Technology was the other) which became universities without merging with any other institution (a few more have now joined it). What should UC do? What should it aspire to become?

I argued strongly that there were many possible 'universities' of high quality and that the University of Canberra had a splendid chance to decide what kind of university it would set out to be.

There is no single model of a university. Universities can teach many things, or few. They can do a great deal of research, or very little. They can be situated in city centres, or in green fields. They can be private bodies, statutory corporations, state instrumentalities, or combinations of these forms. They can have only undergraduate students, or only postgraduate students, or a mixture. They can be very wealthy, or very poor. They can be very big, or very small. They can be very old, or very new. Their essential character is that they have students, and that the students have teachers. The other essential characteristic is that in some sense universities are knowledgeable about the present limits of knowledge. (Aitken 1991, pp.1–2)

The great danger, it seemed to me, was that the University of Canberra would, like some of the other new creations, try to imitate the older models, and for the wrong reasons. In comparison with much of the rest of the world, Australia lacks important ethnic, linguistic, religious and class cleavages, and status rivalries therefore assume great significance. The Universities of Sydney, Melbourne, Adelaide and so on were the 'top' universities, mostly through social cachet but all of them were nineteenth century models which were having varying success in coping with change. The colleges of advanced education were a much more recent model, and plainly successful in attracting students. They emphasised good teaching, relevance to the community and research which was needed by someone. If one looked ten or twenty years ahead, surely it would be better to mobilise strengths like these than to try to attain the status of the older institutions by following them in what they had been doing since the mid-1960s: 'pure' research and the training of doctoral students.

That, at least, was my argument and it seemed to capture the mood of the university, whose members were generally ready to plan and build provided that they knew why they were undertaking all this activity. A taskforce set up to look at the university's academic program produced, among other things, a recommendation that the university proclaim its central mission to be 'the education of people for professional careers, carried out in a professional way'. Shortened to 'educating professionals, professionally', this slogan gave the new institution a clear sense of what it was for with the understanding that the slogan was one for the moment and would change as needs changed. The slogan had the great advantage that it drew attention to, and built on, what the university had done before and was good at and made no inflated claims.

The university would also move purposefully to become the university *for* Canberra and its region and emphasise this by seeking the transfer of its legislation from the jurisdiction of the Commonwealth to that of the Australian Capital Territory. That was a mission which fitted the new institution's name and its activities. It also differentiated it from the ANU, whose name and mission were plainly national in focus and whose teaching and research endeavours were much less aligned with those of the needs of Canberra itself than were those of the University of Canberra. So this shift in focus was not objected to by the ANU and received bi-partisan support in both the relevant parliaments.

Unfortunately, the business of actually transferring the legislation has still not been completed, not through malice but because the enabling bill has never had sufficient priority to get into the government's legislative program in the ordinary way; an embarrassed Labor government, recognising the sin of its earlier inanition, tried to get the bill through all stages in both houses at the very end of its last term but failed by a few hours. Paradoxically, UC does not by any means draw all of its students from the surrounding city. Like the ANU, it is a member of the Universities Admissions Centre of New South Wales and the Australian Capital Territory, and about a third of its students come from elsewhere in Australia (mostly from NSW) or from overseas.

Creating an identity

The slogan 'educating professionals, professionally' was in harmony with several other elements of what was a new 'identity'. CCAE had been well known and widely respected for what it had done; the newly-stated mission was quickly owned by the staff of the university because it accurately reflected what had been essentially unsaid in the institution's first twenty-five years. But would it lose all this by becoming a 'university'? There were many staff who would argue with force that the college had been a 'university' all along – indeed, that the college had anticipated university initiatives in areas like environmental science, sports studies and aspects of education. Yet the college had gone and in entering the new domain there were risks to run as well as gains to make. Accordingly, the emphasis was to be on understatement, not on the bold claim. An early rule was that the university would make no public claims about its quality or surpassing virtues. That was for others – the university's graduates, clients and community in particular.

The corporate style of the university was to be 'cool, elegant and understated', qualities that were in keeping with its built environment.

There was to be no resort to the College of Heralds for a coat of arms or a Latin motto. That would be to look to the past, whereas the new university should look to the contemporary environment and its needs and then to the future. The university's logo, therefore, built on the circular interlinked 'C' (for Canberra) that the college had made its own, and subtended vertically the initials 'UC'. This trademark soon appeared on the university's stationery, its advertising, its vehicles, its publications and even on new markers at its entrances. That, of course, was only half the task. The rest came in getting people to use the new name and abbreviation, and years later there are still staff who refer to 'the college' without realising that they have done so, or who use 'UCAN' or 'U of C' as the short form. What can be said is that while the university was planning for the future, it was proud of its origins and in no danger of forgetting them.

Building a new sense of community

Universities are complex organisations which do not necessarily pull together, even though the need for them to do so is usually great. The jibe that 'universities consist of academics united in opposition to the administration's parking arrangements' can be unpacked for some time. Because academics are trained in critique, it is much easier to know what they are opposed to than what they are for. The need to build a new sense of community seemed very great in 1991. Not only was a sense of despair and of hurt widespread but the preceding six years had known three Principals who came and went quickly. I had not been there long before I learned that I too was not expected to stay – I would be off to some better place! I tried to dispel that feeling by pointing out that my record showed that I was not someone who was prone to the quick flit.

The mission, slogan and corporate identification emphasised the continuing purpose of the institution. To them could be added some more concrete contributions. The first taskforce was set up to provide recommendations about the university's academic program, but its very establishment served the purpose of community-building since its 24 members were drawn from across the faculties and administrative sectors. It was given a major task and a decent amount of time in which to discharge it. The virtually unanimous adoption by the university council of its recommendations made clear that the representative taskforce was a good model for university policy making and it has become an annual practice, which is good both for policy formation and for the university's sense of community. Subsequent taskforces developed policy dealing with the university's environment (1992), its administrative philosophy and structure (1993), its residential accommodation and the principles which should govern access and management (1994), and the university's international dimension (1995). In 1994 representation on the taskforce was widened to include postgraduate and undergraduate students. In 1996 an exploration began of the taskforce principle and its success in practice.

The first taskforce made a number of recommendations that went beyond simple academic policy. Two which were taken up quickly were proposals that the university have a decent newspaper reporting on the life of the 10,000 or so who made up the university community and that there be a staff club. The university newspaper, *Monitor*, made its first appearance before the end of 1991 and, two years later, was awarded the prize for the best university newspaper in Australia. The staff club took longer to bring into being because space was in great demand, but when established it proved an instant success – in part because the club's governing body chose an inspirational cook to run the kitchen.

A related decision moved all the commercial activities – banks, the post office, the travel agent, the book store, a pharmacy and so on – into new purpose-built premises in the centre of the university and linked them to a new and most attractive café, a new theatre and new premises for the student bar. Called 'The Hub', the commercial centre provided a focal point for social interaction and, in doing so, assisted in the task of developing a new, positive community feeling.

Internationalising the University

CCAE had been an early practitioner of TESOL – a widely used short form for 'Teaching English to Speakers of Other Languages' – and it developed through that expertise a strong association with Vietnam, Laos and Cambodia (hundreds of Vietnamese civil servants learned their English in Canberra) and with universities in Japan and China (which exchanged their students seeking fluency in English with CCAE's students seeking to strengthen their Chinese and Japanese). These contacts began in the early 1970s and, on that basis, the new university began to build a constituency among those from other countries seeking a university education which emphasised practical skills founded on a strong knowledge base.

An early pair of strategic directions helped to secure a good outcome. The first ensured, by doubling the university's residential accommodation for students, that there would be more places for those coming from outside Canberra. The second, by encouraging faculties to seek out students from other lands who would have an interest in specific faculty programs, helped to ensure that foreign students were not concentrated in one or two programs in one or two faculties. By 1996 the university had nearly 700 foreign students from 66 countries, and they made up about 10 per cent of total student load. The great majority were from the countries to the north of Australia.

Entering the domain of higher degrees by research

If there were two decisive differences in practice between universities and colleges in the old binary system, they could be seen in the inability of the colleges to offer honours training to their undergraduates and doctoral training to their postgraduate students – who were restricted to degrees at the masters level. The first handicap meant that the colleges lost their best students to the universities and found it hard to develop any sense of the need for 'excellence' in the undergraduate programs. Final honours years (an additional fourth year for courses with three-year degrees) or four-year degrees assessed and awarded at the honours level (in engineering, architecture and the like) were added to the program slowly but steadily.

The university's capacity to do this was, of course, connected to the second handicap because the inability to offer doctoral programs reduced the intellectual range demanded of a set of academic staff, reduced the number of bright young people in a school and reduced its capacity to offer honours degrees. The university had already taken some sensible steps in this field before my arrival by developing a set of rules governing the admission, supervision and examination of research students, which was based on what seemed to be the best practice around the Australian higher education system. (The revised version of this document was highly commended as an example of best practice.) And, following good principle as well as good practice elsewhere, the university confined doctoral enrolment to areas within the university which had both demonstrated prowess in research and possessed a decently large cohort of staff with doctoral degrees themselves. It put considerable effort into ensuring that supervision arrangements were satisfactory.

By 1996 the university had graduated only a dozen PhDs and had a few score doctoral students enrolled, but at least it could be said that the first PhD had won a prize for her thesis and that the university's standards were becoming as high as anywhere in the system. By far the majority of postgraduate students were enrolled in what the institution had for twenty years shown it had real strength in: graduate certificates, graduate diplomas and masters degrees by coursework in professional fields which improved people's professional standing or allowed graduates in one field to move for employment into another. By 1996, also, the university had devised a system of 'professional doctorates', based on a mixture of advanced coursework, research and advanced professional practice, to provide appropriate doctoral degrees for many of its professional programs.

Research

The university had some real research strength in applied science, the social sciences, computing and education, which had been unrecognised in any measurements of Australian research performance until the end of the binary system because the colleges were deemed not to be doing research! The decision of the government that all universities would have to develop and publish a 'research management strategy' imposed no great difficulty on the university since developing such a strategy had been a necessity in any case. The research management strategy of the University of Canberra was one of the earliest to be published and applauded by the Commonwealth as an example of best practice.

There was no great rush to research, which was quite explicitly not defined as the primary mission of the university. Its place was in a supporting and derived role and academic staff were not all expected to be undertaking 'cutting edge' research, a traditional (though somewhat silly) position set forward by most of the older universities. Those areas of research which were strong were, so far as practicable, strengthened. By 1996 the university was the lead academic partner in one Co-operative Research Centre and equal lead academic partner in another, while other staff members were attached to two other CRCs headquartered elsewhere. The CRCs were a major Commonwealth innovation in the early 1990s intended to bring together the best researchers in the universities and the world of government laboratories in partnership with the major likely end-users of research, and to be prominent in one was a straightforward measure of excellence in research in that area. The university was also the home of a major national research centre in social and economic modelling funded by the government, and of several other centres which existed largely on funds generated by successful research for clients. Seeking prowess in the field of 'competitive Commonwealth grants' – those awarded by the Australian Research Council and the Medical Research Committee of the National Health and Medical Research Council – was not seen as a primary element in the university's mission, although the university's record in gaining such grants was not in any way a poor one.

Integrating the undergraduate curriculum

The first university taskforce had been given a difficult task: that of reforming the university's undergraduate program, which, by 1991, was too large for the number of staff available and too complex for anyone, especially an entering undergraduate, fully to comprehend. The college had, since its foundation, used the American system of units and credit points to develop a program which would, in theory, allow any student to design a degree course which suited his or her background and experience. The flexibility of this approach made CCAE attractive to many students, especially those of mature age whose earlier experience of formal education had not equipped them well for traditional arts or science courses. It also encouraged teaching across the faculties rather than within them. It meant, of course, that the university offered many units which had very small enrolments.

The cost of this approach was clearly evident once the university was over-enrolled, as it was in 1990 and 1991: a flexible degree structure was affordable while funds were rising ahead of enrolments, but a great burden when funds were static or declining relative to enrolments. The 1991 taskforce recognised the problem but found solutions too hard to propose. But the problem did not go away, even though the university managed its enrolment process effectively from 1992 onwards. The Commonwealth had been happy to set up a new and large higher education system but proved decreasingly happy to fund it properly and, as the 1990s advanced, the pressure on available funds (a subject worthy of a chapter in itself) kept attention focused on the problem of the program.

At length, the Vice-Chancellor's Advisory Committee – the university's senior management group – decided at the end of 1994 to reduce the university's listed units by at least 30 per cent. Before very long that decision had been overtaken by another which was much more positive: to redesign the university's academic program so that it emphasised the things that the university did well, at the cost of the flexibility which had been characteristic of the program up until then. The outcome, sixteen months later, was an undergraduate program designed on different principles which encompassed about half the units and credit points that had been theoretically available in the past and about three-quarters of the actual offerings in 1995.

The process of change was not, this time, undertaken by a taskforce but by a representative steering committee which generated six major papers on the change, its rationale, dimensions and consequences – each paper other than the first being built on the reactions of academic staff to its predecessor. The Vice-Chancellor and the senior staff member most directly involved in the transformation went round the university's sixteen schools expounding the logic of what became known as 'The New Academic Program' and addressing questions and objections from staff. The opportunity to start afresh captivated some schools to the point where their own new programs are, arguably, the best being offered in Australia. At the time of writing, a similar process is being undertaken with the postgraduate program, with a 1998 starting point now firmly in place.

The arrival of competition

The account so far may have suggested that the University of Canberra was afloat in a some kind of benign policy ocean, able to chart its course without much regard to wind or tides, let alone to other shipping. In fact, the 1990s have not been like that for any Australian university. The same dilemmas, in a general way, must have occurred in every university. Hardly a university was untouched by what became known as the 'Dawkins Reforms': old universities took over advanced education institutions; some of the latter merged to form very much larger new universities; one merger came unstuck; there were extended periods of tutelage for some new creations. On every side came the questions: What do we do now? What are we for?

One thing was certain. The 'Unified National System' set up by the White Paper was a much more competitive system than the binary one, where everybody knew their place. Competition was a new experience for every institution and some enjoyed it more than others. The government made it clear that it wanted the 'market', whatever that was, to do most of the regulating of higher education. More and more Commonwealth money was to be allocated competitively.

The city of Canberra, containing 300,000 or so people, became a fiercely competitive ground for higher education, with two universities (the University of Canberra and the Australian National University), a small, élite university college for military officers which possessed a large postgraduate enterprise open to civilians (the Australian Defence Force Academy, a college of the University of New South Wales), a small campus of the Australian Catholic University, one of the clinical medical schools of the University of Sydney, and a small but high-quality theological activity affiliated with Charles Sturt University. Other universities had links with the Canberra Institute of Technology, a Technical and Further Education (TAFE) institution which itself had ambitions to become a degree-granting body and had links with Cornell University in the USA in its hotel management school. The five universities which had extensive distance education capacity all secured students from the city. Never had there been such attention to demand or such catering to student choice!

The drive for 'quality'

Though committed to the work of market forces, the government was not above giving competition a little boost. In 1993 it began a three-year experiment in quality assurance and enhancement through which all universities were exposed to external assessment. At stake was the annual allocation of around A$70 million in addition to the operating grant; at risk was the reputation of the university. There was no compulsion to participate but it was universally felt that a university which avoided the exercise would be seen as having something to hide.

The quality exercise could not have come at a less appropriate time for the newer creations. They were busy designing themselves and did not have the benefit of years of 'proper' funding. Moreover, in every case they had lost the name and reputation of their predecessor body or bodies, whereas the older universities in every case retained theirs. The

University of Canberra had to decide whether to adapt a recently devised ten-year strategic plan to this new imperative or stick to its plan. It chose to do the latter and, in retrospect, was probably right to do so. Some universities spent lavishly in both resources and the time and energy of staff in presenting an enhanced appearance to the quality assessors. But in the case of UC there were few resources to use, and there could be no concealing the university's relative youth and preoccupation with planning.

The outcomes were, broadly speaking, what any set of reasonable people with some knowledge of the system would have produced. The set of Australian universities was pronounced to be 'excellent', with a range from 'really and truly excellent' to 'decently excellent, all things considered'. If you put together the results of all three rounds, and summarised the separate inquisitions of reputation, teaching, research and community service, Australia seemed to have three broad groups of universities, with the University of Canberra well placed in the middle group, which was a most respectable place for it, given its youth and funding.

Structures and people

In 1991 the new Vice-Chancellor received a good deal of advice that his first task should be a thorough change of the university's faculty structure and, less frequently, that the university needed a transfusion of 'new blood' at the top. The university had six faculties, which covered some 28 professional programs and wide possibilities for general higher education in the arts, social sciences and natural sciences. Its senior people were, in large part, experienced, competent and dedicated to the institution. The academic staff had, for a former college of advanced education, a notably high proportion of doctoral and appropriate higher degrees. There was, on the face of it, no great need to shift areas of study from one faculty to another or to reduce or increase the number of faculties. Having had working experience of different types of university organisation in five universities in three countries, as well as of the civil service and the military, I was not one of those who believed that changing structures was an essential first step in change. Rather, I believed that almost any structure could be made to work well, provided that there was an appropriate vision and that staff understood where the organisation was going and why. The early concentration on mission, goals, objectives, strategies and communication was, therefore, appropriate to the university's needs and to my own sense of priorities.

Yet as the years passed it became clear that one structural modification was needed if the academic program were to be better integrated. This was the creation, or shaping, of 'schools' as the basic academic unit of management beneath the faculties. There were schools in 1991 but their purpose differed from faculty to faculty, as did their structure and powers. In 1995 the university introduced rules for the appointment of Heads of Schools and proceeded to differentiate the powers of those Heads and those of the Deans. The school was to become the locus of responsibility for a defined academic program (for example, the set of awards which related to Nursing or Accounting) and the faculty the provider of corporate services, infrastructure and co-ordination for a set of schools.

In 1991 the university was administered by its Vice-Chancellor, assisted by three Assistant Vice-Chancellors, who embodied the roles of Registrar, Bursar and Director of Planning which were traditional in the older universities. Three years later the three Assistants had become two Deputies, one for academic matters, the other for administrative matters. The university continued to have a notably flat structure with four levels of management (VC, DVC, Dean, Head of School), compared with five or six in most other Australian universities. In my view the flat structure, a good thing in any case, helped to build the sense of identity and community which seemed missing and essential in 1991. In 1994 the administrative side of the university was reformed into three broad divisions – one for academic services, one for administrative services and one for information services. In charge of each division was a Divisional Manager who reported to one of the Deputy Vice-Chancellors or (in the case of information services) to the Vice-Chancellor. The senior management group consisted of the Vice-Chancellor, the two Deputies, the six Deans and the three Divisional Managers. A similar, smaller Vice-Chancellor's Advisory Committee had existed in 1991, but, six years later, VCAC was a great deal better in exercising collective judgment in the interests of the university as a whole and the quality of the people was generally agreed (by competent outside observers, if not always by the staff!) to be of very high quality.

Relative to the older universities, the University of Canberra was notably short of senior academic appointments in 1991. It had not converted its principal lecturers to professors but to associate professors, and only a small group of 'College Fellows', who were paid at professorial rates and had been appointed after external advertisement through processes identical to those used by the older universities in filling chairs, received the title of 'Professor'. The council of the university agreed that the proportion of senior academic staff was very low and authorised a doubling at both professorial and associate professorial levels over the next five years.

Such an outcome could be achieved at the associate professorial level largely through promotion; the university was not at all short of talent and the performance of staff was manifest. Criteria for promotion were established which stressed both excellence in teaching and a real contribution (not restricted simply to research and scholarship in the traditional sense) to the knowledge base of the discipline or professional area from which the applicant gained his or her living – a pairing which grew in importance as the new university explored how it was different to the older creations. Community service, in all its forms, was as critical as teaching and scholarship. In choosing Professors, some resort was had to the possibility of appointment to 'personal chairs' (technically, 'special professorships') but most came from outside, as did four new Deans. Increasingly, we looked for a 'UC type' among the applicants, someone who, above all, was interested in education, likely to mentor younger staff, attracted by the distinctiveness and purpose of the university and outgoing in personality. We could take for granted an impressive research record, given the fields for academic jobs in the 1990s, but felt no obligation to pick the outstanding researcher if he or she lacked the more important human and moral strengths. The performance of the new appointees amply justified the decision to adopt these criteria.

In slow and subtle ways the culture of the university seemed to be changing. It was successful and, therefore, staff grew more confident that its chosen path was an appropriate one. New senior appointees emphasised that path, provided leadership and built networks around the university and between it and other places of higher learning and industry and community organisations. Appointment and promotion procedures had a general effect on aspirations and, therefore, on the mood and activity of the university. The continuing high quality of the best of the students reassured staff that the university could afford to be selective and that they themselves were among the leaders in their own fields. The university had really only just begun but it was beginning well, and that was a source of pride.

Concluding thoughts

For a few years after the 1988 White Paper some commentators referred disparagingly to 'Dawkins universities' when dealing with some of the newer creations. This was an inappropriately selective use of the term for some 31 of the 36 universities in the Unified National System were changed through the amalgamation and renaming process, and all owed their new existence to the processes set in train by John Dawkins. In time, the use of the term died away, save for one or two dedicated critics – Dawkins by now having long since left Parliament. There was still resentment within the system but it was generally agreed that the new system was, on the whole, a success and was here to stay.

The competitive context was not to everyone's taste but it allowed for many winners in many different competitions. Some of the older universities did not perform well in the research game once they were subject to intense competition but, on the whole, the oldest universities had kept their place throughout the quality exercise and the annual ARC and NHMRC grant rounds. Some of the former colleges and institutes of technology had apparently lifted their games quite perceptibly, while some of them, especially those in the regional areas, found building research prowess from a small base a fearful difficulty at a time when every nerve and resource seemed to be needed for basic institution-building. Australia's universities were now very much at the forefront of Australian social life, constantly in the press, highly political though rarely partisan and involved in deals with corporations, foreign governments, the World Bank and other international agencies and community organisations. Research 'breakthroughs' were an almost daily occurrence. A keen observer could notice that virtually all the universities were involved in these activities. Certainly the bigger ones were mentioned more often, but the range of activities covered by the modern university is now so large that no Australian university can be involved in them all. Selectivity, combined with an Australian passion for competition, plus a shared feeling that excellence and achievement are all-important have given each university if not a place in the sun, then a degree of warmth.

As for the University of Canberra, the most obvious conclusion to draw is that it had been a 'university' all along. Once given the title, it made few false starts. Like a good diver it entered the waters of the university system with scarcely a splash. Within the system it was plainly doing well, never at the bottom of any ranking, usually somewhere in the middle, occasionally to the fore. Within its own city, perhaps the most competitive marketplace for higher education in the nation, its relative success was pronounced. Its press and media treatment was consistently positive and, in quantity, not far behind the ANU, which was three times bigger in people and four times bigger in money. A methodologically somewhat shaky comparison of the academic quality of entering students placed the ANU second in Australia out of the 36, but also placed UC ninth. Long-serving UC staff had regained their confidence while newer appointments liked what they saw and made few comparisons with the ANU, which had quite a different mission and certainly had its own problems.

The University of Canberra, in retrospect, weathered its first few years reassuringly well and its success suggested that it would continue to flourish in what is a most uncertain environment for Australian higher education. But more, its success suggests also that the UC model – a university dedicated to preparing people for skilled service in the community and to solving through research the problems experienced by the community which it serves – is a university model thoroughly relevant to contemporary Australia. My own experience suggests that this is the model being adopted overwhelmingly in the developing countries, and that may help to explain why it is that the University of Canberra finds it easy to form good working relationships with universities in Thailand, for example, and to assist these universities in the same task in which we are involved: building a successful, democratic nation.

Appendix

The University of Canberra at a glance

Mission Statement: There is no contemporary mission statement. From 1991 the university has had as its principal concern 'the education of professionals, carried out in a professional way'. In 1996 the need to expand or vary this slogan was under discussion.

Staff: Expressed in terms of 'fulltime equivalents', there were, in 1995, 815 staff – 342 academic staff members and 473 general staff members. If all casual and part-time staff members are counted as staff members, the university has around 1500 staff during term.

Students: In 1995 the university had 8655 students, of whom 63 per cent were full-time. There were more women students than men (55:45) and four undergraduates for every graduate student (80:20). Two-thirds of the students came from the immediate hinterland of the university but there were substantial proportions from other NSW regional districts (13%), Sydney (9%), overseas (8%) and other Australian States (4%). The more than 600 foreign students came from 66 countries. Some 44 per cent of the students were aged between 20 and 24, and another 29 per cent were older than 30. Approximately 1100 lived on campus in university accommodation.

Faculties: Applied Science, Communication, Education, Environmental Design, Information Sciences and Engineering, and Management.

National Outreach: The university is home to a number of national endeavours in higher education, including the Australian Mathematics Trust (which runs the Australian Mathematics Competition, with more than 500,000 entries), the National Science Summer Schools and the National Short Story Competition. It also has a number of centres which conduct research and consultancy activities with a national focus, including the National Centre for Social and Economic Modelling, the Australian Centre for Regional and Local Government Studies, the National Centre for Corporate Law Research and the National Centre for Cultural Heritage Science Studies.

Expenditure: Expenditure in 1995 was A$77 million, of which 57 per cent went to teaching and research, 15 per cent to academic support services, 7 per cent to student services, 6 per cent to buildings and grounds and 15 per cent to administration and overheads.

Chapter 4

Queensland University of Technology

Lawrence Stedman and Peter Coaldrake

The forces that have been, and still are, shaping higher education in Australia are familiar to those working in higher education around the world. Foremost among these forces is the view of higher education as a vital component of national economic development and the consequent transition from an élite system to one which is required to pay heed to national priorities and to educate far larger and more diverse groups of students. Higher education has become more competitive, outwardly focused and international, both in teaching and research. At the same time, governments have expected the higher education sector to follow regimes of greater efficiency and accountability.

In Australia this agenda was realised most dramatically in the latter part of the 1980s with the so-called 'Dawkins revolution', which saw the demise of the binary system of higher education and its replacement by a Unified National System.

This 'revolution' was, in fact, the culmination of several converging developments, occurring both within and outside higher education. The binary system was under increasing strain; as the Colleges of Advanced Education (CAEs) grew in size, accounting for the major part of growth in higher education student numbers over the previous decade, so too did pressures grow for access to research resources and an enhanced status for a broader range of vocational education. Some State governments had already bestowed university status on CAEs, beginning with the formation of the Curtin University of Technology in Western Australia in December 1986. While the Commonwealth government wished to expand the higher education sector for national economic purposes, it was instituting public sector management reforms which required all areas to demonstrate results, achieve efficiencies and operate in a strategic manner. As Charlesworth (1993) put it: '...if (Dawkins) hadn't existed it would probably have been necessary to have invented him.' (p.7).

A key aspect of the establishment of the Unified National System, announced in the Commonwealth government's 1988 White Paper (Dawkins, 1988), was the reformation of 19 universities and 44 Colleges of Advanced Education into 35 (now 37) universities, whose educational profiles[1] were subject to annual negotiation with the Commonwealth Department of Employment, Education and Training. The stated purpose of these amalgamations was to achieve educational benefits in terms of a more comprehensive range of course and program options for students, greater scope for credit transfer, wider career options for staff and an 'enriched research and scholarly environment'. The White Paper also set out to achieve institutional efficiencies by establishing size criteria, expressed as minimum student load benchmarks, for participation in the Unified National System.

The view from Canberra that there were benefits to be derived from institutional amalgamations is, perhaps, not surprising given that following the 1987 election the federal government reorganised its machinery of government to reduce the number of departments from 27 to 16, including the consolidation of the education, employment and workforce training functions into a single Department of Employment, Education and Training. The real reasons for the amalgamations of government departments were complex and derived to a significant degree from political considerations as much as from the publicly stated concerns with co-ordination and administrative efficiency (Wanna, O'Fircheallaigh and Weller 1992). So too the reasons for requiring amalgamations of higher education institutions are likely to be more complex than set out in the government's White Paper, and would include concerns about the inherent potential for duplication in a larger system and the difficulties, given the considerably more direct role played by the federal government in the new Unified National System, of dealing with a group of 63 institutions as opposed to 35.

In any case, the flurry of merger proposals that followed the 1988 White Paper owed more to the desire to survive under the Unified

---

1   The educational profiles were developed as the basis for defining an agreed role and funding arrangement for each university with the Commonwealth. They set out details of strategic plans, including plans in relation to equity, resource management and research, and details of student load targets.

National System than it did to sound educational objectives. Some commentators expressed concerns that the resulting institutions would, under the homogenising influence of the Unified National System, either all seek to become replicas of the older, research-oriented universities, thereby diluting national standards (Karmel 1990; Penington 1990), or that a new binary system would emerge where a few universities would undertake research while the rest would be driven to become predominantly teaching institutions (Lowe 1990). The former view has recently resurfaced in the guise of the self-styled 'Great Eight' group of universities. This group of predominantly older and larger universities has actively promoted the view that the Unified National System has diluted resources for research across all universities. With the rhetorical aim of building institutions of international excellence, it has asserted that research funding should be more selectively targeted.

Many of these concerns about diversity failed to recognise that more was being reformulated than simply institutional structures. The transformation of higher education, continuing at present and for the foreseeable future, involves fundamental changes in the nature of academic work and the relationship between universities and the communities with which they are involved (Higher Education Management Review 1995). The binary system was unsustainable, but not in the sense that the advanced education sector would aspire to emulate the role of the university espoused by the Martin Committee, which recommended the formation of the binary system of higher education in 1965 (Australian Universities Commission 1964/5). Rather, it was inevitable that both sectors would change, evolving under the pressures that have affected the rest of society.

The Queensland University of Technology (QUT) is one of Australia's newest and largest institutions. Its transition to university status and subsequent experience provides a useful case study of the effect of the higher education reforms of the late 1980s and early 1990s.

Formation of QUT

Prior to 1989 the two institutions which became QUT operated under the State Education Act 1964–1987 which governed the activities of all institutes of advanced education in Queensland through the Board of Advanced Education. The Board acted as intermediary between the institutions and the State and Commonwealth governments and exercised considerable control over academic activities within each institution.

During 1988 the Queensland Institute of Technology (QIT) applied to the Queensland State Government to become a university, arguing that the range and depth of its activities warranted this move and that greater autonomy in its operations and more direct dealing with governments was necessary for it to develop properly in the future. A visiting panel drawn from academic, government and professional groups provided advice to the State government and, in January 1989, QIT was formally re-designated the Queensland University of Technology. QIT was one of the five major institutes of technology which had been formed following the report of the Martin Committee in 1965. It had taken over the professional level courses previously provided by the Brisbane Central Technical College and operated from the central-city campus which the college had occupied since 1914.

In late 1988 the Brisbane College of Advanced Education (BCAE) also sought university status in its own right from the Queensland government. Following an assessment by an external panel, this was not granted – principally because its more limited range of offerings did not warrant the creation of a fourth metropolitan Brisbane university. This led, during 1989, to options for the amalgamation of BCAE and QUT being developed.

BCAE had been formed in 1982 during an earlier wave of amalgamations within the advanced education sector. It comprised four campuses which had their origins in colleges of teacher education, although it had since developed significant activity in business education, social sciences and the visual and performing arts. Memoranda of Agreement were signed by QUT and BCAE for the amalgamation of the southern campus at Mt Gravatt, which was situated adjacent to the main campus of Griffith University, to join with Griffith University in August 1989, and in October 1989 for the amalgamation of QUT with the three remaining northern campuses. The Mt Gravatt amalgamation took effect from January 1990, while the QUT amalgamation came into force in May.

The new university retained the name Queensland University of Technology, notwithstanding the inclusion of distinctly non-technological elements from the former BCAE. Over the years the university has developed a national and international reputation under this name, which also serves to remind those within and outside the institution of its practical and applied mission. There are no moves afoot to change it.

The amalgamation process of the newly-designated QUT with the BCAE has been described in detail by the former Deputy Vice-Chancellor (Dixon 1990). In summary, the process was overseen by a Consolidation Implementation Committee (CIC) comprising six members drawn from the two institutions and chaired by the Vice-Chancellor of QUT. The CIC established three working parties, including an Academic Organisational Structure Working Party. This working party chose to adopt an approach based on what was termed 'reflective consultation', whereby extensive consultation took place around a series of questions posed to the university community about principles and possible structures. These consultations generated a considerable response, particularly so when in July 1990 the working party circulated to the university and unions a range of options based on nine or six faculties. Ninety-seven full submissions and 171 letters were received in response, following which an 'eight-faculty' model was developed. A further round of consultation generated 76 submissions and 66 letters. In September a revised eight-faculty model was agreed by the CIC, with some changes to the locations of particular schools, and this model has remained unchanged to the present day.

Reflecting on the process, Dixon (1990) commented:

> the decision to follow an extended process of reflective consultation was wise. In retrospect, the length of the process, January to October, was too great. After a certain time, length adds bitterness without adding wisdom. It is also necessary to make clear the difference between consultation and voting as a method of decision making. A working party must make a decision upon its own estimate of the wisdom of the decision, not upon the number of letters which an active lobby generates, and this fact must be clearly understood (if not universally accepted) within the university community. (p.60)

Notwithstanding these reservations, it is clear that the amalgamation process for QUT contributed to a greater degree of acceptance and institutional identity than might otherwise have been the case. Organisational questions were tackled openly and early: the amalgamation of two institutions amounted to more than simply bringing them side by side. In the case of the Faculty of Education – a major component of the BCAE – areas such as physical education were moved to the new Faculty of Health while arts, drama and music education were moved to the newly-formed Academy of the Arts within the Faculty of Arts. Where feasible, the disciplinary components of secondary teacher education, and some components of primary teacher education, were delivered by teachers in faculties other than Education (Cumming 1994).

One of the principles strongly adhered to was that component parts of the university would not be granted substantial autonomy, in the form of college status or self-governing campuses. The latter point had been a bone of contention within the BCAE since its formation in 1982 and aspirations for autonomy have been a significant source of friction in some of the network universities established in the Unified National System. This principle came to the fore during 1990 when negotiations over the proposed amalgamation of QUT with the Queensland Conservatorium of Music, which occupied a building on the site of QUT's city campus at Gardens Point, reached an impasse with the conservatorium wishing to retain status as a college and the university requiring its amalgamation as a component academic unit on a par with the faculties. It was also a deciding factor in the decision of a working party established by the Queensland government to look at amalgamation options for the Queensland College of Art. Both the conservatorium and the college of art subsequently amalgamated with Griffith University.

Substantial work remained in 1990 and 1991 in integrating the two administrative and support systems across five campuses. By 1992 these had largely been bedded down.

Setting the directions for the new university

QUT began the 1990s with a period of rapid growth. Student load grew in line with national prescriptions: by 10 per cent in 1990 and 4 per cent in 1991 while within the institution substantial work was being done to upgrade the inadequate information technology infrastructure of the university and to upgrade the level of buildings and facilities. A capital development plan was drawn up to address a backlog of A$15–20 million that had been identified in building maintenance and to guide an ambitious program of major capital works on the Gardens Point and Kelvin Grove campuses.

Alongside this growth, the university needed to come to terms with its emergence as a fully-fledged university of considerable size, the sixth largest in Australia, and to develop a shared sense of direction and purpose for its future development. Aware of the emerging quality agenda from Canberra, it embarked on an extensive process of strategic planning.

The CIC Working Party on Mission and Goals reported to Council in May of 1990, at which meeting Council adopted a mission for the new university 'to bring to the community the benefits of learning in technology and the arts'. Three goals were agreed:

- teaching: 'to ensure that QUT graduates possess knowledge, professional competence, a sense of community responsibility, and a capacity to continue their professional and personal development throughout their lives'

- research: 'to advance and apply knowledge germane to the professions and to the communities with which QUT interacts and relevant to the enhancement of economic, cultural and social conditions'

- service: 'to contribute to the development of Australia's international responsibility and competitiveness, to enhance QUT's relationship with the professions, and to increase community awareness of issues through professional service and social commentary'.

In 1991 the mission statement was changed to read 'to bring to the community the benefits of teaching, research, technology and service'.

From the outset QUT has established a distinct niche in Australian higher education. Like many of the other newer universities, it emphasised its role in strategic and applied research and placed considerable weight on teaching as well as on the development of a research profile. The defining characteristics of the university were enunciated by the Vice-Chancellor in the preface to a five-year vision statement for the period 1992–1996:

QUT has a rich history of achievement, strategically located campuses and quality staff who have responded energetically to the challenges of higher education reform. During the next five years QUT will secure its local and international reputation for teaching that prepares beginning professionals for work and research that answers questions relevant to the community.

During 1991 two residential staff retreats were held to develop plans and strategies for the university. The first, in March, was attended by deans and senior executives and the second, in August, by 72 senior and middle-level academic and non-academic managers. A cycle consisting of five-yearly plans and one-yearly action plans for each faculty and division was instigated, shaped by annual planning guidelines issued by the Vice-Chancellor. This system has been progressively refined over the past five years to improve its quality and focus.

Organisation and structure

Following the upheavals of the amalgamation process, the university entered a period of relative stability in terms of its academic and physical structures. This was a deliberate move, designed to test the value of the new structures. The first major organisational changes occurred in 1995 within the Faculty of Business, with a comprehensive restructuring of degree programs at both the undergraduate and postgraduate levels and the transfer of the School of Media and Journalism from Business to the Faculty of Arts.

The central city location of the Gardens Point campus was a prominent feature of the former QIT, while the Kelvin Grove campus of BCAE was also located in the inner metropolitan area (Figure 4.1). Over the next five years it was agreed that the university would close the Kedron Park campus, located approximately six kilometres to the north

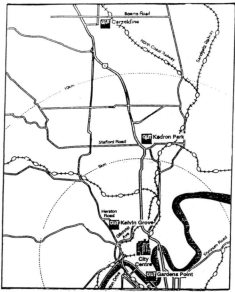

Figure 4.1 Location of QUT campuses
Source: QUT

of the city and divest itself of residual activities on the Sunshine Coast some 100 kilometres to the north. A separate Sunshine Coast University College was developed under the umbrella of QUT, taking in its first students in 1995, with the intention that it would become fully independent in the near future.

The remaining northern campus is at Carseldine, some 14 kilometres to the north of the city. Although relatively small, with around 7 per cent of QUT's student load, this campus is of considerable strategic significance to the university and is well placed to take advantage of the rapid growth in population in Brisbane's northern corridor. Plann- ing has commenced for its development over the rest of the decade.

QUT has, therefore, retained its position as a predominantly inner metropolitan university. While some distance education is offered, this is localised within three faculties and amounts to around 6 per cent of total student load.

Staffing

The new university comprised some 2500 full-time equivalent staff in 1990. The move to university status raised several staffing issues which required early attention. During 1991 Council approved a range of policies for the new university on matters such as professional development programs for academic and general staff, personal appointment for senior lecturers, associate professors and professors, and academic staff development.

A priority in academic staffing was the building of a strong professoriate and the interlocking of professional and management roles. A significant number of new senior academic staff were recruited in the initial years of the university.

The greatest percentage growth in staff numbers has been in those who undertake research activities only, including both academics and research assistants. However, their numbers remain small in absolute terms – the university enshrined its expectations that all academics would undertake both teaching and research activities in its definition of the four areas of achievement against which promotion would be assessed: academic leadership; teaching performance and leadership; research, scholarship and other creative activity; and professional leadership.

Both academic and general tenured staffing has increased by around 20 per cent over the period 1991–1995. However, there has been a notable difference in the growth in casual and limited-term staffing.

Academic casual and limited-term staff comprised just under half of academic full-time equivalent staff in 1991, and their number has remained stable. On the other hand, casual and limited-term general staffing has increased by 74 per cent, around half this increase being due to research-only staff. One consequence of the greater mobility of general staff is that, despite the substantial changes, the age profile of general staff has not changed significantly over the past five years, with an even spread across the different age groups. However, QUT has a steadily ageing academic cohort, with the proportion of academics under the age of 40 falling from 27 per cent in 1991 to 22 per cent in 1995. Early retirement was used sparingly until 1995 (Cumming 1994). Again, the pattern is not uniform across all faculties.

Looking back over the past five years it is clear that staff at QUT have experienced pressures common to academics around Australia, but the transition to university status has not been accompanied by substantial and ongoing dislocation or dissatisfaction with academic roles. The university has not experienced the level of industrial unrest that has occurred on some other campuses. In part, this relative peace may be a legacy of the approach taken to the process of amalgamation; it is also likely to owe something to the fact that QUT was born of two former teaching institutions, thereby avoiding the problems inherent in integrating former advanced education staff into an environment dominated by research-oriented universities (Mahony 1994a). QUT has also made efforts to understand and address the needs of various groups of staff. Most recently, the university established a project to examine the needs of part-time academic staff.

Academic developments

While the former QIT and BCAE received no fixed funds from the Commonwealth government for research, both institutions had been developing research activities throughout the 1980s. The BCAE had five research centres in 1988, while QIT had established ten.

Following amalgamation, the new university quickly set about building up its research profile and structures. The first Research Plan was developed in 1990 and, shortly after amalgamation with BCAE, a Division of Research and Advancement was established to bring together areas responsible for external contact, including the co-ordination and promotion of research. A national presence was rapidly established with QUT increasing its funding from the Australian

Research Council by 112 per cent in 1991, becoming the most successful of the post-1987 universities in attracting such funds.

Encouraged by early growth, the university set a target for itself to be within the top third of research universities by 1996 in terms of attracting competitive research grants. In the event, this target proved overly ambitious and was later set back to 1999. By 1995 QUT was ranked 14th for publications, 16th for grants from industry and other funds, 19th for grants from other public sector funds, 22nd for grants from competitive funds, 22nd for research degree completions and 21st on the overall research composite index. Nevertheless, the rapid growth of QUT's research performance and processes was acknowledged by the 1995 round of quality assessment by the Commonwealth government when QUT received top rating for the 'research management' and 'research improvement' categories.

From 1990 QUT adopted an explicit policy of concentration and selectivity in research, which directed earmarked resources towards selected areas of strength within the university. The most visible aspect of this policy has been the encouragement of progression from research concentrations to school and university research centres and nationally competitive centres. In 1991 QUT listed 25 Research Centres. However, an upper limit of 12 was subsequently set for University Centre status. Since 1990 five research concentrations were upgraded to research centres and three centres were supplanted by others after independent review of performance. PhD students are normally attached to research centres or concentrations, although the Research Management Committee may accredit qualified individuals outside such areas to supervise PhD students. The twelve centres currently in operation are listed in Table 4.1, clearly showing the inheritance of applied research from the former QIT and BCAE and the continuing mission of the university to develop this strategic focus.

The tensions inherent in the introduction of research expectations and research staff into an institution based almost entirely on teaching were identified from the earliest days of the establishment of QUT (Evans *et al.* 1989). However, there was an imperative to build a research infrastructure appropriate for a university while government funding continued to shift away from general operating grants to targeted research and capital support. At the same time, student load grew significantly: over the period 1991–1995 it increased by 21 per cent from 17,040 to 20,713. As a consequence, student-staff ratios increased across the university, albeit not in a uniform manner. It is noteworthy that over the period 1992–1994, student-staff ratios only

Table 4.1 QUT Research Centres in 1996

Australian Centre in Strategic Management (est. 1989)

Centre for Applied Studies in Early Childhood
(est. 1995, formerly a School Centre in the Faculty of Education)

Centre for Eye Research (est. 1988, became a Collaborative Centre in 1991 through the University of New South Wales)

Centre for Instrumental and Developmental Chemistry (est. 1992)

Centre for Mathematics and Science Education (est. 1990)

Centre for Medical and Health Physics (est. 1989)

Centre for Molecular Biotechnology (est. 1989)

Centre for Statistical Science and Industrial Mathematics
(est. 1993)

Cooperative Research Centre for Diagnostic Technologies
(est. 1995)

Information Security Research Centre (est. 1990)

Physical Infrastructure Centre (est. 1990)

Signal Processing Research Centre (est. 1991)

Source: QUT

rose in the newer universities (Curtin, Royal Melbourne Institute of Technology, QUT, Swinburne, the University of South Australia, the University of Technology Sydney and the Victoria University of Technology). The sole exception to this rule was the University of Tasmania. While the reasons for this have not been systematically studied, it is likely that the common need to develop a research profile while taking part in the national expansion of student numbers was a significant factor.

The perceived higher status of research over teaching has been acknowledged in Australia and overseas. Deliberate efforts were made by the university to accord teaching an equivalent standing to research in the course of building up the research profile. A Division of Academic Affairs was established alongside the Division of Research and Advancement and internal grants programs for teaching development were provided in parallel with internal grants for research.

Building on its historical legacy, QUT's approach to education has remained strongly vocationally oriented. Employers and professional bodies are closely involved in course planning through Faculty Advisory Committees and also in lecturing.

The new university moved quickly to establish postgraduate courses and to upgrade undergraduate education in nursing and teacher education to three-year degree level, replacing the former diplomas. The range of postgraduate courses has grown to encompass both coursework and research offerings – the former representing a major area of growth over the past five years, rising from 13 per cent of enrolments in 1991 to 16.2 per cent in 1995. Growth in research enrolments has also been significant, but only in line with the capacity of the university to provide adequate supervision and facilities. In 1995 higher-degree research enrolments accounted for 2.9 per cent of total enrolments, with slightly over half of these being doctoral students.

There has been some concern that the proliferation of units and courses, particularly at the postgraduate coursework level, has outpaced acceptable levels of demand, despite agreement by the university at the beginning of the decade that it would seek to rationalise the number of courses and units on offer. The initial distribution of academic activities undertaken by the CIC Working Party provided for a substantial amount of service teaching, where discipline-based subjects comprising part of a course in one faculty would be taught by specialist staff in another. This situation has been under pressure due to concerns within some faculties about the quality of teaching undertaken outside, and as a result of the general expansion of activities. In all but one of the faculties the proportion of unit load taught outside the faculty has steadily diminished. The situation has become of greater concern to the university as resources grow ever more tight and is being closely monitored.

QUT also moved early to embrace strategic development and quality assurance in relation to its teaching efforts. This was reflected in it being the first Australian university to promulgate a teaching and learning development strategy and to commission an independent academic audit of its undergraduate and postgraduate teaching and supervision. Its standing in relation to teaching has been recognised in being ranked in the top band in the Commonwealth Government's 1994 round of quality assessment and in the designation of QUT as the inaugural 'Australian University of the Year' in 1993 by the *Good Universities Guide* (Ashenden and Milligan 1993). The university has consistently recorded the highest number of first preferences for first degrees in the

State of Queensland and by 1995 it was the fourth largest university in Australia in terms of undergraduate student load and fifth largest in overall load.

Like most other universities, the student population of QUT has become greatly more diverse. In large part this is due to the rapid expansion in the population of fee-paying overseas students. This group increased from around 500 enrolments in 1990 to over 1400 by 1995, making QUT the seventh largest provider of higher education to overseas students in Australia. The university is one of the two or three largest Australian providers to Singapore. The bulk of this growth has occurred in the business and technology fields of the university, increasing the ethnic diversity of the student body considerably in the faculties of Business, Built Environment & Engineering, and Information Technology. In the latter faculty, overseas student enrolments have grown from 3 per cent of the total in 1989 to over 14 per cent in 1995. Students born in Asia or the Middle East accounted for less than 6 per cent of the student population in 1991, but 27 per cent of the growth in student numbers since that time. Now, one in four students at QUT were born overseas.

The proportion of female students has risen steadily from 50 per cent in 1990 to 54 per cent in 1995. Growth in the proportion of female staff, both academic and general, has been modest but steady – 55 per cent of QUT's general staff are women and 40 per cent of academic staff.

Conclusion

Studies that have been undertaken of individual institutions in the period since the inception of the Unified National System (Bradley 1993; Mahony 1995) confirm the view that 'individual university futures will be determined by their institutional legacies, their declared missions and the impact of a range of external stimuli' (Mahony 1994b, p.311). This is certainly true of QUT.

In many respects the Queensland University of Technology is a model of what was intended for the Unified National System. Two comparable former teaching institutions amalgamated successfully and logically, building on former strengths to establish a new type of university, not a replica of the pre-1987 universities. QUT has fostered a more diverse student population and actively pursued the development of high-quality vocationally-relevant education at the undergraduate degree and postgraduate level. It has maintained a policy of selectivity and concentration in its development of a research profile. The university has embraced the national and international quality agenda and has developed comprehensive strategic planning processes across the range of its activities.

Many of the pitfalls encountered by other institutions after amalgamation were avoided by resolving organisational questions at an early stage, allowing the building of a coherent vision for the university and by supporting the various faculties across the various campuses.

The institution was quick to adopt the structures, processes and research profile of a university and to move on from its past in the advanced education sector; in the course of examining internal structures, the term 'college' was considered but discarded on the grounds that it was de-valued by the recent ending of the binary system (Dixon 1990). Nevertheless, the new university has been heavily influenced by its earlier incarnation, not least in its research activities and in the substantial ongoing cohort of academic and general staff who have stayed with the institution from the previous decade.

Significant challenges remain in the years ahead for QUT. The most obvious and immediate is the prospect of needing to adjust to even tighter restraint in Commonwealth funding. Such restraint has, to date, been more gradual in Australia than many other countries and has chiefly consisted of shifts in funding mix rather than overall levels of support. However, the response to financial imperatives encompasses several issues of longer-term significance for the university.

While QUT remains popular with domestic students, it is well-positioned to benefit from possible future increases in student contributions to financing their study. However, in an institution the size of QUT it is inevitable that there is a range in the quality of courses and services. The university is faced with the task of maintaining or improving the accessibility, relevance and attractiveness of all its offerings while also improving academic standards. To some, this task appears to be a reconciliation of opposites. Its resolution poses challenges to traditional conceptions of the relationships between students, academics and the professions, and for the internal culture and management of the university.

In the case of overseas students, significant contributors to QUT's non-government income, significant challenges will also be posed to the university by greater competition and the prospect of future changes, particularly in the South-East Asian region as some countries aspire to become more self-sufficient in their provision of higher education.

The Commonwealth government has signalled that it will be paying greater attention, and providing more resources, to the vocational education and training sector. The boundaries between this sector and higher education are already overlapping and indistinct. The end of the binary system of universities and CAEs reflected the inexorable movement of education for a wide range of vocations into the university arena, including nursing, teacher education, engineering and business. Professional status and 'qualification creep' in the workplace will continue to push the sectors closer together. QUT, with its strong vocational mission and history, will need both to identify areas of common interest with the broader vocational education and training sector and to differentiate itself as a provider of higher education and relevant research.

QUT must also face a number of issues as it builds its research profile over the coming years, particularly in the areas of science and technology. Key among these is the need to match expanded activity and grant income with suitable infrastructure in the form of equipment, facilities and information technology support.

The emerging promise of information technology raises similar issues of the balance between new activity and providing proper infrastructure. Expectations and demands from students and staff for the services of computer networks which provide on- and off-campus access to e-mail, the Internet, information service and teaching and research resources, are growing rapidly and beyond the capacity of the university to provide from its own resources.

The growth of both research and information technology has implications for the future of teaching. In part, this is a matter of ensuring a suitable balance of resources, but, more importantly, QUT also needs to tackle the developing agenda of flexibility in teaching and, in particular, the rapidly-growing promise of information technology applications. The latter is a field where QUT has established an initial reputation in computer-based education, provided on closed networks on campus or through stand-alone packages. These developments will require not only additional resources, at least in the short term, but also have broader implications for the future of QUT as a provider of vocational education and life-long learning in an inner metropolitan context.

Finally, the next decade will see the retirement of an increasing number of the cohort of academic staff who began in the former QIT and BCAE. As they are replaced by people from other universities, other States and other countries, QUT will inevitably be transformed.

It is too early to predict with confidence how all these factors will change the university. What is certain is that QUT has emerged from the dissolution of the binary system as a fully-fledged university, uniquely shaped by its grounding in the advanced education sector. This ground has been seeded by a steady influx of new people with new interests and from different backgrounds. The future growth of the university will depend on the interplay between these conditions and an external environment which is complex and constantly changing. The evolving university will undoubtedly share many characteristics in common with other institutions and will just as certainly be different in other respects. What is more important is that it must achieve excellence, both in research and teaching, and that it must meet the needs of the communities it will serve.

Appendix

Queensland University of Technology at a glance

Mission statement: The mission of QUT is to bring to the community the benefits of teaching, research, technology and service.

Structure: QUT has three campuses, all within the Brisbane metropolitan region. The largest is in the city central business district, while the Kelvin Grove campus is located 2.5 kilometres from the city centre and the Carseldine Campus at the northern urban outskirts, some 14 kilometres from the city centre.

Staff: In 1995 QUT employed 3100 equivalent full-time staff, of whom 41 per cent were academic staff. Twenty-five per cent of academic staff were employed on a casual basis. Of the 1834 general staff, 9 per cent were casual. Forty per cent of QUT academic staff and 65 per cent of general staff were female.

Students: In 1995 QUT enrolled a total of 27,097 students, of whom 59 per cent were full-time. Nineteen per cent were postgraduate students and 54 per cent of all students were female. Sixty-nine per cent of students were drawn from the immediate area of Brisbane, with a further 23 per cent coming from elsewhere in Queensland. Some 7 per cent of students enrolled under distance education programs. The university does not provide on-campus accommodation but does provide assistance to overseas students to secure appropriate accommodation. The number of overseas students studying at QUT has been rising rapidly, to 1510 in 1995. Thirty-four per cent of students were aged between 20 and 24, with another 23 per cent aged over 30.

Faculties: There are eight faculties: Arts, Built Environment & Engineering, Business, Education, Health, Information Technology. Law and Science.

Expenditure: Total expenditure in 1995 was A$256.7 million, of which 58 per cent was directed to teaching, research and service, 12 per cent to academic support services, 7 per cent to student services (the library and other information services being included as academic support), 12 per cent to the building and maintenance program, and 11 per cent to administration.

Part III

Britain

Chapter 5

The Reform of Higher Education in Britain

Ronald Barnett and Svava Bjarnason

For some thirty years, since its inception in the mid-1960s, the higher education policy of successive UK governments was built upon a binary system, essentially of universities and polytechnics. (Polytechnics as such were confined to England, Wales and Northern Ireland but comparable non-university institutions existed in Scotland.) Throughout much of that time the Directors of Polytechnics had pleaded a case that polytechnics should be renamed universities. Many of their institutions, after all, so grew in size that they came to rival and to surpass universities in the number of undergraduates enrolled on first-degree courses. And although the funding system for supporting research was unhelpful, most had established a significant research capability. Governments, however, implacably resisted those overtures from the polytechnic directors, seeing in the binary system the basis of their higher education policy.

Suddenly, at the beginning of the 1990s, that 30-year-long policy approach was overturned. A White Paper, *Higher Education: A New Framework* (DES 1991), proposed that polytechnics could take on the title 'University' within a new 'unified' system of higher education. Within a year the UK possessed around 100 universities; polytechnics and their like disappeared from the higher education landscape (see Appendix 5.2 for detail). How might we account for such a complete and dramatic policy reversal?

In what follows, rather than taking a strictly chronological approach (which can be found in Appendix 5.1), we shall develop our account under a number of themes. The story of the change in national policy over higher education is a complex of stories – these include the emergence of a mass higher education system, changing conceptions of the welfare state and the development of a quasi-market in higher education, the insertion of higher education more into the national economy and changing notions of what it is to know the world and of the relationship between higher education and the world of work. By themselves, none of these elements would have produced the apparently sudden and dramatic policy shift, in which the binary system was replaced by a so-called unified system. Together, however, they presented a situation in which that change was simply its inexorable logic.

The arrival of mass higher education

The arrival of mass higher education in the UK has two components. The first is that of size – or, to be more accurate, the composition of the higher education system. The second is that of its character, its substance and its texture. Inevitably, there are connections between the two issues.

On the size of the system, it has to be recognised that the UK system of higher education has undergone dramatic growth. From an age-participation rate of 12 per cent in 1979 and 19 per cent in 1991, it reached 30 per cent by 1993 (see Appendix 5.3 for detail). This rapid growth, by itself, was bound to exacerbate tensions already present in the binary system. In a small system tensions might be containable, but the sheer growth in the two systems were bound to exacerbate the disturbance in the system (see Appendices 5.4 and 5.5 for growth in student numbers). The administrative burden of trying to manage two sectors of higher education, supposedly separate but equal, with different financial structures and different quality arrangements was going to be difficult to sustain. However, the associated task for the state of trying to preserve distinctive but complementary missions between the two sectors, was bound to prove impossible to fulfil as, over time, the two sectors increasingly overlapped in their course profiles, student intakes and research interests. All of these tendencies were reinforced through the transformation of the relative sizes of the two sectors, with the public sector (containing the polytechnics and other colleges) being encouraged to grow so rapidly that – during the period in question here – it overtook the university sector in sheer size. The proportions of the sub-groups were also significant, with the universities retaining by far the larger proportion of postgraduates and the polytechnics continuing to enrol the overwhelming proportion of undergraduates and below-degree level students.[1]

Behind these points stands a separate issue of the relationship of the state to higher education. The period in question is one of conflicting stories. On the one hand we have witnessed attempts by the government to promote more of a market in higher education, giving the students a significant share in the funding of higher education. On the other hand, through a series of administrative devices – reducing the power of the local education authorities (LEAs) over the public sector, abolishing the funding structures and instituting new national bodies[2] directly accountable to the Secretary of State both for funding and for quality control – the state took on an increasingly *dirigiste* stance in relation to higher education.

With the arrival of mass higher education, this more interventionist stance became more overt. Indeed, the arrival of mass higher education in the UK was not happenchance but was itself an explicitly intended part of government policy. We shall say more about this in a moment, but, here the point is that the government, having ushered in a startling growth in the size of the system[3], was bound to want to ensure, so far as it was able, that the new system was responsive in the ways envisaged for it. The key issue before us is that of the sudden change in policy on the part of the state in abandoning its binary policy. The point here is that the arrival of the mass higher education, as a result of state policy,

1   Numbers of students enrolled in England in 1991 were:
     first-degree students: polytechnics 307,000
                            universities 237,000
     postgraduates: polytechnics 50,000
                            universities 100,000
     below-degree level: polytechnic 254,000
                            universities 10,000
2   The formation of these bodies is discussed in more detail in the section 'Quality and Standards'.
3   The White Paper, *Higher Education: Meeting the Challenge* (DES 1987), envisaged a rise in the age-participation index of 18–19 years olds entering higher education from 14 per cent in 1985 to 18.5 per cent by the year 2000. This was subsequently revised upward in the 1991 White Paper to 20.5 per cent. The actual figures grew to over 30 per cent participation by 1993 (CVCP 1995b).

created problems of state management and steerage which the binary system, with its separate structures and separate sector missions, exacerbated.

Against this line of argument it may be suggested that the comparative evidence is entirely the other way. Unified systems are the exception rather than the rule. Australia and the UK possessed binary systems and then abandoned them, but, more commonly, governments (such as in the USA, France, the Netherlands, Switzerland, Germany and Scandinavia) have sought to sustain binary systems or to develop other forms of differentiation within a mass system of higher education. This is so, but our argument is that in the UK the State has played a particular role in driving through a process of transforming higher education, a role in which a unified system becomes both a policy and a political imperative.

The logic that we are pointing to which led to the abandonment of the binary policy in the UK was a logic that derived precisely from the exceptional part being played by the State in the shaping of the newly-emerging mass higher education system (Salter and Tapper 1994). The suddenness of the emergence of the mass higher education system was a State policy with the agenda of supporting the repositioning of the economy in global markets. The logic that we are describing here was a logic characteristic of the particular combination of factors in the UK. That it is unusual in no way undermines the use of the term 'logic' in this case: this was a social and political logic borne of the UK situation in which the State saw in higher education a vehicle for assisting its wider plans for the reshaping of the UK economy and its human capital.

We said earlier that there were two sets of features of the UK mass higher education at work in the changing State policy: those of size and composition, and those of its character, substance and texture. Having said something about the former aspects, we now turn to the latter sets of issues.

Changing conceptions of higher education

The sense of 'changing' in the sub-heading is ambiguous. Conceptions of higher education have been changing. They have been changing in any case as a result of the arrival of mass higher education, but they are also being changed deliberately as a matter of State policy.

These changes are occurring at a number of levels. In a mass higher education system what it means to be a student changes as a result of falling staff-student ratios[4] and reduced State resources flowing to the students[5] (see also Appendix 5.6). Those developments, in turn, are taking place amidst changes in the global economy such that the labour market is more volatile and further training is needed very often even to secure an entry into a career pathway. In a mass higher education system, too, the economic value of a degree is likely to fall as more graduates seek employment and turn increasingly to what have hitherto been non-graduate forms of employment. All these factors act on the total system, although admittedly affecting institutions differently. (An honours degree at an élite university still retains both extra economic and cultural capital.) Accordingly, what it is to be a student takes on new dimensions across the system as a whole.

These factors are largely unintended consequences of features of the external environment. To these have to be added intended consequences of government action. In the UK, perhaps more than in any other country, the State has been active in attempting to modify the nature of the higher education that students receive. Both indirect and direct approaches have been followed in fulfilment of two sets of aims: shifting the curriculum more in the direction of skills for the labour market and in reducing the power of the academics as producers.

Indirect approaches have included the establishment of national quality evaluation mechanisms which, as well as looking at course quality as such, have introduced into their agendas talk of 'transferable skills'. Such generic skills, straddling all courses, are not yet required but they are liable to be pursued in depth wherever a university claims to be developing them. Another indirect strategy has been to give institutions encouragement in introducing modular systems, especially those which offer students credit. In this way, in theory at least, students can be more mobile, not only across but within institutions, thereby reducing the power of the academics, who no longer can count on a captive audience.

4   In the university sector the SSR was 9.3 in 1979/80 and 10.7 in 1992/3; the polytechnic SSR over the same period was 8.1 in 1979/80 and 12.9 in the early 1990s.
5   Public funding has fallen 25 per cent per student between 1989/90 and 1994/95. In England full-time student numbers increased by 61 per cent over that period, while funding per full-time student fell by 25 per cent in real terms over the same period (CVCP 1995b).

Direct measures on the part of the State have also been introduced. The Enterprise in Higher Education (EHE) initiative was launched in 1987. This has been a system-wide government initiative sponsored by the (former) Department of Employment in which institutions have been encouraged to work with employers to develop 'enterprising' proclivities among their students. Grants have been made available for whole-institutional strategies involving the drawing-in of employers and staff development programmes. A feature of its development has become the attention given to the acquisition on the part of students of transferable skills. Around 56 projects (34 in former polytechnic institutions and 20 in universities) have been funded over a six-year period.

No substantive evaluation has been conducted of the impact on the dispositions being developed among students through the initiative, but the point here is that it is a system-wide initiative – the funded projects being distributed evenly across the total sector. In other words, the State makes no overt distinction between institutions so far as its expectations of teaching outcomes are concerned. The higher education system is a system: the State is increasingly looking to every institution of higher education to produce graduates with common sets of skills for the labour market. If there is no divisibility in its expectations of different institutions in this respect, then again the case for a divided system of higher education weakens.

The significance of this initiative for our story should not be underestimated. Implicitly, the binary system of UK higher education was founded in the 1960s precisely on such a distinction. In establishing the polytechnics, the universities were chided by the then government for being insufficiently 'responsive'. As well as their other key quality of providing opportunities for access to higher education and so widening the latent demand for higher education, polytechnics were to provide 'vocational' education – so leaving universities implicitly to focus on their more theoretical and non-worldly offerings.

It is tempting to read the abolition of the binary system as a recognition of the failure of the educational apartheid which was embedded within it. That is to say, through a process of academic drift, polytechnics came more and more to resemble universities in their educational missions. A more telling reading, however, is that the policy has been abandoned because it was no longer appropriate for a higher education system now being reoriented by the State towards a global economy. In the global economy there are no hiding places.

Accordingly, the skills to be imparted by a higher education have to be universal across the sector. The cross-sector operation of the Enterprise in Higher Education initiative is, therefore, a nice indication that the days of the binary system had to be numbered. There can be no educational apartheid in the higher education system of the current age; *all* institutions of higher education have to be seen to be making their contribution to the realignment of the UK economy.

But the point, of course, has a further twist to it. Since the polytechnics had manifestly been falling in with that mission since their inception, and since the overwhelming proportion of their courses had an overt orientation towards the world of work, the abandonment of the binary system has to be seen as an injunction on the universities to continue to adapt their offerings along the lines of the polytechnics. The reading that opens, therefore, both of the Enterprise in Higher Education initiative on the one hand and of the abandonment of the binary system and of permitting the polytechnics to take the title 'university' on the other hand, is not that the polytechnics were becoming universities but that universities were becoming like polytechnics, and were being encouraged to be so.

Quality and standards

That in the abandonment of the binary system the universities were being enjoined to become more like the polytechnics, is given further support in the matter of quality. The Council for National Academic Awards (CNAA) had been a feature of the public sector – or polytechnic – side of the binary divide almost since its inception. It was a recommendation of the Robbins Committee[6] that the CNAA be established, and it had, in fact, predated the binary policy as such by two years. Robbins had seen the CNAA purely as a short-term measure to enable the regional colleges, as they were called, to bring them to the point where they could join the university club. But its presence was integral to the idea that the polytechnics should form a sector of higher education different, but equal in standard and status, to the universities. The CNAA – not the polytechnics – possessed the powers to award degrees to students taking degree courses at polytechnics (and other

---

6 The Committee of Inquiry into Higher Education under the Chairmanship of Lord Robbins was set up in 1961 to review the pattern of higher education in Great Britain. See Appendix 5.1 for more detail.

colleges of higher education). And, in order to satisfy itself that the standards of course provision at polytechnics and other colleges were appropriate, it developed an elaborate set of systems of review and validation both of individual courses and of institutions. But with the growth of that sector, with the arrival of mass higher education, system-wide problems of State steerage opened up. The binary policy was needed no more; nor was the CNAA, which was accordingly disbanded in 1992.

By the mid-1980s, therefore, the public sector of UK higher education had long been accustomed to external evaluation of its work and it was surely inevitable that in its restructuring of the higher education system the State would look to see some form of evaluation extended across the university sector. The Committee of Vice-Chancellors and Principals (CVCP), sensing that such moves were on the way, attempted to head them off by establishing its own Academic Audit Unit in 1990. Rather than looking at courses as such, this Unit sought to satisfy itself as to the rigour of universities' quality assurance systems. The strategy to establish a system of quality evaluation under the control of the universities failed on two counts, both as a result of the Further and Higher Education Act of 1992.

First, under the Act, a new national body was established – the Higher Education Quality Council (HEQC) – to audit the quality assurance arrangements of every institution of higher education. *Prima facie*, the establishment of this council could be read as an endorsement of the work of the Academic Audit Unit, which it now subsumed. The council has a board of directors appointed by the Committee of Vice-Chancellors and Principals and other representative bodies of institutions of higher education and its members are drawn entirely from universities and other institutions. However, the council has a basis in statute and formal responsibilities to advise the Secretary of State for Education on particular matters (such as on applications from institutions seeking degree-awarding powers), and the Secretary of State is increasingly looking to the HEQC to assist the government in assuring and in improving standards in higher education.

Accordingly, although the control of HEQC lies *de jure* with the academic community, *de facto*, the State is coming to play an increasingly influential role in shaping the agenda to which the HEQC works. In other words, the establishment of the HEQC could be seen as the academic community maintaining control over its own affairs, but, in reality, has come to reflect the advance of 'the evaluative state' in UK higher education (Neave 1990). The HEQC is a nice example, as we might put it, of *negotiated surveillance*, in which a professional community and the state form a working set of practices which do some justice to their respective agendas (of autonomy and of 'accountability').

The other way in which the 1992 Act represents a rebuttal of the intentions behind the formation of the Academic Audit Unit is that it heralded also the establishment of new bodies (Funding Councils for England, Scotland and Wales), each of which possessed a quality function. There have been differences in their detailed operation but each Funding Council has developed a review methodology which assesses the quality of courses as such and, in doing so, assembles teams – often led by non-academics – which directly inspect teaching practices. External evaluation, directly accountable to the Secretary of State, now finds an *entrée* into the hitherto intimacy of teacher-taught interactions.

For our purposes, the point of this excursion into the current quality arrangements is clear and simple. The whole system of higher education is now subject to a common quality evaluation framework. Old or new, large or small, specialist or multi-faculty, liberal or vocational, there is no hiding place for any institution. Every institution of higher education falls under the same arrangements. These arrangements stem from an evolving policy agenda on the part of the State overtly to ensure 'value for money'. But that phrase contains more hidden agendas, for what is to felt to constitute 'value'? The answer has to be placed in the context of the realignment of and the deliberate expansion of UK higher education in support of a more vibrant and changing economy competing in world markets and at a time of an intended reduction in State expenditure on public services. The sudden appearance of a massive and State-driven evaluation system has to be located in such wider considerations. Admittedly, the tensions produced by having two parallel sets of quality arrangements – HEQC's and those of the Funding Councils – are such that a new unified body is now being formed. But the emergence of such a single, and, therefore, powerful, agency is further testimony to the development of a single system of higher education, all of which is to fall under a common policy agenda in which the State now becomes clearly the dominant player.

Given that every institution of higher education will have to fall within that policy framework (the new quality arrangements being just one instrument to deliver that policy agenda), again there is no reason to have a difference in nomenclature between the major institutions. It

re, entirely logical that the 1992 Act, in developing the new
ality evaluation arrangements, should also move to allow
ιics to take the title 'university'. The possession of a single
name (now 'university') to embrace all the larger institutions of higher
education reinforced the sense that every institution was operating
according to the same policy agenda as did the formation of a single set
of quality arrangements.

The idea of a university

The real question before us is not 'why was the binary system of UK
higher education abandoned?' nor even 'why were polytechnics allowed
to call themselves universities?' but rather 'why were universities not
required to call themselves polytechnics?'

Universities embody clusters of ideas. In the Western tradition there
is at work a value background which informs our idea of a university.
Certainly, there are spurious claimants to the title: private agencies call
themselves 'universities' which clearly do not live up to the promise of
the title but their doing so underscores the point. In calling themselves
universities they are doffing their cap to the symbolic weight and
promise that attaches to the title. Certainly, too, in a mass higher
education system there will be many legitimate interpretations of the
term; what counts as a university can justifiably take on different hues,
shapes and patterns. But it is not a case of 'anything goes'. There
remains, stubbornly, a core of ideas that provide a horizon of meaning
within which institutions can work out their separate missions.

The value background of 'the university', the constellation of ideas
that generates our expectations of institutions bearing the title, would
include notions such as: that there should be an institutional
separateness ('academic autonomy') to allow the university space in
which to develop and advocate ideas; that truth matters (even if there
are different interpretations of truth); that universities should bring
about the highest forms of human learning in which students come to
have their own, but self-critical, hold on their own ideas and their
expression; that conceptual schemas can help us in understanding the
world and that universities, through their world-wide networking, are
invaluable in advancing and in imparting such conceptual schemas; that
ethical qualities – such as respect for persons, integrity, honesty and
sensitivity to others in communicating seriously with them – attach to

the pursuit of truth; and that the more senior members of a university ('lecturers') should have significant measures of freedom in admitting students and in determining the character of the educational experiences put their way.

This may be thought to be straightforward or, alternatively, an overly narrow and traditional sense of a university. But it will be noticed in that suggested constellation of ideas behind the Western university that there is no mention of research or teaching but there is mention of learning. In other words, universities are genuinely learning communities. This conception of the Western university allows for many kinds of interpretation in which, doubtless, terms such as teaching and research might well play a part. The idea of the university is not given in any tight sense and is and always has been negotiable.

The question for us here, against those reflections, is how we might construe the changes in nomenclature in UK higher education which have accompanied the abandonment of the binary policy. To repeat the earlier question: instead of permitting the polytechnics to title themselves universities, would it also have made some kind of sense to require the universities to be named polytechnics? Or, to put the question another way, what, if anything, is to count as a university in a mass system of higher education?

The argument here has been that, through a combination of funding, quality and structural arrangements, a unified system of higher education – at least, on the surface – was engineered in the UK by the government over the period in question in this book. The engineered similarities went deeper than superstructural issues of finance and accountability measures. Commonality was engineered in the deeper character of universities. Changes in structure and process have changed the character of academic work so that any earlier sharp divisions between polytechnics and universities were dissolved. The significant changes, however, were just as much a matter of universities taking on the character of polytechnics as it was polytechnics taking on the character of universities. If the 1970s were characterised by fears of academic drift, the 1990s should be more properly characterised as a time of steerage in the direction of the world of work accompanied by external surveillance – a dual orientation with which the polytechnics had long been identified. At the same time, other characteristics of a mass higher education system with which the polytechnics had been identified were also enjoined on the universities. The changes were of two kinds: of academic labour and of its epistemologies.

The ending of academic tenure[7] was, at one level, significant but was, in reality, only a symptom of the deeper changes in the character of academic labour that were being effected as the total higher education system in the UK was brought round towards playing its full part in economic regeneration. The more substantial strand in these changes was a reduction in the power of the academics as producers, a greater voice being given both to the world of work and to students as 'consumers'. Three other elements were significant. First, that academics now have to be entrepreneurs, generating income directly through their knowledge services ('consultancies'). Second, that universities have become organisations – notwithstanding that the corporate world has seen the development of flat management structures, universities have moved in the other direction, attempting tightly to organise their academic labour through internal mechanisms of accounting for work performed, tighter financial controls (for example over external earnings) and the introduction of modular systems of course design, so making the teaching function more transparent and more susceptible of managerial control. Third, to the external quality control systems we noted earlier, most universities have now added their own internal quality assurance mechanisms.

All of this spells a reduction in the autonomy of the academics. Halsey (1992) has described these developments as the 'decline of donnish dominion' and has suggested that we are witnessing a process of 'proletarianisation'. In less value-laden terms we can talk not just of a change in the nature of academic labour but, indeed, of the emergence of academic labour as such. No longer are the conditions of work almost entirely framed by the academics themselves, rather they are now significantly circumscribed by others, including the university's management team, the State, the students as consumers and the world of work.

The point here is that, again, these features are common in that they bear on the whole system of UK higher education. Certainly, their significance varies both across institutions and across subjects. Pure subjects – physics or history – in élite institutions fare differently from more work-oriented fields in the newer universities. But the emergence

7   Under the 1988 Education Reform Act no new tenured appointments can be made. Academics already in post retain their tenure only so long as they do not move to another university or accept promotion within their present university (Mackinnon and Statham (1995)).

of academic labour is a feature of the system as a whole. Again, too, this development isn't happenchance. It has been deliberately orchestrated so as to reduce the power of the academics. And, if this was an undeclared policy, it made sense to have the polytechnics named 'universities'. The existing universities could not then say, with a straight face, that these developments were fitting for those other institutions but were inappropriate for us, the universities.

Knowledge within the university

The other shift of note affecting the whole system is the change in the social epistemology of the academic world. By 'social epistemology' we mean the underlying conceptions of knowledge that frame the academic life. As higher education has been exposed to the wider world, especially the world of work, so its epistemologies have widened. Theories of knowledge are social in character: they are socially sustained and perform social functions. The theories of knowledge that the academic class took unto itself emphasised its separateness from the world. Both the correspondence theory of truth (as propositions which correspond to an external world) and the coherence theory of truth (as propositions which hang together in a meaningful way) gave a privileged position to the knower and to her separateness from the world. Now, we are seeing a range of epistemologies which tie in the knower to the world and, indeed, deny that there is a separateness in the knowing act. Three versions of this knowledge-in-the-world are now to be seen in academic life.

First, knowledge is now understood to be created in the world. This so-called Mode 2 knowledge is precisely that: not pure discipline-based and propositional knowledge (Mode 1) or even applied knowledge but knowledge created immediately in the world in response to problems in the world (Gibbons *et al.* 1994). The problems are practical and not theoretical in character. The interest behind the knowledge takes on a pragmatic edge. This is interdisciplinary and team-based, but it is essentially practical. Second, and related, is the notion of reflective practice (Schön 1987). It is different from our first category in that this knowing is captured in action itself. Certainly, to count as knowing, the act has to be complex, typically that of professional life, but the knowledge is embedded in the action itself. And it is refined through 'reflection-in-action', by the person concerned, rather than through a concerted and organised attack on identified problems. Third, there is a sense, too, that personal knowledge, experiential knowledge, tacit knowledge and what might be termed emotional knowledge are crucial, especially in certain professions – such as the caring and health professions – but are of value more generally in the world of work. The crucial point about these forms of knowing is that they are irredeemably tacit and cannot be made explicit and become the focus for formal interrogation. But they are real enough for all that. People can simply come to know how to do things and handle themselves in situations with very little of it being available for systematic reflection.

Academic epistemologies, then, are taking a pragmatic and action-based turn. It may be said that the former polytechnics were always in this knowledge game, that many of the older universities had also been sensitive to these ways of knowing (both through their interest in preparing for the élite professions and through the 'sandwich' courses put on in engineering and other courses oriented towards the industrial and manufacturing world). Equally, in many institutions of higher education there had been imaginative efforts – for example through study service – to broaden the exposure of students to different experiences and to enable them to 'know' the world in a wider array of ways (Goodlad and Hirst 1989). That may be true to some extent, although many of those experiences were impregnated by academic notions of applying propositional knowledge to the world rather than experiencing it in a more unmediated way. But the point is that these three ways of knowing the world pragmatically are now finding their way into the curriculum such that the pure disciplines of the academic world are having a hard time in maintaining their hegemonic position.

Fields of study built around Mode 2 knowledge in the world (business studies, tourism studies, transport studies), new methods for learning, included supervised work experience which is now assessed in some detail – the students being required to keep logs or diaries of their practical experiences, role play, presentations by students and profiles of their achievements over a range of non-propositional forms of experiencing the world: all these and many others are testimony to the way in which knowing the world is now much more complicated than it was. Again, while there are differences across subjects and across institutions – with the newer universities being more ready to take on these wider forms of knowing through their more intimate insertion into the world of work – the whole of the UK system of higher education is being expected to move in this direction. Again, therefore, a binary

policy makes no sense if major – essentially cultural – cʲ
kind are sought from the whole system.

Back to differentiation

We have been arguing that the logic of the situation presenting the then
government in the 1980s was such as to make inevitable the
abandonment of the UK binary policy. Higher education came to be
seen, especially amidst unflattering international comparisons, as a
significant feature of the transformation of the UK economy. A labour
force which was highly skilled, adaptable and able to go on developing
itself had itself to be highly educated. To produce such an end, certain
changes were required to and in higher education. These changes
included a massive increase in participation rates, a curriculum more
oriented towards the world of work, a significant diminution in the
autonomy of the academics, an epistemology more rooted in the world
of action rather than contemplative knowing, a separation of research
from teaching (since all students needed to be taught but, arguably, not
all students needed to taught in a context of high-level research),
external evaluation of the quality of higher education (to ensure, in a
hard-pressed welfare State, 'value for money') and tighter internal
managerial controls over the considerable resources of institutions.
These were all system-wide desiderata and, therefore, there needed to
be a 'unified' system to which these policies should apply. The binary
system, accordingly, while an understandable policy development in
the 1960s as an attempt to end the hegemony of the universities, was
now past its sell-by date and had to be abandoned.

However, the sought-after unified system has not yet fully arrived –
and nor will it. In a mass higher education system recruiting over 30 per
cent of the population there will inevitably be significant differences
between institutions. There remain not just vertical differences of kind
(institutions having different 'missions') but differences of actual and
perceived value. The amount and kind of research, the intensity and
reputation of the scholarship, the extent to which institutions have an
international orientation, the insertion of a university in its regional
economy, the student profile of each institution (not only in students'
ages but in their values, expectations and economic independence), the
economic independence of each university and the mix and character of
the courses offered: all these are, and are likely to be, enduring features
of diversity in the system.

As we have just implied, some of these differences are differences of actual and perceived value. The value, in purely instrumental and economic terms, that individual institutions offer will differ. An institution, which looks to the State for less than 50 per cent of its recurrent funding, has a significant centre of research in, perhaps, a score of subject areas, sees its students passing easily into the graduate labour market and is a substantial player in various overseas markets (in attracting students and providing consultancies) could be said to be generating more value than another institution which looks to the State for more than 80 per cent of its funding, has little of a research profile, sees its students passing into the graduate labour market with some difficulty and into less prestigious and less-well remunerated careers and has become active overseas largely through 'franchising' its awards to institutions in other countries.

Intimately tied in with the differential economic value is the perceived value of such institutional profiles. Education is a cultural good as well as an economic good and there develops, in any mass higher education system, a pecking order of institutions in terms of their public reputation.We know little about the basis for such differential estimations of 'quality' in the public mind but, presumably, factors such as age, subjects offered, research profile, public profile and more intangible links to deep-seated cultural sentiments such as rural-urban resonances, the church (especially the Anglican church) and separateness from the world of work are all present. In other words, just as the dominant policy of the State is to drive through to a unified policy, so there are tensions within the system for differentiation.

To be sure, some of the now emerging countervailing pressure for differentiation is coming from the State itself. In the context of a welfare state which is being restrained, if not diminished, the idea of the university is being examined by the State itself. Does a university have to conduct research? A policy of selectivity, it will be noticed, will be attractive both to the State (so as to limit the overt demand for research funds) and to the 'élite' universities which secure over 70 per cent of State funds for research. But the question is not susceptible to an easy resolution. It may just be that teaching in the context of research is more likely to produce the inquiring minds which advanced capitalism requires than teaching conducted without that environment. (Unfortunately, that research is not yet conclusive in its findings).

Further pressures for differentiation arise from within the system. The emergence of the so-called 'Russell Group' (a small informal group

of universities which see themselves as th
and which wish to protect that status) is ii
within the system to accept that a un
protection of these universities' cultural
public prestige, has to be seen as part of th
cultural capital has economic return: to
sense) shall be given. Especially in an age (
for higher education, cultural capital ha:
earn its interest every bit as do the phys
universities.

policy of perm
are maintai
The ke
future
of v

Conclusion

The abandonment of the binary policy is already past history in the modern story of UK higher education. What we are now seeing develop is the emergence of differentiation within a unified framework; of diversity within a single system of higher education. That is easily said but it is analytically weak. What elements are to count under the heading of 'unity'? What elements are to count under the heading of 'differentiation'? And what are the relationships between those two sets of elements? How much differentiation might be permitted before we lose any semblance of a unified system? Fortunately, in this essentially historical essay we do not have to answer these questions, but some observations may be in order.

The State is faced with policy goals which are in tension. On the one hand it seeks to bring the total system of UK higher education into a common framework so that the entire system is adding maximum value to the general aim of regenerating the economy and on the other hand subsidiary tensions reduce the extent of commonality. For example, being an international commodity as well as promoting regional economic well-being; maintaining the research and development capacity of higher education but restraining that expenditure as part of the wider governmental restraint on public expenditure; looking to all graduates to have a common platform of 'transferable' skill but having a sense that the modern economy not only requires some specificity of high-level functioning but – and more seriously for a unified higher education policy – that it requires different levels of symbolic competence (broadly, symbolic creationists and symbolic technicians): all these tensions felt by the State are prompting a much more subtle

...ssible 'diversity' while some elements of commonality
...ied.

...y strands of commonality which will remain in the foreseeable
...are: that higher education should be oriented towards the world
...ork; that universities should maximise their own sources of income;
...at students should bear a significant proportion of the costs of their
education (but never the full part for that would introduce too much
volatility into the system); that the costs per student will continue to fall;
that all courses should fall within a common framework of credit
accumulation; and that all institutions will be subject to external (that
is, State orchestrated) evaluation of their work.

Within this common framework diversity will be permitted and even
required in the domains of research, consultancy, subjects studied,
student profile, modes of attendance, sites of study, regional and
international profiles, the extent to which programmes of study are
actually situated in the world of work, the encouragement given to
students to be creative and independent and the freedom allowed to
academic staff within the internal and external expectations and even
demands on academic life (that is, varied conditions of work across the
system).

A modern system of higher education requires diversity: it has so
many tasks to perform and some of those tasks are, in any case, likely to
generate more value through a policy of selectivity. On the other hand,
there are general parameters which supply an overarching common
policy into which all forms of diversity are expected to fit. These
parameters derive from the aims of bringing the higher education
system into the service of securing the regeneration of the UK economy
and of ensuring value for money through external evaluation of the
system as a whole. Two subsidiary parameters of reducing the power of
the academic community over the services that it provides and living
prudently within ever-reducing State-provided per capita funding are
also at work in support of the two dominant parameters. Providing that
these four paremeters are observed by every institution, diversity is to be
welcomed and, as we have seen, in some areas, to be required.

In crude terms, therefore, all the institutional changes and the policy
developments that we have noted can be reduced to the following
formula for the medium term: that a common policy for UK higher
education consists of a continuing and ever-widening orientation of
institutions to the world of work and that institutions should
demonstrate their effective and prudent use of public resources but

that, within this common policy, diversity is to be permitted. This is a new hybrid policy for higher education – of diversity within commonality.

As in all hybrids, there is a mix of progenitors and this particular combination allows for all kinds of institutional hybrids to proliferate within the general policy framework. The next twenty years will be characterised by experimenting with the possible forms of institutional life permitted by the framework. Some forms of institutional life will no doubt raise queries as to whether we are seeing 'higher education' at all. That is the nature of hybrids, they test the boundaries of our definitions and assumptions. Higher education will straddle all kinds of borders in the future. It is a nice example of border life.

Appendix 5.1
Chronological List of Significant Legislation and Reports

1963   *Committee of Enquiry into Higher Education* – The Robbins Report

Key points include: Raising the percentage of the age group receiving full-time higher education from about eight per cent to about 17 per cent by 1980; setting up of a new Ministry of Arts and Sciences; teacher training to be removed from local authorities and integrated, administratively, into the university pattern.

1981/83 The Leverhulme Inquiry.

Organised jointly by the Society for Research into Higher Education and the Leverhulme Trust, the inquiry resulted in a series of ten monographs and a final report. A number of themes were examined, including the need for increasing access to higher education, a need to reform the content and structure of courses and a need for more professional management.

1985   *Report of the Steering Committee for Efficiency Studies in Universities* – The Jarratt Report

Key points included: recommendations that universities examine their structures and governance with a view to becoming managerial oriented, including development of performance indicators, delegation to budget centres, utilising fewer committees and developing academic and institutional plans. Further recommendations related to government intervention and funding structures as well as a call for support from the Committee of Vice-Chancellors and Principals on behalf of institutions.

1987   *Review of the University Grants Committee* – The Croham Report

Key points include: restructuring of the University Grants Committee (see below) and recommended creation of a body that involved more 'lay' people representing business and industry. The new council was to be more managerial in approach and, in effect, remove the 'buffer' between the government and funding mechanisms.

1988   Education Reform Act – *Higher Education – Meeting the Challenge Cmnd. 114*

Key points include: LEAs' duty to provide facilities for Higher Education removed; existing institutions to become legal entities in their own right. The National Advisory Body for Public Sector Higher Education to be replaced by a Polytechnic and Colleges Funding Council and the University Grants Committee to be replaced by the Universities Funding Council.

1992   Further and Higher Education Act(s) – *Higher Education: A New Framework Cmnd. 1541*

Key points include: three Higher Education Funding Councils (England, Scotland and Wales) established; details the dissolution of the Universities Funding Council and the Polytechnics and Colleges Funding Council with transfer of property to the Higher Education Funding Council for England; power to award degrees, to change the name of the educational institution within the Higher Education Sector and use the title 'University' with the approval of the Privy Council. Also provides for the dissolution of the Council for National Academic Awards.

1994   Education Act

Key points include: setting up Teacher Training Agency and Training as a Career Unit; funding for teacher training and definition of Students' Unions and their management.

1996   National Committee of Inquiry into Higher Education

Established by the Secretaries of State for England, Scotland and Wales, the Inquiry was chaired by Sir Ron Dearing. The terms of reference for the inquiry were far reaching, including examination of the 'purposes, shape, structure, size and funding of higher education, including support for students, should develop to meet the needs of the UK over the next 20 years, recognising that higher education embraces teaching, learning, scholarship and research'. The Committee was to report by the summer of 1997.

Appendix 5.2
Number of institutions

Number of institutions (as at 1 August 1996)

	*Universities**	*University Institutions*	*Colleges of Higher Education***	*Total*
England	72	93	48	141
Scotland	13	13	9	22
Wales	2	7	6	13
Northern Ireland	2	2	2	4
Total United Kingdom	89	115	65	180

* = Includes University of Buckingham

** = Includes teacher-training colleges

There are 115 university institutions in the UK, counting separately the constituent colleges of the federal universities of Wales and London. If Wales and London are counted as single institutions, the total is 89. There are also higher education students studying at a number of further education colleges.

Source: The Committee of Vice Chancellors and Principals of the UK Universities. Higher Education Statistics Autumn 1996.

Appendix 5.3
Students

Participation rates

	1985/86	*1990/91*	*1993/94*	*Percentage 1995/96**
GB Age Participation Index (API)	14	19	30	30–32
API Scots-domiciled students	–	26	38	–
Northern Ireland participation in Higher Education	–	27	39	44

GB API = Under 21 home initial entrants/average number of 18- and 19-year-olds in the population

API Scots-domiciled students = under 21 Scots entrants to full-time undergraduate courses in the UK/population of 17-year-olds in Scotland in the previous year

Northern Ireland participation in higher education = Full-time new entrants to higher education in Northern Ireland, Great Britain or the Republic of Ireland/18-year-olds in Northern Ireland population.

* = projected

Source: The Committee of Vice Chancellors and Principals of the UK Universities. Higher Education Statistics Autumn 1996.

Appendix 5.4

Home undergraduate students by mode of attendance, Great Britain

	Full-time (000s)	Part-time** (000s)	Open University (000s)	Total (000s)
1988/89	516	233	82	831
1989/90	551	242	85	877
1990/91	596	249	89	934
1991/92	673	257	92	1024
1992/93	771	267	94	1130
1993/94*	853	288	97	1238
% Growth 1988/89 to 1993/94	65	24	18	49

* Provisional

Sources: DFE Statistical Bulletin 13/94, DFE Budget Briefing (CVCP 1995a).

Appendix 5.5

Home postgraduate students by mode of attendance, Great Britain

	Full-time (000s)	Part-time (000s)	Open University (000s)	Total (000s)
1988/89	47	59	3	109
1989/90	49	66	4	120
1990/91	53	75	6	134
1991/92	64	87	7	158
1992/93	71	104	9	184
1993/94*	78	115	11	204
% Growth	66	95	267	87

* Provisional
** Includes overseas part-time students
Sources: DFE Statistical Bulletin 13/94. DFE Budget Briefing (CVCP 1995a).

Appendix 5.6
Finance

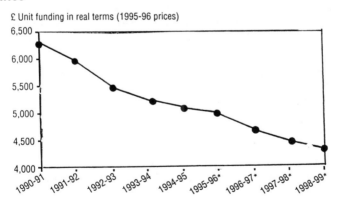

£ Unit funding in real terms (1995-96 prices)

Higher education: recurrent and capital public funding per student, England, 1989–90 to 1998–99

Source: DFE (CVCP Higher Education Statistics 1996) * = projected

Chapter 6

The University of Humberside

David Foster and Roger King

During the second half of the twentieth century central government in the United Kingdom has taken a progressively greater interest in higher education, stimulated by its ever-increasing demands on the public purse. The reforms of the late 1980s and early 1990s have seen the culmination of that process with the subordination of universities, the take-over of advanced institutions from their original providers – both municipal and religious – and the creation of a unified system.

As a local authority college until incorporation in 1989, Humberside belonged to the advanced further education sector. This sector had been developed in the 1960s, as one of the strategies for modernising higher education as an alternative to the universities and, in particular, making it more responsive to the needs of the economy. Prior to incorporation the institutions in the public sector had been characterised by their close connections with the economy of their regions, which was reflected in an accessibility to students of a wide range of ability, and by their municipal origins and links, which had encouraged a sense of accountability rather than autonomy. This accountability was widened to a national context with the advent of the National Advisory Body for Public Sector Higher Education (NAB) in 1981.

One of Britain's 'new' universities, Humberside has undergone considerable evolution in the last twenty years. Founded by the new Humberside County Council from a merger of six independent institutions in the city as recently as 1976, it was known as Hull College of Higher Education. Seven years later it was enlarged to Humberside College with the addition of advanced-level work from Grimsby College of Technology as part of a regional restructuring of further and higher education provision by the local authority. During that period the college had campaigned for polytechnic status, though no new polytechnics had been created since 1973. This objective only became capable of realisation following the introduction of national planning for the polytechnics and colleges sector during the 1980s with the advent of the NAB.

In 1989, as a result of central government reforms, polytechnics and colleges were given corporate status and the college was detached from its historic links with the local authority. National planning in the sector was now taken over by the NAB's successor, the Polytechnics and Colleges Funding Council (PCFC). The PCFC was charged with expanding student numbers as cheaply as possible and the handful of colleges seeking polytechnic status responded to the challenge as a means of achieving their goal. In addition, the PCFC laid down criteria for the designation of new polytechnics, which included minimum size and an appropriate range of work, and these enabled the college to bid successfully for the polytechnic designation which was granted in 1990. Further change came within the short space of three years when government policy enabled all polytechnics to apply for the title of university, and Humberside Polytechnic seized the opportunity to become a university immediately.

Governance and management

Prior to incorporation the college was governed, under an Instrument and Articles, within a regulatory framework which enabled the local authority to control all aspects of its work, including the crucial areas of finance, employment and estates. However, strong civic pride which the Humberside County Council had in the college led to very supportive relationships and to the eventual *de facto* delegation of a range of responsibilities to the college. Both governance and management took place within a culture of participation and shared responsibility between the Governing Council, dominated by local authority and college members, and senior management and representatives of the staff operating through Academic Board and its committees.

With incorporation, the reforms of 1988 and 1992 stimulated a more professional and business-like approach to the government and management of colleges by replacing a regulatory bureaucracy with the authority of a corporate body, and by introducing a culture of power relationships into the polytechnics and colleges, investing in both the Board of Governors and the Director powers which had hitherto rested with local authorities. In the new context, the board, on which independent members were to be in an absolute majority, was directly and solely responsible for the educational character and mission of the college, for the effective and efficient use of its resources and its solvency and for the employment and conditions of service of all staff. Central government anticipated that the dominance of independent members would introduce a culture of efficiency to institutions.

Equally crucial was the strengthening of the role of the executive at the expense of elected academic representatives in determining the strategic direction of the institution and in its management. The Director, later Vice-Chancellor, strengthened considerably in his role as chief executive, was responsible for implementing the decisions of the board and carried full responsibility for making proposals concerning the educational character and mission to the Board of Governors. This reduced the role of Academic Board to that of advisor. He held executive responsibility for the organisation, direction and financial management of the college, and the management of staff, with direct control over senior postholders and student discipline.

Two major devices, common to most corporations, have developed to assist the Director in the management of the institution. The widespread concept of a senior management team in pre-incorporation institutions, often carrying out considerable iteration with the Academic Board, evolved into a more formal executive committee structure which has become not merely the dominant unit but the major locus of power and authority within the institution developing policy and practice independent of the traditional academic channels. At the centre has been an inner cabinet consisting of the Director/ Vice-Chancellor and his immediate colleagues, each of whom exercises portfolio responsibilities under the supervision of the chief executive. The executive has also made considerable use of specially appointed sub-committees or working parties, with a limited life, usually led by a member of the Executive Board to drive forward the work of the institution. Thus the major task of converting the university's academic portfolio to a modular structure in 1993/94 and the establishment of a new international strategy in 1993 were carried out by such groups. The position of management was also strengthened on the new Academic Board which was reduced from 50 to 29 members, of whom 16 were ex-officio and two co-opted. Its powers were also to be exercised in an advisory capacity to the Director and confined to two areas: quality and academic standards.

It has been suggested that the corporate model of governance and management, where power is located and exercised only at the centre, runs the risk of alienation, develops a management style which is political and tactical rather than strategic, operates within a short-to-medium-term time-frame and is best suited to crisis situations (McNay 1995). Certainly, the marginalisation of the Academic Board from the decision-making process produced a feeling of disenfranchisement amongst staff. Recognition of the longer-term difficulties which may ensue from this issue led the university to seize the opportunity offered by the 1992 Act to increase the size, though not the responsibilities, of the Academic Board.

More recently, in response to the university's audit report from the Higher Education Quality Council (HEQC), further steps are in hand to encourage greater iteration between the Executive and Academic Board without surrendering the Vice-Chancellor's legal responsibility for the academic development of the university. Accusations of short-termism can, in Humberside's case, be refuted by the energy which has been devoted to the production of five-year strategic plans, but such is the context of permanent change – largely, though not exclusively, produced by central government policy – that medium- and longer-term planning can appear to be undermined. Whilst the word crisis is inappropriate, the incorporation of the college did present new and significant challenges. The move to more efficient management and strategic planning had been foreshadowed by the NAB, established in 1981 to plan and control the development of higher education in the public sector. Nonetheless, the scale of reform required urgent and dramatic change and it is arguable that centralisation of power was the only means by which energy necessary to achieve the objectives could be harnessed.

One of the most immediate and important impacts of incorporation on the college was the ability to carry forward money from one year to the next, to earn interest on its balances and to create a reserve out of revenue income if it wished. Furthermore, it was required to assume a wider responsibility for those elements of work, such as finance, estates and personnel management, which previously had been carried out by the local authority. Therefore, the central plank of the college's financial strategy after 1989 was support for the academic plan within the confines of a balanced budget, coupled with an intention to make a contribution towards the establishment of reserves and to minor works.

In the period since incorporation a strategy involving close control of costs, thorough internal estimates and budgetary procedures by senior managers with Governing Council support, enabled the college to create a healthy, even robust, financial platform from which to support its academic plan (Appendix 6.3). The most obvious measure of its success in this area is the fact that not only has the academic plan been fully underpinned but major improvements have been made to the estate and judicious investments have strengthened corporate support services such as estates, finance, personnel and administrative computing. Moreover, a surplus has been achieved every year and reserves of some £15 million have been created.

Academic developments

One of the dominant themes of the 1989 reform was the provision of autonomy to institutions which was to be exercised by strong local management within a framework of government centralisation. Control was exercised through the Polytechnics and Colleges Funding Council (PCFC), whose task was to implement government policy which saw the sector making a major contribution to the social and economic needs of the country by expanding access for mature students, recruiting more students in science, engineering and vocational subjects, increasing links between industry and education alongside a more constrained view of research funding, and emphasising delivery and accountability in the context of decreasing public funds. This influence has been particularly evident in the area of academic development and curricular reform. In keeping with the attempts to create more business-like institutions, institutions have been required to produce mission statements and develop strategies to accomplish them, invited to open their doors to ever wider constituencies and urged and given incentives to revise their curricula to make students more responsive to the economic and social requirements of the nation.

Mission and strategy

Since PCFC's objectives were similar to those which many public sector institutions had pursued prior to incorporation, Humberside's initial development plan, of 1989, inevitably contained large elements of continuity with what had gone before. It was based on the offer of accessible, vocational higher education to its region, and it also sought to capitalise on its well-established European experience. But it also contained an unfulfilled ambition to become a polytechnic, which had

been thwarted for some dozen years or more. The college's case was based upon its existing character and achievements and its potential for development. Its academic case was based on the size, spread and balance of its academic portfolio, which compared favourably with a number of the smaller polytechnics, its accreditation by Council for National Academic Awards (CNAA) in 1986 and its recognition externally for innovative programmes, particularly in the European area. Its potential for growth was strong in a region of almost one million people, traditionally under-provided with vocational higher education, and was based principally on its favourable geographical location as a major seaport on the east coast of England in the light of the emergence of a unified European market in the early 1990s.

Since their creation in the 1960s, public sector institutions had been at the forefront of the provision of professionally- and vocationally-oriented courses to a wider group of students and at a significantly lower cost than in the universities. Firmly located in this tradition, Humberside contributed to the emerging system of mass higher education occurring largely through expansion in the former public sector (Trow 1989; P. Scott 1995). Central to the college's mission was a strategy of growth in student numbers from an existing 6500 to 8000 students, most of whom would be in the vocational areas of Information Technology, Computing and Mathematics; Business and Management; Humanities and Social Science; Art, Design and the Performing Arts; and Teacher Education. This target for planned growth of some 23 per cent over three years was ambitious. However, PCFC advice to the Secretary of State was that new polytechnic designations should be made only where an institution had at least 300 full-time higher education students in a majority of the council's nine programme areas, a higher education enrolment of at least 4000 full-time and a substantial number (c.1500) of part-time students and have over two-thirds of its full-time higher education students on degree level courses. Consequently, there was a degree of inevitability about the college's dash for growth which was finally rewarded by the granting of polytechnic status in June 1990.

By the time that the PCFC required a new strategic plan to cover the period 1992–97, the educational environment had changed substantially. The impending disappearance of the binary system and the creation of a sector containing over eighty universities and a number of other major colleges challenged the institution to position itself more clearly in a system which was meant to have the potential for greater diversity than had previously existed. The government's planned increase in the participation rate, both numerically and socially, provided new opportunities for growth, though the achievement of those targets with little additional resource would pose its own challenges in terms of curriculum content, delivery, student support, modes of attendance, flexibility and pace of study. Furthermore, it was apparent that any growth would have to be achieved in the face of a declining unit of resource, thus placing strains on institutional finance.

Government, therefore, sought to provide a context within which greater institutional diversity might develop by offering universities the opportunity to define their character within the framework of a market managed by government control of overall funding. Against this background, Humberside's decision to become an institution providing mass higher education emphasised that conversion to university status would not deflect it from its primary commitment to providing relevant and vocational-oriented higher education to the region and to Europe, and it looked forward to continuing overall student growth from 10,700 to 14,000 which meant increases in all academic areas except in-service teacher education. Given the problems of capital funding, growth would be achieved primarily by widening access to a range of approved study centres throughout the Humberside region and through the expansion of formal agreements with local and European colleges, some of which would be able to obtain associated status.

In a number of respects Humberside has sought to create for itself a distinctive role within the national system and, through its emphasis on access to vocational higher education, to avoid convergence with the old universities. However, despite government intention to stimulate the development of a more diversified and differentiated system of higher education, a number of pressures have operated to cause convergence, thus helping to maintain some of the homogeneity of which the system has long been proud.

Government attachment to the 'gold-standard' of entry qualification (Advanced level of the General Certificate of Education) and to the concept of a national standard for degrees, the apparent desire of most if not all universities to maintain the three traditional elements of research, professional training and collegiate ethos and the relative conservatism of the student application and graduate recruitment market all militated against differentiation of the system. In Humberside, as elsewhere, this has meant a subtle shift from a teaching-only university to a teaching-first university in order to facilitate research and, therefore, prestige and income in particular niche areas; encouragement of professional education, particularly through the Enterprise Project; and the search for devices to maintain the intimacy of élite, collegiate systems.

Similar developments have occurred in what might be termed the paraphernalia of higher education. In common with other CNAA-validated institutions, the college had held traditional awards ceremonies prior to incorporation and continued to do so after 1989. Equally important, a number of developments suggested that, at least at the image level, attempts were being made to imitate the traditional universities. The power to award its own degrees obliged the university to create its own academic dress for graduands, but the opportunity was also taken to create ceremonial robes for the Vice-Chancellor, though not for other senior colleagues. The imitation was complete in May 1995 with the installation of a mace and of the university's first Chancellor, Dr J.H. Hooper, who has chaired the Board of Governors since the formation of Hull College of Higher Education in 1976. In a similar vein, the college decided, prior to incorporation, to introduce professorships, though this did not occur until after 1989.

Mass higher education for the region

The advent of mass higher education, defined as between 15 per cent and 40 per cent of the age group, occurred in the United Kingdom as recently as 1987–92, and the polytechnics and colleges made by far the greater contribution to that achievement. It is widely believed that a major contribution to this growth had been the access policies in the so-called public sector which had opened higher education to previously disadvantaged or under-represented sectors of the population, such as members of the working class and ethnic minority groups. However, recent work has suggested that growth has been based primarily on the exploitation of existing constituencies of students with significantly increased participation by women, but no great progress with mature students or socially-disadvantaged groups (P. Scott 1995).

Humberside has had a commitment to access through its promotion of courses in the local colleges of further education from 1980 but it is clear that, in so far as there was any conflict, the dash for growth to achieve polytechnic status to 1990 took precedence over access policy. In achieving the growth elements of its strategic plans, the institution was extremely successful in the period from incorporation until 1994/95, when overall student numbers increased by 106 per cent, though the growth was confined largely to full-time (208%) and, to a lesser extent, sandwich students (89.9%) (Appendix 6.1). Crucial to the attainment of the early targets, which helped to achieve polytechnic status, was government encouragement to recruit fees-only students because it lowered overall unit costs, creating greater efficiency. Humberside achieved 2834 students in 1990/91 and 2718 in 1991/92 in this category. However, during the same period the number of part-time students remained stubbornly stable with a growth of only 12 per cent (Appendix 6.2). During the five years under consideration the proportion of women on university courses has remained steady at 48.6 per cent and the proportion of mature students has been slightly higher at 50.05 per cent.

Mass higher education implies not merely growth in numbers but greater accessibility to the education available and Humberside has sought to reform its academic structures and awards with this need in mind. At the centre of this reform was a search for greater efficiency and flexibility, particularly in facilitating student choice – which assumes greater importance the more that the system feels the impact of market discipline. The major change has been the conversion of courses to a modular structure which enables students to study subjects singly or in combination, at major and minor levels, for a range of named awards. Inevitably, in a context where resources are declining, the range of subjects on offer must be controlled and students are offered planned choice in a range of subjects which the Executive Board determined to be essential to enable the university to fulfil its overall mission. The range of choice for some students is widened by the opportunity to apply for accreditation of prior learning, either individually or through in-company staff-training schemes, and an education for capability is offered to all students through the internal requirement that all modules be designed on the basis of the learning outcomes which students can hope to achieve on successful completion of their courses. Wider opportunities for part-time students as well as greater efficiency in the overall use of resources is also offered through the simple device of combining classes popular with both part-time and full-time students in the twilight zone, 4pm to 7pm.

A further measure of the accessibility of an institution lies in its ability to serve its region, and in this respect Humberside has enjoyed a marked degree of success. This is indicated by the continued recruitment of over 64 per cent of its students from the north of England in each year for which reliable records exist, with at least 35 per cent of the total student body coming from the county of Humberside, though there has been a small but steady decline in that proportion over the last few years (See Appendix 6.2).

However, recruitment to courses on its main campuses is but one indication of the university's commitment to its region. The expansion of access to learning had been a major plank in the institution's strategy since 1976. Initially, this took the form of preparatory courses for mature students who wished to enter higher education but lacked the traditional entry qualifications. These courses were devised by the then college in partnership with local further education colleges and successful students were able to find places in higher education. This practice developed rapidly in many parts of the country and eventually the work of access courses was co-ordinated nationally by an Access Courses Recognition Group which encouraged areas to develop their own formal organisations for the approval and recognition of their courses. Locally, the Humberside Polytechnic and Partners Authorised Validating Agency received national approval in 1990/91. Access was also improved through the franchising of a number of courses, primarily at first-year level, initially in part-time and later in full-time mode, to local further education colleges and the local college of agriculture, the latter becoming an associate college of the university in 1993. Between 1990 and 1995, 547 of the students graduating from local access courses went on to higher education and 3876 students had enrolled on franchised courses in the period 1992–95.

The county of Humberside has one of the lowest higher education participation rates in the country and the university sought to address this problem through a number of initiatives involving Humberside schools. In 1992/93 the university's Enterprise in Higher Education Project launched a student tutoring scheme, by which students of the university spend time in local schools as part of their degree courses encouraging pupils in their studies and trying to motivate them to continue on to higher education. Another initiative in this area was the establishment of a scheme whereby young people from local inner-city schools in Hull and Grimsby, not traditionally associated with progression to higher education, should be encouraged to do so. A College Studies programme was set up, which produces a record of achievement to be taken into account in offering a university place at Humberside alongside the results of studies leading to the more traditional school-leaving award, the Advanced Level of the General Certificate of Education.

Other important contributions to regional development saw the university active in seeking to improve the skills base of the region. Major progress in this area was made with the 1989 launch of a linked Engineering degree with British Aerospace; a Professional Updating for Women returning to Work course, supported by the Training Agency and local education authority and by the European Social Fund in 1991/92; the establishment of the Food Innovation Centre in Grimsby, funded jointly by the university and the Ministry of Agriculture, Food and Fisheries as part of the latter's initiative to stimulate innovation and the transfer of technology within the food industry; and the introduction of the first part-time masters' degree in Fine Art in collaboration with other regional providers. In turn, these initiatives have led to reciprocal sponsorship of students on the modular Food Studies degree by local companies, substantial donations to the specialist food technology library in Grimsby by local food companies, the sponsorship of two chairs by local companies and an increasing number of prizes donated to outstanding students in a range of areas for presentation at the annual Awards Ceremony.

Towards a new curriculum for the twenty-first century

The development of mass higher education, with its emphasis, especially in Britain, on education for capability, implies reform of both curricula and teaching and learning strategies. The enrolment of increasing numbers of students wishing to study at their own pace in a variety of modes, perhaps using widely dispersed centres, requires a revolution in approaches to teaching and learning in which technology will be only a part, albeit an important one. Core capabilities are at the heart of the university's search for a vocationally-oriented curriculum and it seeks to distinguish between generic, occupational and professional competence. The latter two imply an ability to perform specific, recognised occupational activities to particular standards and are redolent of a narrow vocationalism which the university seeks to avoid. Generic competence is, however, more conducive to higher education in that it encourages a convergence between knowledge and intellectual development on the one hand and particular skills on the other (Gaskell 1989). It is, perhaps, better described by the term 'capability', which implies an integration of knowledge and skills within one person.

In the 1980s, government criticism of higher education's failure to make a significant contribution to the economic needs of the nation was uncompromising. In particular, criticism focused on higher education's failure to produce sufficient graduates with the skills and competencies required by an enterprise society. Government did, however, acknowledge that some institutions in the public sector had recognised their responsibility in this respect (DES 1985 and 1987) and it was no coincidence that in 1987 the Department of Employment's Manpower Services Commission, later renamed the Training Agency and, finally, the Training, Enterprise and Education Directorate, established the Enterprise in Higher Education Programme (EHEP).

The EHEP was one of the means by which government sought, through specially dedicated funds, to exercise greater influence over the direction and content of higher education. But the attempt to transform higher education, and universities in particular, into suppliers of suitably-trained students did not meet with universal acclaim. Critics saw it as a means by which the government sought to control the values and the content of higher education through the application of a market model which some rejected as incommensurable with higher education (Prickett 1994; Tasker and Packham 1994). The envisaged partnership between higher education and industry to ensure that the former became more responsive to the demands of the labour market and its rapidly changing needs, and became more accessible to an increasingly varied clientele by providing courses which met their needs rather than those of the suppliers, was not unfamiliar to the polytechnics and colleges. Their experience of degree-level studies, carefully blending knowledge and competence, confounded critics of the EHEP who feared the development of a narrow vocationalism.

The major focus for the development of a new curriculum at Humberside has been the university's participation in the national EHEP 1990–95 and the establishment in the university of the privately-sponsored British Petroleum Strategic Development Fund (BPSDF) in 1991. The former supported work to the tune of £1 million over the five-year period of the project, which itself attracted business support worth an additional £4.5 million. The latter consists of an endowment, also of œl million, which, in the first six years, is providing an annual income of £50,000, at least doubled in each year from the university's own funds.

The juxtaposition and overlap of the two projects have enabled the university initially to establish its commitment to the philosophy and application of enterprise and to continue and refine it in the BPSDF. In this context the decision to focus the first BPSDF project on a five-year programme to harness modern media and technological developments to the development of mass and vocational higher education was crucial to the emerging mission of the university. Humberside's EHEP, however, did not signal a major transformation of its educational rationale and philosophy, nor herald major changes in its work and course portfolio. Rather, it provided an impetus to develop existing work and to expand it to academic areas less traditionally associated with employment, thus underlining the congruence between the national EHEP and the college's mission.

The aim of the national enterprise initiative was to re-direct the education process towards the development of personal qualities, effectiveness and key skills so that students might become more enterprising, better communicators, life-long learners and experienced in the world of work. However, this was to be achieved not through the promotion of a narrow vocationalism, nor by the replacement of high level expertise in specialist areas, but through individual empowerment and the integration of new objectives with existing educational provision (EHE 1989). Embracing the flexibility inherent in the EHEP, the college emphasised the need to develop students' potential by a transformation from tutor-centred to student-centred learning involving independence, team work and partnerships with employers, closely matching the overall intention 'to become an enterprising, accessible and highly regarded Polytechnic'. The Learning Development Initiative established through the BPSDF set out to develop a new learning environment focusing specifically on equipping students with the skills for independent and lifelong learning, and work on this project continues.

However, in addition to the continuity which the university forged between the two projects, there were important contrasts which were significant in promoting success. There was an important difference, perhaps crucial in the long run, in the organisation and management of the two projects with the BPSDF having a far stronger central direction than the EHEP. Both projects recognised that success depended on a marriage of central management and local ownership but it is arguable that the organisation and management of the two were both children of their times. The launch of EHEP in late 1989/early 1990 came at a time when bureaucratic and pseudo-collegial ideas of management still prevailed, whereas the BPSDF was established two years later when the institution had a more developed form of central managerial direction and control.

Both projects had central and active management committees, including institutional and business personnel, but there was a significant contrast in actual membership and function. The EHEP Management Committee, which included both chair and vice-chair of the Board of Governors and a range of business and academic interests in the region, consisted of around twelve members at any one time and had a total of 27 members over its five-year existence and offered a broad supervisory role in the project. In contrast, the BPSDF was managed by a small but influential steering group consisting of the Director and a Deputy Director of the Polytechnic, the Works Manager of the local BP operation and the former Works Manager, who was also vice-chairman of the Polytechnic's Board of Governors. They were to be joined by the Professor of Learning Development on appointment. The steering group gave focus and direction to the project, thus ensuring that its work was consonant with the aims of the polytechnic.

There was a similar contrast at the organisational level. EHEP had a small central Enterprise Office headed by a senior member of staff as Project Director, whose ex-officio membership of Academic Board and the Senior Management Group ensured that EHEP had a high profile with the senior executive and academic management in the college. Local ownership was achieved through an Enterprise Team of staff drawn from every school, appointed by open competition and promoted to principal lecturer grade for the duration of their association with EHEP. They were responsible for identifying school objectives and contributions within the framework of the overall project and for forming links with a number of employers to facilitate other aspects of the project. This bottom-up approach to the organisation and management of the project gained the commitment of staff throughout the college and the enthusiasm with which Enterprise Managers undertook their work localised ownership of EHEP work and encouraged staff to innovate. In contrast, the BPSDF was established through a central Learning Development Unit (LDU) whose task was to drive the project forward; staff development activity was concentrated initially on those staff seconded from schools who were centrally involved with specific projects approved by the steering group, with the consequence that enthusiasm for and commitment to the establishment of a new learning environment has been more limited in the early stages of the project.

What progress has been made to the development of a new curriculum? Whilst the completed EHEP, which played a major role in raising awareness of the need to revise curricula and teaching/learning strategies in the light of mass higher education and the needs of the economy, is more susceptible to evaluation than the continuing BPSDF initiative, it is already clear that the BPSDF initiative will have a greater long-term impact on the university's work. Considered separately, each project has specific achievements to its credit. Designed as a change agent with respect to curriculum and university-employer relations, the national EHEP has been represented as a series of lost opportunities (Brown and Sommerlad 1992). But, in terms of managing changes at institutional level, EHEP assisted Humberside's transformation into a more efficient organisation by highlighting and supporting its vision, by requiring it to foster critical but supportive external advice and by enabling it to achieve its goals more quickly and easily (Crothall 1994).

Courses are now designed with student learning outcomes as the key organising principle. Client need has replaced supplier definition as the prime engine of development and independence in learning and transferability of skills are central objectives of teaching and learning strategies. At the moment, the enterprise competencies seem to be fairly well embedded into Humberside curricula, though work needs to be done on establishing criteria for use in the validation of new courses and in the assessment of those competencies. With respect to employer links, Humberside's EHEP exceeded expectations by involving all major and numerous smaller employers in the region with £4.45 million being contributed against a target of £3.3 million, though a number of elements require further development. The input by employers to course design and review is more variable than might be desired and their role in the assessment of students' work, particularly placement and live projects, is limited – at least, in part, by the time which companies can afford to devote to collaborative work.

At the time of writing, the development of the New Learning Environment (NLE) is at an early stage but it is clear that, like all revolutions, it will be embraced by the enthusiastic and resisted by the sceptical. During the early stages of the project programmes based on open and distance learning materials were developed and individual schools produced a range of interactive and student-centred learning materials. But such piecemeal experimental development, even though it conformed to the criteria established by the steering committee, was unlikely to lead to a transformation of the learning environment of the whole university without wider evangelisation.

The creation of a new learning environment to meet the needs of mass higher education and achieve the objectives implicit in the concept of education for capability requires substantial changes in the traditional approach to higher education and an extensive programme of development has been put in place to achieve the re-professionalisation of the roles of some staff. Initial reactions suggest that although more flexible course structures have been introduced, there is a need to consolidate the learning outcomes work begun with the EHEP, particularly in the design of content and assessment strategies to be compatible with learning outcomes. Plans are under consideration to include within every student's programme a competence strand assessed through a portfolio which demonstrates particular capabilities, though this seems to be perilously close to the bolt-on studies which the national EHEP wished to avoid.

The NLE, and the EHEP before it, are predicated on the necessity for universities to respond to and satisfy the needs of the market-place, though the latter concept is not easy to define. Certainly, the demands of employers for students with capability is being addressed widely throughout the system and not only at Humberside, but the needs of students and their reaction to the diet on offer is less certain. It is true that the advent of many schemes to introduce more independent and work-related learning in schools will help students adjust to the university's approach, but as long as government continues to adhere to the 'gold standard' of the Advanced level of the General Certificate of Education for the majority of entrants, student reaction to the NLE is uncertain. It is clear that new students will require intensive introduction to the approach to learning which they will confront, particularly if they have come from cultures where a didactic approach is favoured. However, it is possible that the advent of increasing numbers of non-traditional entrants who are likely to have undergone more varied experiences of learning will reduce the severity of this problem.

In 1995 the university developed and piloted a Learning to Learn project which enables students to identify their own learning styles and any development required, introduces the range of learning and assessment methods in use in the university and offers advice on how to benefit from them. It also provides an introduction to core and subject-specific study skills which will be beneficial throughout students' courses. At the time of writing, it is too early for any evaluation of the project but it seems set to become an important element in students' introduction to higher education, either in its present or an amended form.

An international university

For traditional universities in Britain, involvement in international higher education has been based upon the twin foundations of academic excellence, whereby networks of scholars push back the frontiers of knowledge through joint research programmes, often aided by visiting fellowships and occasional international conferences, and assistance with social and economic development, whereby universities accept an obligation to assist in the development of other societies by training students from developing countries. Such students were able to study in the UK on subsidised fees. For British students, the main involvement in international education has been through exchange programmes within the developed world which are thought to have enhanced the value of their educational experience, thus increasing their employability. During the last 25 years the enhancement of staff and student mobility by international economic groupings, such as the European Economic Community and the European Free Trade Association, has led to the design of courses which are more appropriate to what has become known as the global economy, and British government policy on overseas student fees has made the training of students from overseas a vital part of Britain's export performance.

Humberside was one of the early pace-setters in the field of joint-European courses. In 1981 its joint course with the Fachhochschule Münster in Germany was established and quickly expanded to include partners in France and Spain. However, it was clear that if the newly-incorporated institution was to gain an outstanding reputation as a 'Polytechnic for Europe', courses would have to be developed and additional partnerships forged to enhance student capabilities in respect of European Community policies, processes and legislation, and to provide opportunities for greater student mobility as well as to promote language facility and cultural awareness.

By 1992 the university had 64 formal partnerships with higher education institutes in Europe and the number of named European courses had grown from one to fifteen and covered all schools.

Forty-five of the partnerships involved student exchange programmes which were normally funded by the ERASMUS programme, a scheme introduced by the European Community to encourage student mobility between member states. In terms of student numbers, the university has had between six and seven hundred European students studying in Humberside each year from 1991 to 1994, a figure in excess of those of its national competitors in this area. There was at that time an expectation that this enrolment would grow considerably, though this has not been realised to the extent that was planned.

Equally important has been the growing external recognition, by the government and its agencies and by the private sector, of the university's strengths in this field. In 1990 the polytechnic was awarded the Cable and Wireless Prize, one of the coveted Partnership Awards – an industry-backed scheme which seeks to recognise innovation in higher education teaching and learning. In 1991 it was selected by the Department of Employment to undertake a major European competencies curriculum project. Contracts in Eastern Europe were obtained under the government's 'Know-How Fund' for the development of business education in Hungary through the College of Foreign Trade in Budapest, and for advice in solving the problems of food distribution in Estonia. In 1994 the Overseas Development Administration awarded a contract to the university for training of Eastern European business people under the Joint Industrial and Commercial Attachment Programme (JICAP) scheme.

Further recognition came from the European Commission, which invited the university to organise, on behalf of the Commission, the inaugural London conference on the EC Memorandum for the Future of Higher Education in the European Community held in the Queen Elizabeth Conference Centre in September 1992. In 1994, under the auspices of the TEMPUS Scheme introduced by the EC to encourage progress towards a Western-style economy in the former Eastern bloc countries, the university was invited to develop an inter-university post-graduate management centre in Sofia with three Bulgarian universities, based on the Bulgarian system but using open learning material developed in-house.

By 1992, European growth, the development of American student exchange programmes and the benefits which polytechnic, and, later, university, designation afforded in the recruitment of international students to Humberside had provided the university with the experience and confidence to broaden its approach and seek to internationalise the institution. Just as the 1980s had seen a concentration on preparing students to work in Europe, so in the 1990s they need to be equipped with the knowledge and competencies to operate effectively in the global economy. Modern graduates will work in an economy without national boundaries and success in the competitive environment will go to those who have both the necessary business knowledge and skills and an understanding of other societies and cultures. It was also recognised that, in the spirit of access, the university must be prepared to take the product to the consumer and develop programmes which were capable of delivery outside the UK in modes which met the clients' requirements.

Thus an approach has been developed whereby the university seeks to build upon its European success by offering products in the wider international market for a specific return, thus helping to broaden the concept of an international university. Recognising that not all British universities will be in the international first division, Humberside's strategy of focusing on delivery and distribution of products created by others as well as itself points to an international university based on high-level, often postgraduate, flexible training, with both staff and students developing capability for operating in international and global markets and societies. These objectives are being achieved through a continuation of existing international activity together with the development of institutional partnerships overseas for the franchise and delivery of courses, particularly open- and distance-learning post-graduate management programmes using highly-structured open learning materials. In consequence, the university is actively involved in partnerships throughout Western, Central and Eastern Europe, Middle East, South-East Asia and Australia.

Quality in higher education

Quality in education has become a major industry in the 1990s and no university can afford to take a relaxed stance on this subject. The reasons for increased interest in quality are both educational and financial. When higher education was confined to a minority of the population, the traditional notions of quality were almost taken for granted, but the movement towards mass higher education has been encouraged by a government which, at the same time, wishes to see academic standards at least maintained and preferably enhanced. Not only has higher education become available on a far greater scale to a student population which includes more adults and part-timers but the range of educational qualifications at entry and the diversity of content offered, especially through modular courses, was undermining the traditional concepts of quality which had drawn strength from the single-subject honours course and the more recent CNAA-inspired approach to course quality. Furthermore, the market climate which government is seeking to create encourages students to define themselves as customers and adopt a consumer mentality. It is no longer adequate for institutions to decide what is good for students. The financial stimulus was premised on the need for accountability in institutions which were in receipt of considerable sums of public money.

Coincidental with the advent of incorporation, Humberside College was accredited by its main validating body, the Council for National Academic Awards, in 1989. It was anticipated that the major institutions, such as Humberside, would develop a relationship with the validating body which would result in virtual self-validation. This arrangement, together with a strengthening of the external examiner system and the continuation of inspection of teaching by Her Majesty's Inspectorate (HMI), would meet the need for the assurance of quality.

However, the reforms introduced in 1992 giving polytechnics and some colleges the power to award their own degrees meant the abolition of the CNAA and a requirement for systems of quality control and assurance which were both externally credible and internally effective. The decision of government to require universities to be responsible for quality control systems, the efficacy of which would be audited by a Higher Education Quality Council (HEQC), but to place quality assessment in the hands of the Higher Education Funding Council for England (HEFCE) produced an inefficient and hybrid system which is currently under review. Perhaps more problematic is the issue of quality for a mass higher education system with its increasingly flexible structures and delivery methods. Courses, standards and awards are still largely based on the traditional system, which was devised for more élitist days, and the extent to which three-year, predominantly subject-based honours degrees are appropriate for a mass higher education system will have to be confronted in the near future.

Whilst participating in quality audits and quality assessment visits with generally satisfactory outcomes, Humberside is seeking to amend its internal quality control structures and systems, which were derived from its CNAA experience and quite suitable for an approach in which the course was the central element to be evaluated, to ones which are more appropriate to an institution offering mass higher education. Issues which require attention in the future include the relationship between the executive's responsibility for academic development and the Academic Board's responsibility for the quality assurance of the resulting programmes, the better integration of the new learning environment initiative into the university's formal mechanisms for the assurance of quality of teaching and learning and the issue of student response.

In common with most institutions, satisfied students appear amongst the objectives of the university but the university does not appear to have undertaken any systematic monitoring of student opinion – though many school-based annual surveys, together with comments made in HMI inspection reports, suggest a reasonable level of student satisfaction. Nonetheless, the changes involved in the work of the university will require serious strategic thought in this area. Is the creation of a new learning environment, with a major emphasis on independent learning, precisely what the students require ? Is the provision of learning resources adequate ? How can the quality of work and experience in a varied range of centres, national and international, be controlled and its standards guaranteed?

The future

Although the revised mission statement was intended to apply to a five-year period from 1992, externally-imposed changes in the system compelled the university to reconsider its position in the summer of 1994. First, government decisions to cap growth in higher education, the decline of 18-year-olds in the population and the emergence of the new further education corporations as providers of certain types of higher education all increased competition and placed a premium on the need to develop a distinctive reputation for high-quality performance. Second, the introduction of league tables, based largely on traditional university criteria, placed universities like Humberside in a less favourable light. Also, it had to be recognised that the university had limited areas of recognised academic excellence, reflecting, at least in part, its low research base and the correspondingly few staff with national reputations – though the 1996 Research Assessment Exercise indicates significant progress in this area. Thus it was necessary for the university to improve its image in the market-place. In addition to the impact of changes in the external environment, the announcement, in May 1995, of the university's involvement in the Lincoln project – which will lead to the creation of the University of Lincolnshire and Humberside with campuses in Lincoln, Hull and, until 1999, in Grimsby – transformed the planning environment.

Thus a combination of external pressures and internal opportunism required an early revision of the university's mission for the remainder of the decade. The new mission, 'to provide our students world-wide with the best employment prospects and to equip them to become life-long learners', seeks to invest for quality whilst maintaining its accessibility and business-like character. Behind this vision are a number of key ideas which will be tested during the next few years. The concept of a regional university involves more than simply operating within a region. Rather, it reflects a commitment to the region and, in particular, to raising the base-line of higher-level skills and to applied research knowledge in support of the region's economic development. An international university is seen as one which prepares increasing numbers of its students to operate in trans-national economies and societies through strategic alliances and joint ventures abroad and delivery of courses overseas, all of which will also assist the reputation of the university at home. Quality vocational learning implies a concern with the whole process of student learning, which will be flexible, responsive and innovative and which will be underlined by applied research which will sustain the concept of a 'teaching-first' rather than 'teaching-only' university.

Clearly, the plans to develop a University of Lincolnshire and Humberside represent high-profile partnership within the region, but other, related, developments based on the new technologies, will further underline that commitment. Despite government intentions to consolidate student numbers, this development will inevitably lead to some growth – associated primarily with Lincoln. But the plan envisages a far greater diversity of student need which will require correspondingly greater flexibility in the provision of vocational higher education. Central to this vision is the new learning environment whereby students will become more responsible for their own learning and progress, and flexible academic structures which include a rationalisation of subject offerings in Hull and Lincoln. This last issue may be the most interesting of all as the university moves towards a position which might involve internal differentiation between its main sites, with the move to Lincoln establishing a more traditional, élitist approach and the campuses in Hull offering mass higher education.

Appendix 6.1

Number of students enrolled

	Full-Time	Sandwich	Part-Time	Total
1989/90	2775	1250	2817	6842
1990/91	3880	1506	2583	7969
1991/92	5252	2186	2903	10341
1992/93	6602	2387	2570	11559
1993/94	7779	2654	2147	12580
1994/95	8553	2374	3155	14102
1995/96*	8712	2046	2941	13699

* Information to date and likely to increase marginally

Appendix 6.2

All students by region of origin (per cent)

	1989/90	1990/1	1991/2	1992/3	1993/4	1994/5
Humberside	54	46.7	41.1	36.4	36.3	34.8
Yorkshire and North of England	14.9		24.7	28.3	28.6	28.9
English Midlands	10.8	46.7	10.9	14.4	15.0	7.9
South of England	6.6		9.6	10.3	10.0	17.9
Northern Ireland, Wales, Scotland, Isle of Man, Channel Islands	2.9		3.3	3.2	2.9	2.9
Europe	7.8	4.4	6.7	5.5	5.5	5.3
Rest of the World	2.7	2.2	1.7	1.9	1.7	2.4

Appendix 6.3

Institutional income and expenditure (£millions)

Year Ending	Income	Expenditure	Surplus
31 March, 1990	17.18	16.42	1.01
31 March, 1991	21.23	19.72	1.89
31 March, 1992	26.78	25.93	1.25
31 March, 1993	37.21	30.51	6.70
31 March, 1994	41.48	37.72	4.73
31 July, 1994*	46.59	42.01	5.80
Total surplus			16.67

* Provisional

Chapter 7

Napier University

James Murray

Napier University, one of three universities in the city of Edinburgh, opened in September 1964 as Napier Technical College. The college was named after John Napier of Merchiston, the Scottish mathematician responsible for the invention of logarithms. The fifteenth-century Merchiston Tower where he was born is now a working part of the Merchiston campus of the university. A study of the metamorphosis of Napier University from craft college to polytechnic and university provides an interesting insight into the ability of an academic community to react to changes in its external and internal environments and also into the educational system of Scotland.

The intention of the City of Edinburgh Council when they authorised the building of Napier College was to provide a craft college that would serve the growing demands of local employers for part-time courses for their apprentices. In 1966, following the receipt by government of the report of the Robbins Committee into higher education in the United Kingdom (DES 1963) and the decision to increase the number of universities, Heriot-Watt College, Edinburgh, changed from being a government-funded Central Institution to Heriot-Watt University and decided to transfer all technician and other courses not leading to awards of the university to Napier College. This influx of new courses, an increase in demand by industry for technicians and a rapid decline in the need for craft skills meant that the staff of the new college had to adapt quickly to a role completely different from that originally envisaged.

The change in status of Heriot-Watt College in Edinburgh and also that of the Royal College of Science and Technology in Glasgow, which later became the University of Strathclyde, meant that Scotland no longer had large technical Central Institutions funded by central government in its two major centres of industry, Glasgow and

Edinburgh. Henceforth the major colleges in these two cities would be funded by the civic authorities, whereas the smaller cities of Aberdeen, Dundee and Paisley had old-established government-funded Central Institutions developed from the nineteenth-century Mechanics Institutes. The decision not to designate Napier College a Central Institution had a profound effect on its development.[1]

Within a short period of its opening, staff from Napier were playing major roles in the expansion of technical education in Scotland, links were being developed with industry and under the dynamic leadership of its first Principal, J. Dunning, the college began to take the first steps towards its goal of being authorised to offer the degrees of the Council for National Academic Awards (CNAA).

Student numbers were expanding rapidly and if the college was to offer undergraduate courses then some rationalisation of course provision would be necessary. In 1969, five years after the opening of the college, all craft courses except printing and a number of lower-level technician courses, with associated staff, were transferred to two recently-built colleges of further education. The name was changed to Napier College of Science and Technology to reflect the type of work now being undertaken.

In 1973 the college was approved by the CNAA to offer courses leading to the awards of the Council. The first undergraduate course to be approved was an interdisciplinary vocational course with two periods of supervised work experience, 'Science with Industrial Studies'. This course was in the mainstream of the Scottish educational tradition and took advantage of the broad curriculum studied by senior pupils in Scottish schools. The course proceeded from a broad base of the study of five sciences and social science in the first year to the specialist study of two sciences and management in the final honours fourth year and involved staff from five departments. The course was the precursor of a number of similar interdisciplinary vocational degree courses that gave education at Napier its distinctive flavour. These courses were

---

1 In 1901, guidelines issued by the Scottish Education Department allowed the establishment of 'Central Institutions' (CIs) which would allow the development and improvement of technical education to take place. The work to be carried out in the new institutions would be of the highest standard and would be strictly vocational. They were seen by the Scottish Education Department as potential 'technical universities' and would also act as the apex of a system of colleges of technical education. The Scottish Education Department also indicated that the management of the Central Institutions should be devolved to governors representative of local interests who would be given considerable freedom in the operation of the institutes.

significantly different from those offered in the other universities in Edinburgh and therefore direct competition in the recruitment of students was avoided.

In 1974 Napier College merged with Edinburgh College of Commerce, which had opened in 1968, to become Napier College of Commerce and Technology and, after one year, adopted the four-faculty structure that it retained until 1996 when it assimilated the Lothian College of Nursing as its fifth faculty. The college continued to expand and develop new undergraduate courses and began to attract some external funding from industry and the research councils but these activities were not viewed with favour by the City of Edinburgh Authorities and the Scottish Education Department. Both bodies felt that the college should remain a teaching institution. This shortage of external funding, the inability to set aside any funds as a reserve and the significant proportion of staff with no research background were later to prove major handicaps.

In 1981 Principal J. Dunning retired and was succeeded as Principal by Dr W.A. Turmeau, the Dean of the Faculty of Technology and one of the Assistant Principals of Napier College. Dr Turmeau shared his predecessor's vision of an enhanced role for the college in higher education in Scotland. He also realised that if this was to be accomplished, Napier College had to become a Central Institution (CI) and gain access to the more generous funding arrangements for buildings, capital equipment, revenue and research which would follow. His views were supported in the report of the Council for Tertiary Education which recommended to the Secretary of State for Scotland, amongst other things, that Napier College should be funded directly by central government, that is become a Central Institution.

When, in 1985, Napier College and its sister college in Glasgow became Central Institutions, the move was not universally welcomed. The trade unions representing academic staff feared a possible loss of membership and the smaller non-technical Central Institutions were afraid that their sector of the education scene would be dominated by the two large newcomers.

The change in control came at a propitious time for Napier as it facilitated, in May 1985, the purchase and refurbishment of a large third campus, Craiglockhart College. This was a former teacher-training college which had been the site of an historic meeting during the First World War between the English war poets, Wilfrid Owen and Siegfried Sassoon, when the building was being used as a military hospital for officers. The purchase of Craiglockhart would not have been possible if the transfer to Central Institution had not taken place, due to the financial constraints on local government. The new campus provided much needed teaching space in addition to housing the increased administrative staff now that the college was responsible for its own affairs. Craiglockhart College had residential accommodation for 187 students and this was an additional benefit as Napier College had no other residences.

Another advantage of CI designation was access to the government-funded SWITCH initiative which was introduced to help students choose courses in engineering and computing. Napier missed out on the first round of this funding despite having the largest number of eligible students in the whole of Scotland and only gained access to later rounds as a result of the change to Central Institution. (Napier benefited to the extent of £660,000 and the salaries of ten academic and eight support staff.) The debit side of the transfer was that the college incurred the extra costs associated with three-site operation.

In December 1985 the report of the Scottish Tertiary Education Council, the body which replaced the Council for Tertiary Education, recommended that there should be a single funding body for all Scottish higher education. This proposal was strongly opposed by six of the universities and was not implemented.

On becoming a Central Institution the Academic Board of Napier College decided to expand its number of sub-committees to allow as many of its staff as practicable to participate in its decision-making processes. The new committees included an Academic Standards Committee, one of the first committees of its type in an institution of higher education in Scotland. This committee played a key role in the subsequent change from polytechnic to university.

The growing stature of Napier College had been recognised earlier by the decision of the Committee of the Directors of Polytechnics in 1984 to invite Dr Turmeau to become the first Scottish member of their committee, although Napier did not at that time have the title 'polytechnic'.

The Principal soon recognised that the college would have to expand and achieve a critical mass of about 6000 Full Time Equivalent (FTE) students to guarantee its long-term survival as a separate institution. Student numbers were expanded rapidly to meet this target. This figure was based on economic considerations and studies of institutions of higher education in Europe and Australia.

The Principal also became aware that the title 'Napier College of Commerce and Technology' was becoming a liability. Many potential customers, including school leavers, industry and commerce, were confused by the title. Newspapers and statements from professional bodies referred to higher education as the universities and polytechnics. One government White Paper referred to the universities, polytechnics and colleges, indicating a clearly defined pecking order. The title 'polytechnic' was seen by many Scots to be alien to the Scottish educational tradition and its use would be another example of the Anglicisation of their culture. The Scottish Education Department was also reluctant to allow the use of the title. However, the logic of the Principal's case was irrefutable and was accepted, although with some reluctance, by the Academic Board. But it required the personal intervention of the Secretary of State for Scotland before the Scottish Education Department agreed to a change of title to 'Napier Polytechnic of Edinburgh'. Since this was a protected title the Secretary of State for Education in England also had to ensure that Napier satisfied all the necessary conditions before giving his agreement. Approval from parliament for the use of the title 'Napier Polytechnic of Edinburgh' was finalised in September 1988. Many people external to Napier saw the change as one of status but it was seen by its academic community as merely one of title and a stepping stone towards gaining the title 'university'.

In 1987 the maturity of the institution was recognised by the CNAA in the report on its Institutional Review. This contained such phrases as 'The overall impression gained was of an institution which had adopted a thorough approach to the management of course development; the strong leadership of senior staff, the careful procedures and the administrative support were developed with a sensitivity to the academic needs of courses and to the academic responsibilities vested in the Academic Board'.

Napier was among the first group of polytechnics and was the first Scottish institution to be granted Delegated Authority by the CNAA in 1987 to monitor and validate its own courses. It was also among the first group of polytechnics in 1988 to receive CNAA Accreditation, giving the institution almost complete autonomy over the operation of all its taught courses. Around this time the polytechnic began to take advantage of the greater freedom offered by the Scottish Education Department with the establishment of a very successful company, Polyed, which was responsible for co-ordinating and increasing the external revenue-generating activities of the faculties and to begin to generate financial reserves and in 1989 the polytechnic appointed its first professors and readers. That year also saw the polytechnic receiving accreditation for research degrees from the CNAA.

In 1991 the publication of the Government White Paper, *A New Framework* (DES 1991), which proposed the abolition of the binary line between the universities, polytechnics and colleges, meant that the lobbying by Dr Turmeau and his colleagues in the Committee of Directors of Polytechnics had been recognised and Napier Polytechnic and Glasgow Polytechnic would become universities. The older Central Institutions, because of their smaller size, did not qualify, but after extensive lobbying the Bill was modified to incorporate Paisley College and Robert Gordon's Institute of Technology (Aberdeen). *The Further and Higher Education Bill (Scotland)* received its third reading in the House of Lords on 12 March 1992 and 15 June saw the official inauguration of Napier University by the Lord Provost of the City of Edinburgh.

The smaller Central Institution, Dundee Institute of Technology, later became the University of Abertay, Dundee. It was to be of benefit to the former Central Institutions that they joined as a group of four when they initially met with representatives of the older universities to discuss the future of the university sector of higher education in Scotland. In practice, the abolition of the binary line in Scotland took place in a spirit of co-operation and the nine existing universities and the four newcomers quickly established committees to look after the interests of their sector. One of the first issues to be addressed was staff salaries and conditions of service. In the Central Institutions these were negotiated nationally for Scotland whilst in the older universities they were negotiated on a UK basis between the university Vice-Chancellors and the Association of University Teachers. It was the view of Napier University management that they should withdraw from the national system at the earliest opportunity. The older universities resolved that salaries should continue to be agreed on a UK basis and that they did not wish a separate bargaining system for Scotland. In September 1995 Napier University and the other new universities withdrew from the national bargaining system and discussion is still continuing on the future of the negotiating system for salary and conditions of service in Scotland.

There was some debate in the academic community of Napier as to the title to be adopted by the new university. Some thought that while there might be short-term gains in retaining Napier in the title, in the longer term a geographical title might be of greater benefit in marketing the institution. This would be important when the university joined the University Central Admission Services (UCAS), the UK-wide system for dealing with applications from applicants for undergraduate courses.[2] The decision to adopt the title 'Napier University' was unanimous after it had been made known that the Privy Council would be unlikely to approve the title 'Napier University of Edinburgh'.

Unlike the older universities in Scotland, the Act setting up the new universities did not propose that they should have a Royal Charter. It stated that they should have articles of governance similar to their articles as a Central Institution and that they should have a supreme governing body, the Court, consisting of a majority of lay members, similar to their current Council.

The draft scheme of governance did not find favour with the academic members of the council due to the limits it placed on the academic community and on the ability of senior management of the university to manage their own affairs. The council appointed a sub-committee consisting of the Registrar, a Vice-Principal and one of its lay members (a senior member of the Scottish legal establishment) to draft an alternative proposal and enter into discussions with the Scottish Education Department, the agents of the Privy Council. A satisfactory instrument of governance was devised and agreed. The instrument was also adopted by the other new Scottish universities. These articles of governance ensure that all academic matters remain the concern of the Academic Board and that the management of the university is the responsibility of the Principal and Vice-Chancellor. The articles are framed in such a way as to obviate any recourse to the Privy Council except in exceptional circumstances.

The Academic Board decided not to adopt the title 'Senate', with its implications for membership of all professors, but to retain its previous title and structure. This meant that the four faculties – Applied Arts, Engineering, Science and the Napier Business School – would continue to have equal representation irrespective of size. The Board would have, in addition to the faculty representatives, ex-officio membership by the Principals, the Heads of certain units and representatives of the Students Association.

---

2 Napier Polytechnic was one of a very small number of institutions to stay outside the
   UK-wide system of applying for places.

The University had to prepare its own 'University Calendar' detailing its procedures and awards prior to the start of the new session. The production and agreement of these procedures in a very short period posed a major problem for the Academic Standards Committee and the Quality Assurance Unit but the deadline for the production of the calendar was met. The university also had to appoint a Chancellor and were pleased that the distinguished Scotsman, Lord George Younger, the former Foreign Secretary, accepted the post.

The change from polytechnic to university for Napier took place concurrently with a number of other significant events in the educational scene in Scotland. These included the impending establishment during session 1992/3 of the Scottish Higher Education Funding Council (SHEFC), the single funding body for all higher education in Scotland. In addition to its funding role, SHEFC is also responsible for reporting to government on the quality of teaching in Scottish higher education. SHEFC has developed its quality assurance role using criteria different from those employed by the Higher Education Funding Council in England.

The bill setting up the new universities went through parliament in parallel with legislation transferring all colleges of further education in Scotland from the control of local authorities to the Scottish Education Department. These colleges now have financial autonomy similar to that enjoyed by the former Central Institutions and many have aspirations to offer higher level courses, including degrees, thereby increasing the competition for students.

Other important factors affecting higher education in 1992, were the impending General Election, the growing difficulties faced by graduates in finding relevant employment and the financial hardship being faced by students as their grant support was reduced. In addition, Napier University faced the immediate retirement of its Vice-Principal, Professor Anderson, and the impending retirement of Professor Turmeau in the summer of 1994. The university decided to appoint a second Vice-Principal for a period of two years to assist the process of transition from polytechnic to university.

Napier University embarked on its new role as the fourth largest university in Scotland with a confidence based on its previous standing as a major polytechnic: its staff were well regarded by its students and the local business community, its courses had a high reputation with employers throughout the United Kingdom, its students had a good record of finding employment after completing their studies and it put emphasis on student care.

The Academic Board had a number of important decisions to take in the first few weeks after becoming a university, of which the first was to produce a mission statement that would provide a clear signal as to the type of university it intended becoming. The statement finally agreed was as follows:

> To develop in students the ability and desire to pursue knowledge independently and to assist them in developing their full potential. To promote excellence in research, scholarship and teaching. To provide benefits to society through the advancement and dissemination of knowledge.

The agreement on the statement was reached after prolonged discussion. It was thought by a substantial number to be too bland but all agreed that its message was clear.

The Academic Board also began to re-evaluate the strengths and weaknesses of the university and to draw up a five-year plan for its future. One important question was whether to follow the example of Heriot-Watt College on becoming a university and transfer from the institution all courses that did not lead to awards of the university. The number of students on these courses was declining but still amounted to about 30 per cent of the total. The loss of this number of students would have caused a dramatic reduction in the funding received by the university. Since Napier did not have a redundancy policy, the loss of these courses would either have meant an introduction of such a policy or the transfer of university lecturers to a college of further education. Senior management of the university was not willing to implement either of these alternative strategies. The decision to retain the technician courses leading to the awards of the Scottish Vocational Educational Council (SCOTVEC) was taken reluctantly, but it was also resolved, wherever appropriate, to replace the SCOTVEC courses with courses leading to awards of the university. The retention of these courses was to impose an additional burden on staff since they are resource intensive, criterion referenced and require separate quality assurance and administrative procedures. But retaining these courses has two benefits: first, they attract funds and second, science and engineering students enrolling on a SCOTVEC course can bridge across to an undergraduate course and many who use this route realise their potential and graduate with a good honours degree after two or three years of additional study.

When it became a university, Napier had a strong Academic Board and a powerful system of executive sub-committees: Academic

Standards, Academic Planning, Research and Consultancy, External Relations, Staff Development, Learning Resources and its four Faculty Boards. These committees enabled a significant proportion of the academic community to participate in the decision-making processes of the institution. In addition, there were two management committees – the Principals Committee and the Principals and Deans Committee. The operation of these committees and management structure allowed the university to face with confidence the prospect of being the first of the new universities in the United Kingdom to have its systems reviewed by the Division of Quality Audit of the Higher Education Quality Council (HEQC). Napier submitted its documentation in November 1992, a mere five months after becoming a university, was visited in February 1993 and was pleased to have its belief in itself confirmed by the receipt of a favourable report.

In 1991 Napier decided, due to constraints imposed by space and the shortage of resources, that the current rate of new course development could no longer be sustained. The legacy of the CNAA, where every course consisted of customised units, was wasteful of teaching resources and there was a need to return to the Scottish tradition of a broadly based first year dealing with fundamental principles and which took advantage of the four years available for undergraduate education to honours. It was agreed that the best way forward would be the adoption of a modular scheme.

The group responsible for devising the scheme made an intensive study of modular systems in operation throughout the United Kingdom and the United States of America and best practice from the schemes studied was included in their proposed scheme. This scheme was radical and innovative and, in addition to assisting in course rationalisation, would place greater emphasis on student centred learning; but it would continue to be course based and thus retain the distinctive nature of Napier courses. The scheme incorporated the concept of 'notionally effective student hours' (NESH), the total student workload including contact time plus directed and private study. It also proposed that the NESH total should be the same for each undergraduate course irrespective of discipline and that the contact time should decrease as the course progressed. As part of the scheme all students take two free-choice electives chosen from a wide catalogue of modules offered by all departments in each year of their course. The elective scheme has encouraged staff to develop modules based on their own specialist interests and allows the introduction of new subject areas.

The proposal was viewed initially with scepticism in some departments where class contact hours had been drifting upwards and where high contact hours gave staff an excuse for not participating in research or consultancy. The decision to proceed with the scheme was taken only after meetings involving all the academic staff, a large proportion of the administrative staff and a heated debate at the Academic Board.

The scheme also involved the development in-house by the staff of the Computer Unit of a comprehensive computer-based modular course management system (MCMS) which records on-line complete details of all students and their academic records. The university, as part of its modular scheme, also decided to switch from a three-term session to one of two fifteen-week semesters with an inter-semester week. The scheme retained the existing pattern of holidays with extended breaks at Christmas and Easter.

Opposition to the scheme came from staff who already had a workload considerably in excess of their counterparts in the older universities and who viewed the change from polytechnic to university as posing enough problems without the added complications of the introduction of semesters and having to redesign their courses in the new modular format. Others equated the reduction in contact time with a drop in standards and a considerable minority objected on the grounds that the modular management system would lead to greater management control.

In Napier the relationship between the senior management and the rest of the staff has always been good but the teacher trade unions, who again were worried about a possible loss of members to the Association of University Teachers, used the introduction of the modular scheme as an additional bargaining counter in the national annual salary negotiations. Most of their members refused to co-operate in the development of the modular scheme and these tactics continued even after the end of the national dispute. Delay for a year was being considered inevitable when the matter was resolved in time to allow the implementation to take place on schedule, but the incident illustrates some of the tensions which existed in the institution at the time.

The modular scheme is one of the success stories of the university, despite teething troubles chiefly associated with the inability of students to gain a place on their chosen electives, the inability to provide sufficient satisfactory study places for students and a computer system that was not initially user friendly. There has been the desired cultural shift towards a greater emphasis on student-centred learning. Staff have produced imaginative learning materials for directed study. Student contact hours have been reduced and the use of library materials has significantly increased. Course rationalisation has taken place and the process is gaining momentum. Pass and progression rates are improving, although more slowly than anticipated, and the level of academic debate across the institution has been raised. The revised system of departmental and course examination boards is now accepted by academic staff who initially found it impersonal. It allows staff to concentrate their attention on borderline and difficult cases and there is a greater consistency in pass/fail and degree classification. Some staff remain critical of the scheme because of its perceived bureaucracy and they feel that it has removed some of their academic freedom. Others complain that the lack of large lecture rooms entails the repetition of lectures and a loss of some of the promised advantages of the scheme. In 1996, following an extensive review of the first four years' operation, the scheme was simplified, a standard size of module introduced and the amount of free choice available to students slightly reduced.

The cultural shift associated with the greater emphasis on student-centred learning was assisted by the receipt of funds totalling £1 million over four years from the government-sponsored Enterprise in Higher Education initiative. These funds have assisted the integration into the modular system of studies that help students develop communication, presentation and self-learning skills.

The change from polytechnic to university presented a number of serious challenges to senior management. The abolition of the binary line should, in theory, have implied the existence of a level playing field for the higher education sector in Scotland. In practice, staff soon discovered that the going was both difficult and uphill. In the audit carried out by HEQC no allowances were made for the distinctive nature of the new universities or that Napier University had only been in operation for a matter of months as opposed to the five hundred years of some of its neighbours. Staff, however, saw advantages in the application of the same criteria across all institutions, despite the short-term problems this caused.

Earlier it was stated that prior to becoming a Central Institution, Napier University had been unable to establish a reserve fund. The college had also been excluded from access to a range of funds, including the research funds and research studentships of the Scottish Education Department and the funds from other bodies such as the Carnegie Trust. It was only in the period immediately prior to becoming a university that the institution began to gain access to a variety of trusts. A grant from the Robertson Trust enabled the building of an extension to the library at the Craiglockhart Campus.

The principal reason for the need for a reserve fund was that under the new funding arrangements the university would receive a one-line budget from SHEFC with no possibility of any additional grant to meet contingencies or capital projects. The university did not qualify for funding under the 'Mac' initiative that provided the older universities with comprehensive and compatible administrative computer systems, but Napier University was expected to participate. The decision was taken to remain outside this scheme as it did not appear cost effective and the scheme appeared to offer no advantages over the university's existing systems.

Another handicap facing the new university was the lack of space, not only for teaching and staff rooms and the increasing number of research students, but, equally important, the shortage of social space and residences. The small number of residential places owned by the university was proving to be a severe handicap, particularly when attempting to attract full-cost overseas students.

The teaching space available, in square metres per student, was the lowest of all the Scottish Central Institutions and well below the norms in the universities. The Merchiston Campus that housed most of the faculties of Engineering and Science was overcrowded and lacked adequate library accommodation. The single-block Sighthill Campus housed more students than the University of Stirling! Therefore, the university was forced into renting accommodation in a number of properties throughout the city to alleviate its space problems.

In 1963 the publication of the 'Robbins Report' and the expansion of higher education in the United Kingdom was accompanied by substantial government funding for the building of new campuses. Thirty years later this generous provision was not available to Napier University and its sister institution in the West of Scotland, Glasgow Caledonian University. These institutions became universities at a time when the government was cutting back on expenditure not only on higher education but also on schools, hospitals and social services. In addition, there was a growing demand in the UK parliament for universities to be more efficient and more accountable for the use they made of taxpayers' money.

The university had for a considerable time been asking the Scottish Office Education Department (SOED, formerly SED) to purchase on their behalf a large but mainly disused Victorian hospital with extensive grounds in South Edinburgh (Craighouse) situated near two of its campuses. The SOED did not agree to purchase but passed the decision to the new Funding Council, who decided to allow Napier University to proceed with the purchase at a cost of £10.5 million – of which they would provide £5 million, leaving the university to raise the rest. The purchase of Craighouse offered an ideal solution to the space problems of the university but also introduced short-term difficulties for senior management – principally how to finance the deal in addition to providing funds to provide new residential accommodation. There were also the additional costs incurred by operating a fourth major campus and the provision of student support facilities including refectory, library and information technology resources.

In the years immediately prior to 1992 Napier realised that pump-priming was required if it was to attract funds from the Research Councils. The number of students reading for higher degrees by research was increasing, but they tended to be concentrated in the faculties of Engineering and Science. Only one department was attracting significant funds from the Science and Engineering Research Council (SERC). The Department of Mechanical, Manufacturing and Software Engineering was consistently attracting substantial funding for Teaching Companies with high-tech companies in Central Scotland. This department was also attracting funds through its training and consultancy activities and these were ploughed back into the department to upgrade its computing facilities and hire support staff. The expanding Department of Civil and Transportation Engineering was also beginning to gain SERC funding and was taking advantage of its ability to recruit new staff with a proven track record in research.

In 1992 the University participated in the UK Research Assessment Exercise (RAE) for the first time. Not all of the 23 departments were submitted and the result was disappointing for Napier with only three departments gaining a rating of two and the university coming near the foot of unofficial league tables. The implications of this were serious for the institution; since SHEFC also allocated additional funding based on RAE ratings, little extra income would be available. This brought home to the university the need for all departments to increase their research activity and publication rate and for the university to reappraise its recruitment and promotion policies. The failure to attract extra funding from SHEFC highlighted one of the principal differences between universities in the United Kingdom. The FTE student numbers in two institutions across the former binary line may be similar but the total income to the institutions may vary by a factor of two or three. The university set out to rectify its deficiencies and progress has been made, but the threshold has been raised for the 1996 Research Assessment Exercise and only departments gaining a rating of three or higher will gain additional funding from SHEFC.

Unlike a number of the newer Australian universities, Napier University has not insisted on those members of its staff without a higher degree improving their qualifications and becoming involved in research. Therefore, the proportion of staff participating in the 1996 exercise remained low in many disciplines. The change in promotion policy means that in putting forward their case for promotion, staff have to be able to demonstrate excellence in two of the following: teaching, administration or research. The adoption of these criteria has led to interesting debate, for example what is meant by excellence in teaching and how can it be demonstrated? There is the feeling among some staff that the only one of the three criteria that matters is research and this has led to a fall in the amount of consultancy activity as departments and staff turn their attention to research.

SHEFC, in 1992, published the criteria they intended to use for the quality assessment of teaching and learning of each cognate area in every institution of higher education in Scotland and stated that they intended making their judgement following a three-day visit to each department being assessed. This proposal was resented by the older universities and the newer universities saw in the scheme a return to the earlier practices of the CNAA. The decision meant that staff who were already trying to increase their research and deal with modularisation and the internal system of course validation and review would have to carry the additional burden of preparing documentation for the visit. SHEFC uses a four-point scale for grading (excellent, highly satisfactory, satisfactory and unsatisfactory) and only the excellent category attracts additional funding. The criteria used by SHEFC consider the total educational experience of the student and include such factors as the quality of lecture theatres, course management, library and computer facilities, counselling, the feedback given to students, whether the courses meet their stated objectives and those of the university, classroom teaching and its underpinning by research. Seven Napier departments were graded 'highly statisfactory' and eight 'satisfactory,' so no extra funds have been obtained.

It had been the belief of staff at Napier University that although their departments had not done well in the Research Assessment Exercise, the majority would be rated excellent in the assessment of their teaching. The documentation which staff submit to SHEFC includes a self-assessment of how each department rates itself in each of fourteen categories. Departmental assessments proved to be much higher than those of the Academic Standards Committee and SHEFC. In their reports, SHEFC highlight the problems caused by the rapid expansion of the institution, the high workloads of staff and the limited research underpinning teaching. Departmental staff point out that many of the factors affecting the rating – such as the quality of teaching accommodation and social space – are outwith their control and require action by senior management if there is to be an improvement in the next round of visits.

Midway through the SHEFC visits it became clear that the quality assurance systems of the university would benefit from a comprehensive revision to satisfy a number of objectives: first, to reduce the administrative load associated with the validation and review of individual courses; second, to place greater responsibility for quality on faculties and satisfy their demands for a move away from centralised systems; and third, to enable the university to monitor the entire work of a department, including its management and quality assurance systems, its approach to research and the total loading on the department. The scheme devised was comprehensive and based on best practice from ISO 9000 and a study of the systems in operation in New Zealand and the United States. It proposed that the activities of each department would be reviewed on a five-year cycle with substantial delegated authority over its affairs between reviews.

The university also decided that, since the efficiency and effectiveness of its operations and the quality of the student experience was based not only on its academic departments but also its administrative and support departments, they too should be reviewed on a five-year cycle.[3]

The scheme was generally welcomed by academic departments who saw its benefits, but some administrative departments were bitterly opposed to any scrutiny of their operations by either internal or external

---

3 On becoming a university, Napier had earlier recognised the importance of its administrative and support departments by treating the heads of these departments on a par with academic heads.

peers. The scheme was introduced on a pilot basis in session 1994/5 for academic, administrative and support departments. In addition to satisfying the objectives listed earlier, academic departments benefit from the rigorous review enabling them to rectify weaknesses identified prior to a SHEFC visit.

Since 1991 each academic department has had to produce a comprehensive business plan giving details of its mission statement, objectives, expected student numbers, new course development and the expected external revenues to be generated from research, consultancy and training. The inclusion of administrative and support departments in the review scheme means that they too have to produce business plans. Their staff have become more aware of the role played by their department in helping the university achieve its goals and they now participate as members of review panels. The third benefit of the new scheme is that it offers staff the opportunity to exchange best practice with their peers. The evidence from the pilot reviews is that although there are short-term costs in staff time and the expense involved with the actual event, the system is welcomed by the majority of staff – who are appreciating their increased participation in the management and decision-making processes of their department. In addition, some of the longer-term benefits are already being realised: the Department of Building and Surveying gained the highest quality rating of any Scottish university in its group.

The other important factor involving the development of Napier as a university was the need to appoint a successor to its Principal, Professor Turmeau. Napier University has benefited in its development through the stability associated with having only two Principals in thirty years. The appointment of the Principal is the responsibility of the Court and their original intention was to form an Appointment Committee that did not include any representation from the academic staff. This situation was not acceptable to the academic community and confirmed some of the fears that existed when the articles of governance were being formulated. The situation was finally resolved by the addition to the committee of one of the Vice-Principals who was not an applicant for the post and the decision that any recommendation regarding the appointment would require to be unanimous. There was debate in the committee as to what background should be expected of the new Principal. Some members expressed the view that since the university was essentially a business, an academic background was not a prerequisite for the post. A list of suitable applicants was drawn up and, after an extensive series of interviews involving applicants from business, public service and academia, the decision was taken to appoint a distinguished academic and engineer who had experience of industry, Professor J. Mavor, the Dean of the Faculty of Science and Engineering at the University of Edinburgh.

Professor Mavor, during his first year, sent several clear signals that things would change. These included statements that he would be placing emphasis on external income generation, research and quality. The Principals Committee was disbanded and the executive management of the university is now the responsibility of a Central Executive Group (CEG) consisting of the Principals and Deans together with the Registrar and the heads of finance, personnel, external relations and the Director of the university company. The post of Dean was made full-time and faculties have been given greater autonomy over staff appointments and the allocation of budgets. Unlike traditional universities, only a few Napier departments are multi-professorial and the post of Head of Department was permanent with responsibility for both the academic leadership and the running of the department. Since 1996 Heads of Department are now on five-year contracts with the possibility of extension. The appointment of full-time Deans has been expensive and added an extra layer to the hierarchy, but they are expected to co-ordinate the activities of their faculty and undertake university-wide duties. It is significant that the university experienced difficulty in obtaining suitably qualified staff to fill two vacant deans' posts. This difficulty of recruiting highly qualified staff with substantial research experience is one facing all the new universities in the United Kingdom.

The Principal also requested that reports should be produced recommending possible changes to the faculty structure, streamlining of the committees of the Academic Board and a review of the administration. The first two reports took almost a year to produce and the delay in their publication caused a great deal of uncertainty in the academic community. A number of heads of department worried that their department might be merged with another. Some members of staff saw possible opportunities for promotion whilst others envisaged their prospects receding. The principal recommendation of the final proposal was that the university should retain its four-faculty structure and that following the reorganisation of health education in Scotland and the successful bid for the incorporation of Lothian College of Health Studies within Napier University in September 1996, it becomes the fifth faculty.[4]

Other recommendations were that there should be a transfer of some departments between faculties, that three new departments be formed and that no staff would either lose their job or be demoted. Naturally, not all staff welcomed the proposals. A series of consultative meetings took place to discuss the implications and the Academic Board saw a heated debate before finally agreeing to their adoption. The restructuring brings together strong subject groupings to allow rationalisation of courses both within and across faculty boundaries. It provides the impetus to bring together 'critical mass' teams to drive forward new measures to improve the quality of teaching and research. However, it also provides a structure that will facilitate the merger of departments if necessary. A similar exercise with administrative departments carried out in session 1995/6 has led to a streamlining of activities and a decision to use contract staff for some duties, for example security.

The restructuring of the committees of the Academic Board from six to three (Standards and Quality, Planning and Services) reflects the devolution of authority to the faculties and significantly reduces the time spent in committees but still retains a system which allows academic and administrative staff at all levels their voice in the decision-making processes of the university.

Money has been made available at the expense of teaching budgets for the establishment of 'research pillars' which are intended to concentrate research effort across the university and lead to increased external funding and an improved research rating. The first pillar to be established is in the interdisciplinary field of transport studies.

During session 1994/5 SHEFC made available funds that offered enhanced pensions to members of staff opting for early retirement. Twenty people, many in promoted posts, took advantage of this offer and a number of others in departments that were overstaffed were persuaded to go early, also on enhanced terms. The scheme has enabled

---

4   The Napier University bid was greatly helped by the fact that the degree courses of the Lothian College were validated by Napier University. The college would not have entered this relationship if Napier had not been a university.

the university to recruit as replacement young staff with a proven track record in research.

Three years on from becoming a university, staff are coming to terms with the costs and benefits associated with their new status. Session 1995/6 saw for the first time in the United Kingdom a decline in the number of school leavers applying for places at university. Napier University found not only a drop in the numbers applying for courses in science and engineering but also for the first time for its business courses. The competition for students among universities has increased and more are living at home and gaining a higher diploma qualification at a college of further education before continuing their studies at university. The government, in September 1996, announced its approval for a new University of the Highlands and Islands and one Scottish university has recently announced that it is considering the introduction of 'accelerated' degrees that may be completed in two years, thus intensifying the competition. In addition, the requirement for all universities in Scotland to make efficiency gains of 10 per cent over the next three years is increasing the pressures on staff, many of whom are feeling stressed. These pressures have been intensified by management entering into discussions with the teaching unions over the introduction of a redundancy policy.

The overall student:staff ratio is now 17:1, leading to a drive by the Educational Development Unit to assist staff devise more efficient methods of teaching and learning. The slowing down of the rate of growth and the decline in student applications have caused staff to consider carefully the position of the university in the market place, the type of courses being offered and to place much greater emphasis on the quality of the educational experience being offered. The income generated by the university company, NUVentures (Polyed), whilst remaining high, has fallen slightly for the first time due to a decline in external training activity and a greater involvement by staff in research.[5]

The university has agreed with each department target figures for the external revenue it expects it to generate. Some departments still have to shake off their dependency culture and make key appointments before they begin to attract substantial external funding.

However, the university has a number of successes to report. Full-time equivalent student numbers have reached over 9000 with the

---

5   The figures for session 1994/5 were: turnover £3.4 million, with £1.5 million remitted to the university.

incorporation of the Lothian College of Health Studies. Alumni in Hong Kong have established a scholarship fund of HK$3 million for students wishing to study at Napier. The first graduation of students studying for a part-time Napier University degree at the University of Hong Kong took place in November 1995. Other Napier courses in Hong Kong and Mauritius are proving successful. Staff are also benefiting from participating in a range of joint ventures in Europe, China, Taiwan, the United States and New Zealand. Many students from the European Community take part of their course at Napier. The university is currently reconsidering its policies on international liaison with a view to maximising the benefits.

The Enterprise in Higher Education Centre at Napier University was one of the most successful in the UK. The funding received has been used to finance a range of developments, including the integration of the teaching of enterprise skills in the modular scheme, staff development, student tutoring in schools, working with voluntary organisations and student projects in the community. The centre has also been attracting significant external funding, often in partnership with another university – for example the establishment in Scotland of a Centre for Entrepreneurial Studies with the University of Stirling and the Robert Gordon University. The external funding for the centre finished in August 1996 but the activities of the centre have been integrated into the mainstream of the university and the staff retained.

The number of postgraduate research students has increased by 75 per cent since becoming a university and the proportion of students on SCOTVEC courses is now only 8 per cent.

The Craighouse campus, potentially the finest new campus in the United Kingdom, situated on a commanding site dominating the skyline of south-west Edinburgh, became operational at the start of session 1996/7 and a major grant of £650,000 has been received from Historic Scotland towards the restoration of the hall in the main building. This, coupled with the recent completion of the thousandth residential place, is enhancing the student experience at Napier University.

Considerable investment has been made in enhancing the planning processes and developing the necessary information technology infrastructure and communication networks to enable the university to move forward during the next decade. External funding from SHEFC has provided networks linking all the institutions of higher education in the East of Scotland.

The university, in common with other new universities, is finding the going tough and now realises that unlike the titular change from college to polytechnic, becoming a university required a major cultural change. External pressures on the university may lead to a loss of the distinctive flavour of education at Napier – for example the interdisciplinary nature of its courses, the periods of supervised work experience and the industrial experience of staff.

The Central Executive Group has difficult decisions to take in balancing the present short-term difficulties against the long-term needs of the university – for example whether to continue to subsidise research at the expense of teaching. There was also the dilemma over the strategy to be adopted for the RAE. The decision was taken to place the emphasis on excellence and submit only departments likely to obtain a rating of three or better. This, naturally, has had an adverse effect on morale in those departments not submitted. In 1996 the university submitted in 13 categories, mainly in engineering and science. The other departments were not expected to gain a rating of three or higher and, therefore, were not submitted.

The university has had a cut in the grant from SHEFC for session 1996/7 in excess of the anticipated 3 per cent and there was a rise in the salaries for staff of 4 per cent. The SHEFC grant and student fees amount to 80 per cent of the total income and staff salaries 75 per cent of expenditure, therefore further shedding of staff appears inevitable.

The university has always realised that its chief asset is its staff and that there is a need to have people with the skills of academic leadership and entrepreneurship leading departments if the university is to prosper. The calibre of the appointments made during 1996 to the vacant heads of department, deans and other key posts will play a crucial role in deciding the future of the university.

Napier University grew from being a craft college to a university through the vision of its first two Principals and the hard work of its staff. It has taken steps to become leaner and fitter. Now that the heady days of becoming a university are consigned to history, staff appreciate how much remains to be done before the full potential of Napier University is realised.

Appendix
Napier University at a glance

The recently-adopted mission statement of the university is:

Napier University's primary goal is to help its students gain the qualifications, personal skills and experience that will benefit society in general, and companies and organisations in particular. It is a goal that promulgates an active and mutually rewarding relationship between all parties concerned – the students, those for whom they carry out projects in the community, industry, commerce and the professions, and Napier University.

The university is multi-campus with three of the five main campuses being situated within a one-mile radius in south-west Edinburgh.

The university has 25 academic departments in five faculties – Applied Arts and Social Science, Engineering, Health Studies, Napier Business School, and Science.

The staff of the university in session 1995/6, expressed in terms of full-time equivalents, was 476 academic staff and 853 support staff.

Student numbers in session 1995/6, expressed in terms of full-time equivalents, were 9165 total, of whom 6927 were full-time. There were 6999 students on undergraduate courses, 1305 postgraduate students and 859 on diploma courses. There are currently almost 60 per cent male and 40 per cent female students. The distribution of students by attendance is: full-time 75 per cent, part-time 24 per cent and distance learning 1 per cent. The majority of the students come from East and Central Scotland. (In addition, in session 1995/6 the Lothian College of Health Studies, which became the fifth faculty, had 1510 FTE students, 124 FTE academic staff and 68 FTE support staff. The incorporation of the Lothian College will make the ratio of male/female students in the university 50/50 in session 1996/7.)

The geographical distribution of the undergraduate students is as follows: Scotland (84%), England and Wales (7%), Northern Ireland (3%) European Union (4%) other overseas (2%). The majority of Scottish students come from Central and East Scotland. The overseas students came from 34 countries.

The university has residential accommodation for 1300 students, most of which has been completed in the last three years.

The current total expenditure of the university in session 1994/5 was £43.2m, of which £22.6m went to academic departments, £4m to academic services, £6.5m to central administration, £3.9m to property costs and £7.2m to other costs. The total income was £44.7m, of which £24.9m came from the Funding Council, £10.3m from tuition fees, £2.1m from research grants and contracts and £4.3m from other services and endowments. The university had an operating surplus of £1.5m.

The university has particular strengths in its links with industry in central Scotland through the Science and Engineering Council (SERC) Teaching Company Scheme, in which the Department of Mechanical, Manufacturing and Software Engineering is working with both high-tech companies and small manufacturing enterprises (sme's).

The university has a strong Transport Research Institute, which integrates the work of its departments in transportation engineering, environmental studies and transport economics and planning.

The university, in collaboration with the University of Dundee, operates the Scottish Film School and runs the Centre for Entrepreneurial Studies with the University of Stirling and the Robert Gordon University.

The university also has strengths in the following areas: banking and finance, biological sciences, environmental management, hospitality and tourism, industrial design, polymer chemistry and technology, software engineering and computing, and printing, publishing and journalism.

Part IV

Hong Kong

Chapter 8

The Reform of Higher Education in Hong Kong

Nigel J. French

For most of the past fifty years Hong Kong's higher education system was 'small and elitist, drawing mainly upon the output of a small number of academically oriented schools'. (Morris, McClelland and Yeung 1994, p.131). During the period from 1988 to 1995, however, this situation changed radically as a result of major government initiatives which transformed the face of higher education in the territory. This paper describes this transformation, and the role played in it by the University Grants Committee of Hong Kong (UGC)[1], from the vantage point of one intimately involved in the process as Secretary-General of the UGC since June 1990. It also describes how and why three of Hong Kong's higher education institutions, two of them originally 'polytechnics', achieved the status and title of 'university' during this period.

Background

Prior to 1963 there was only one university in Hong Kong, the University of Hong Kong (HKU, founded 1911) (Mellor 1980). In

---

1 The University Grants Committee of Hong Kong, established in 1965, is a non-statutory advisory body appointed by the HKSAR Chief Executive (formerly by the Governor) to advise on the development and funding needs of Hong Kong's higher education sector.

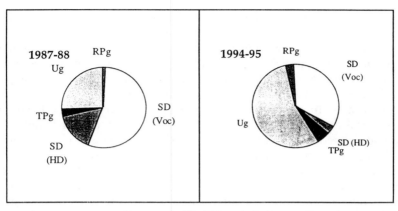

SD (Voc) = Sub-Degree (Vocational); SD (HD) = Sub-Degree (Hons Diploma *et sim*)
Ug = Undergraduate; Tpg = Taught Postgraduate; Rpg = Research Postgraduate)

*Figure 8.1 Student enrolments (fte) in post-secondary and tertiary
education institutions in Hong Kong 1987–88 and 1994–95*
Source: University Grants Committee Secretariat

1963 the Chinese University of Hong Kong (CUHK) was established
by bringing together three former post-secondary colleges – New Asia
College (founded 1949), Chung Chi College (1951) and United
College (1956). A fourth college, Shaw College, was founded in 1986.
These were, in 1988 (indeed prior to 1991), the only 'universities' in
Hong Kong, both offering a range of first and higher degrees in a wide
range of disciplines. There were, however, other post-secondary and
tertiary education institutions.

In 1972 the Hong Kong Polytechnic (HKP) was established, taking
over the work of the former Hong Kong Technical College and offering
full-time and part-time courses leading to higher diploma, diploma,
higher certificate and certificate qualifications. In 1983, on the
recommendation of the UK Council for National Academic Awards
(CNAA), the polytechnic was permitted to offer courses leading to first
degrees. Also in 1983, a former post-secondary college, the Hong Kong
Baptist College (HKBC), was incorporated as a tertiary education
institution. From 1986 the college was empowered to award degrees, in
addition to its former higher diplomas, subject to their being validated
by the CNAA. In 1984 a second polytechnic, the City Polytechnic of
Hong Kong (CPHK) was founded, offering, initially, higher certificate,

diploma and higher diploma courses, but with the expectation, realised in 1986, that it would also offer degrees validated by the CNAA.

There were also two registered post-secondary colleges: Lingnan College (LC), founded in 1967, offering government-funded two-year Form 6 courses and post-Form 6 courses, and Shue Yan College, registered in 1976, offering self-funding four-year diploma programmes. In addition, the Hong Kong Academy for Performing Arts (APA) was established in 1985 to offer foundation and diploma courses aimed at providing students with complete and integrated training for a professional career in the performing arts.

The Vocational Training Council (VTC), established in 1982, operated eight technical institutes offering courses at craft and technician levels, leading mainly to awards from the UK Business and Technician Education Council, and 16 training centres offering off-the-job basic and updating training for specific industries. Finally, the four Colleges of Education and the Institute of Language in Education, all established under the Education Department, offered between them initial teacher education courses at sub-degree level and a range of in-service training and refresher courses for serving teachers.

Table 8.1 Full-time equivalent student enrolments in post- secondary and tertiary education institutions inHong Kong – academic year 1987–88

Institution	SD (Voc)	SD (HD)	Ug	TPg	RPg	Total
HKU	23	–	6121	1223	281	7648
CUHK	–	–	5975	674	264	6913
HKP (PolyU)	8562	2553	2090	–	–	13206
HKBC (HKBU)	65	1753	751	–	–	2569
CPHK (CityU)	1420	976	1134	93	–	3623
LC	707	238	–	–	–	945
Shue Yan	–	4040	–	–	–	4040
APA	422	–	–	–	–	422
VTC	20688	–	–	–	–	20688
Cs of Ed (HKIEd)	3246	–	–	–	–	3246
Total	35133	9560	16071	1990	545	63300

Source: University Grants Committee Secretariat and Institutions

Table 8.2 Full-time equivalent student enrolments in post-secondary and tertiary education institutions in Hong Kong – academic year 1994–95

Institution	SD (Voc)	SD (HD)	Ug	TPg	RPg	Total
HKU	–	–	8768	1465	919	11152
CUHK	–	–	9381	785	798	10963
HKUST	–	–	4367	306	430	5103
PolyU (HKP)	4763	–	7378	819	196	13156
HKBU (HKBC)	–	–	4006	176	54	4235
CityU (CPHK)	4070	–	6473	685	151	11379
LC	–	538	1409	–	–	1947
Shue Yan	–	2483	–	–	–	2483
APA	170	–	182	–	–	352
VTC	16669	–	–	–	–	16669
HKIEd (Cs of Ed)	4132	–	–	–	–	4132
OLI	637	–	7088	–	–	7725
Total	30441	3021	49052	4236	2548	89296

Source: University Grants Committee Secretariat and Institutions

In the academic year 1987–88 enrolments in these various institutions (as at January 1988) totalled about 63,300 full-time equivalent (fte) students (see Table 8.1). However, in terms of access to higher education only some 7 per cent of the relevant age group (17–20 years) could gain admission to a first degree place in a Hong Kong tertiary education institution, although a further 3.4 per cent could enter professional or honours diploma courses, which were of nearly equivalent standing.

Developments 1988–1995

By the academic year 1994–95 the scene had changed dramatically, with first-year first-degree places available for 18 per cent of the relevant age group and total student enrolments (as at January 1995) in the above institutions (some having also changed their status significantly), the Hong Kong University of Science and Technology (HKUST) (opened in 1991)[2] and the Open Learning Institute of Hong Kong (OLI, established in 1989) totalling some 89,300 fte students (see Table 8.2). There were three separate government policy initiatives that contributed to these developments:

- establishment of the Open Learning Institute of Hong Kong
- expansion plan for 1991–94 triennium
- revised expansion plan for period 1991–95.

Establishment of the Open Learning Institute of Hong Kong

Following a recommendation of a visiting panel headed by Sir John Llewellyn,[3] the UGC had been invited by the government, in July 1983, 'to consider fully the question of an Open University in Hong Kong'. The government had in mind an Open University modelled on that in Britain and distinguished from a traditional university in four ways: less rigorous entrance qualifications, study conducted away from a campus as a norm, the majority of students being in employment and distance learning methods being employed. However, standards of attainment were to be similar to those of traditional universities.

After careful consideration, the UGC decided, in July 1984, to recommend against the development in Hong Kong of a higher educational institution modelled on the UK Open University (UPGC 1984). The committee had concluded, from all the evidence studied during the intervening twelve months, that the minimum continuing constituency required to produce a viability in cost terms for such an institution was around 70,000 – 100,000, which it did not think would be forthcoming. Moreover the committee considered that most of the necessary academic and technical expertise required to staff such an institution would not be found in Hong Kong, yet a knowledge of the needs of the territory in educational terms would be essential to success. Furthermore, the need to teach in both Cantonese and English and the lack of an appropriate environment for home study in Hong Kong

---

2 Planning for the construction of a 'Third University' began in 1986, following advice and recommendations of the UPGC in 1982 and 1985. The fascinating, and at times controversial, story of the planning, design and construction of HKUST falls outside the scope of this chapter. For a full account see Walker (1994).

3 In the panel's report *A Perspective on Education in Hong Kong* (1982).

would give rise to unacceptably high costs for bi-lingual preparation of teaching materials and the provision of a network of study centres.

On the other hand, the UGC did recommend that a very high priority should be given by the government to the further development of 'open education'. By this, the committee did not imply a single method or system of education or training provided through an institution devoted to reaching non-traditional students. Rather, it meant 'Distance learning by correspondence courses combined, as appropriate, with radio and television programmes, part-time attendance at existing recognised institutions, external degree and diploma programmes offered by a university, polytechnic or recognised college and short courses – particularly those aimed at providing continuing education.' The UGC further recommended that 'The development be based on all the institutions providing higher education and that this development be a co-operative and collaborative venture, with a minimal co-ordinating machinery…' (UPGC 1984, p.3).

The government referred the matter back to the Education Commission, which recommended (EC 1986) the establishment of a consortium of tertiary education institutions in Hong Kong to offer open education at the post-secondary level:

- to provide a second chance for those who had to forgo, or were denied the opportunity of, further education when they left school, or whose requirements for further education develop relatively late in life

- to provide continuing education to update and enhance the training of those who completed their further education at the beginning of their careers

- to provide retraining for those who need to change or extend their career or vocational skills later in life to adapt to technological, economic and social change.

The Education Commission further recommended the establishment of a planning committee, on which all participating institutions should be represented, to survey the principal areas of demand and need for open education, establish the availability of contributory effort within participating institutions, assess the immediate availability of material from overseas institutions and produce a detailed implementation plan.

After extensive public consultation on the Education Commission's recommendations, the Governor in Council approved, in September 1987, the establishment of a Planning Committee for an Open Learning Institute, along with a set of planning guidelines. In his speech at the opening of the 1987/88 Legislative Council session on 7 October 1987 the Governor, referring to the decision to form a Planning Committee, said: 'The provision of an Open Learning Institute, which will be Hong Kong's sixth degree-awarding institution, will considerably increase the opportunity for tertiary education. The Institute will offer degree and sub-degree courses. It should admit its first students in 1989.'

Based on the advice of the Planning Committee, the Open Learning Institute of Hong Kong (OLI) was established by law in May 1989 as a tertiary institution with the power to confer academic awards in its own name, but operating as a consortium with the existing tertiary institutions funded through the UGC. The setting-up and initial operating costs of the OLI were supported by the government but the institute was expected to become self-financing in about four years through income from tuition fees and other sources. Enrolment in the OLI's programmes started in late 1989.

The initial concept of the OLI as a consortium has not worked particularly well and the institute has required further injections of government funding to keep it afloat, but its enrolments have increased steadily, after early setbacks, so that its enrolment stood at about 17,400 (headcount) in 1994/95.

Expansion plan 1991–94

In September 1988 the government approved indicative student number targets by level of study and year for the then existing or planned tertiary degree-awarding institutions (CPHK, HKBC, HKP, CUHK, HKU and HKUST) for the 1991–94 triennium and noted their planning projections for 1994–2000. The student targets and planning projections were conveyed to the institutions by the UGC in October 1988 in the form of 'start' letters which invited the institutions to initiate action on the preparation of uncosted Academic Development Proposals (ADPs) for 1991–94.

Incidentally, in June 1988, on the recommendation of the Education Commission (EC 1988), the government had decided that at all tertiary institutions funded by the UGC all students should be accepted for first degree programmes after Secondary 7, following a two-year sixth-form course leading to the Advanced (A) Level Examination or to a combination of A and Intermediate levels. This structural change, which had particular implications for CUHK because of its previous

Table 8.3 Student number targets (in fte terms) 1991–94

	Academic Year		
Institution	*1991–92*	*1992–93*	*1993–94*
CPHK (CityU)	8900	9800	10800
HKBC (HKBU)	3000	3000	3250
HKP (PolyU)	13500	13500	13500
CUHK	8250	8475	8700
HKUST	700	1840	3450
HKU	8470	8790	9100
Total	42820	45405	48800

Source: University Grants Committee Secretariat

practice of taking most of its entrants after one-year sixth-form courses, was to be implemented by 1996-97.

The institutions' uncosted ADPs were considered by the UGC in January 1990. The committee decided that the 1991–94 academic planning exercise should be carried through separately from the further expansion plan for the period 1991–95 (see below). Accordingly, formal 'allocution' letters in respect of the institutions' 1991–94 ADPs, including the UGC's specific advice on the various academic programmes and initiatives put forward for the original triennium, were issued to the institutions in February 1990. These 'allocution' letters confirmed student number targets for the 1991–94 triennium, as shown in Table 8.3.

Revised expansion plan 1991–95

In the meantime, however, the government had, in October 1989, announced its decision to undertake a massive expansion of tertiary education. This included the policy commitment that first-year first-degree (FYFD) places planned for the 1994–95 academic year should be increased to no less than 18 per cent of the relevant (17–20) age group, or approximately 15,000 places. (This figure was later revised to 14,500 in accordance with a revised projection of the population in the relevant age group.) The UGC was invited to advise on how to meet the revised student number target and to submit its recommendations to the government in 1990. In March 1990 the institutions were invited to submit revised ADPs for the expansion for the period 1991–95, based on targets tentatively proposed for consideration by the UGC.

On the advice of the UGC, the government agreed, in July 1990, that the target should be achieved by:

- expanding further HKU and CUHK to 11,500 fte students each, achieving a total provision of 6240 FYFD places
- reaffirming the previously-approved target of 5070 fte for HKUST, leading to the provision of 1990 FYFD places
- increasing the percentage of degree level places offered at HKP and CPHK to 65 per cent each, so that the two polytechnics would provide altogether 4970 FYFD places within a total population (degree and sub-degree) of 25,200 fte students (13,500 fte at HKP and 11,700 at CPHK)
- bringing forward plans for expanding HKBC to achieve a student population of 4000 fte, providing 1110 FYFD places
- upgrading LC to a degree-awarding institution with a total population of 2000 fte students, offering 690 FYFD places.

To tie in with the expansion for the period 1991–95, the UGC recommended, and the government agreed, that a two-phase grant assessment exercise should be undertaken on the basis of a single grant year for 1991–92, with the next triennium running from 1992–95. Costed academic proposals for 1991–92 and 1992–95 from the seven UGC-funded institutions (including LC) were considered at the September meetings in 1990 and 1991 respectively. The UGC's grant recommendations in respect of the two phases of the exercise were approved by the government on 10 November 1990 and 22 October 1991. Following the approval of funds by the Finance Committee of the Legislative Council, recurrent grant 'allocation' letters for 1991–92 and 1992–95 were issued on 20 February 1991 and 31 January 1992 respectively.

The actual student numbers provided by the seven UGC-funded institutions, expressed in full-time equivalent (fte) terms, corresponded closely with the student targets and were as shown in Table 8.4.

Table 8.4 Student Numbers – targets and actual enrolments 1991–95

| | Academic Year | | | | | | | |
| | 1991–92 | | 1992–93 | | 1993–94 | | 1994–95 | |
Institution	Target	Actual	Target	Actual	Target	Actual	Target	Actual
CityU	8934	9395	9663	10162	10375	10801	11042	11379
HKBU	3261	3445	3395	3695	3527	3915	3655	4235
LC	1350	1310	1504	1489	1657	1719	1797	1947
CUHK	8900	9225	9641	9873	10265	10460	10832	10963
PolyU	13599	14542	13349	14028	13053	13364	12743	13156
HKUST	700	770	1797	2144	3361	3668	4930	5103
HKU	8765	8793	9433	9800	10156	10618	10796	11152
Total	45509	47480	48782	51190	52394	54544	55795	57935

Source: University Grants Committee Secretariat

The targets for first-year first-degree places over the period 1991–95 as shown in Table 8.5.

Table 8.5 First-year first-degree places targets 1991–95

1991–92	1992–93	1993–94	1994–95
10086	11007	12520	14500

Source: University Grants Committee Secretariat

In accordance with the government's advice on special manpower requirements, priority was given to the expansion of provision at degree and sub-degree level of courses in social work, information technology and computer engineering, electronic engineering and building services engineering, business administration and management, hospitality management; expansion of provision at degree level of courses in primary education, English and Chinese; and expansion of provision at postgraduate level of courses in education.

Recurrent grants for 1991–95, updated to take account of salary increases approved during the period, were as shown in Table 8.6.

Table 8.6 Recurrent grants 1991–95

| | *Academic Year* | | | |
| | 1991–92 | 1992–93 | 1993–94 | 1994–95 |
Institution	HK$m	HK$m	HK$m	HK$m
CityU	720	865	981	1018
HKBU	254	351	424	408
LC	84	128	154	163
CUHK	964	1388	1620	1771
PolyU	915	1228	1333	1245
HKUST	302	681	1003	1232
HKU	1113	1515	1774	1888
Total	4354	6156	7290	7726

Source: University Grants Committee Secretariat

Table 8.7 Capital grants 1991–95

| | *Financial Year* | | | |
| | 1991–92 | 1992–93 | 1993–94 | 1994–95 |
Institution	HK$m	HK$m	HK$m	HK$m
CityU	355	356	127	60
HKBU	21	59	255	82
LC	20	24	96	293
CUHK	139	292	230	158
PolyU	165	115	110	52
HKUST	875	900	250	226
HKU	298	252	339	257
Total	1873	1999	1406	1129

Source: University Grants Committee Secretariat

The capital grants approved for the institutions during 1991–95 amounted to just over HK$6400 million, as shown in Table 8.7.

The revised structure was, in the event, fully implemented, with CUHK having completed the transition from admitting students predominantly after one year in the sixth form to admitting all their undergraduate students after Secondary 7, three years ahead of schedule in the academic year 1994–95. The expansion package was achieved on schedule in 1994–95.

University title for HKP, CPHK and HKBC

In its Special Report covering the period October 1965 to June 1976, the UGC devoted Chapter Three to 'Differences between Institutions', highlighting the characteristics of those tertiary institutions which the committee was then most concerned with: universities and polytechnics. The differentiation between these types of institutions was based on the propositions that:

- there is 'a large block of tertiary level work in which the advanced education element is more accentuated (compared with Technical institutes, Colleges of Further Education, etc., which are not funded by the U(P)GC) but without losing the training element, a block which is spanned by Universities as well as Polytechnics'

- there is also 'a smaller block of top tertiary level work which, while still maintaining the training element, continues the educational element to become the advancement of learning, i.e. a University' (UPGC 1976, pp.10–14).

These propositions also indicate the committee's perception of the comparative sizes of the two 'blocks': the 'polytechnic' requirement being larger than the 'university' requirement.

In 1983, when the HKBC became a tertiary institution publicly funded through the UGC, the committee indicated that the college was expected to be a smaller size institution (than the then universities and polytechnics) and would fulfil 'a clearly differentiated and distinctive role as a College of arts and sciences in which provision is made for a liberal education, albeit with an orientation more towards preparation for employment than for post-graduate education' (UPGC 1983, p.29). A similar 'college' role was subsequently expected of Lingnan College when it became a UGC-funded tertiary institution in 1991.

The UGC considered that these distinctive and complementary roles of the tertiary institutions suited the community interests, making the best use of available resources. Indeed, the committee had already for many years adopted as planning guidelines that:

- the development of particular interest areas and the offering of courses in these areas will depend upon many factors, among which are innate ability, student needs, employers' needs and the possible future requirements of the community. Overlap in areas of study and in the level of course work is necessary

- one of the responsibilities of the universities is the recognition and education of the relatively few students of outstanding merit. Their activity in providing for the general body of students enables them also to support the few outstanding students by appropriate means

- in between the universities and a mixture of post-secondary institutions (such as technical institutes), and overlapping with both, are the polytechnics (and colleges). The major overlap will be with the universities because in the nature of things there will be little to distinguish the abilities of many polytechnic students, and there will be common employment opportunities in many cases.

Accordingly, when HKBC submitted a formal request for 'university status and title' in 1989 it did not gain the UGC's support. As advised by the Chairman in his letter to the President in April 1989, the overriding concern of the committee was 'the need to ensure the continued development of the College as an institution providing primarily a first degree education based on the liberal arts and science with a vocational emphasis'.

The planning guidelines outlined above were reviewed by the UGC during 1991 but the committee maintained the view that the institutions should continue to fulfil their differentiated roles with the aim of achieving a higher education system that has an appropriate balance between programmes at different levels and in different areas and in which different institutions make differing contributions to the community. Meanwhile, however, the committee had received representations from HKP, CPHK and HKBC in various different contexts, including Institutional Review Visits, Academic Review Visits, etc, seeking both institutional accreditation and the award of university status and title.

The three institutions argued that they should be awarded university status (or at least the title) on the following grounds:

- expansion of student numbers – both polytechnics had reached a size comparable with, or larger than, that of the universities (in the case of HKBC, expansion of its student population was envisaged up to 4000 fte by 1994–95 and possibly up to 5000 fte eventually)

- increases in first degree work – HKBC had been admitting only degree-level students since 1990 and the percentage of degree level places at the polytechnics was to be increased to 65 per cent by 1994–95

- development of postgraduate work – both polytechnics had already developed postgraduate work in selected fields and it was expected that in each case the percentage of postgraduate students (taught and research) would be increased to 8 per cent by 1994–95. In the case of HKBC, the college had initiated a taught postgraduate programme and was planning to expand it further to the extent of 4 per cent of its student population whilst developing a postgraduate research programme for 1 per cent of its students

- academic accreditation – the external validation by the UGC/HKCAA[4] had confirmed the suitability of the polytechnics and HKBC for offering first degrees and for gradual development/extension of higher degrees. The institutions therefore believed that the stage had been reached when they should be considered for institutional accreditation

- precedents in other countries – there were said to be 'good precedents' in Australia and North America for the term 'university' to be applied to institutions similar in nature to the polytechnics and colleges in Hong Kong. Moreover, the recently published UK White Paper *Higher Education – A New Framework* (DES 1991) sought to abolish the binary line between universities on the one hand and polytechnics and colleges on the other, and provide for the extension of the title of university to those polytechnics which wished to use it

---

4   The Hong Kong Council for Academic Accreditation was established in 1990 and took over work in Hong Kong formerly undertaken by the UK CNAA.

- recognition problem – due recognition of the academic standing of the polytechnics and HKBC had, it was claimed, been hampered by their non-university status. For example, they were excluded from membership of the Association of Commonwealth Universities (ACU) [albeit they were subsequently granted associate status]. In Hong Kong the general public was also said to associate degree qualifications only with the universities

- recruitment of staff/students – mainly because of the recognition problem discussed above, the non-university institutions felt that they were at a disadvantage with regard to retention and recruitment of qualified staff and students.

Although not totally convinced by all of these arguments, the UGC agreed that, taking into account developments elsewhere, there was a *prima facie* case for abandoning the titles polytechnic and college, subject to certain conditions.

The committee agreed in September 1991 that the granting of university title should only follow:

(a)   implementation of common salary scales and the principle of parity of funding,

(b)   acceptance by the institutions of the principle and terms of a differentiation of roles and missions, and

(c)   successful institutional accreditation.

As regards (a) above, the UGC had submitted a recommendation that academic staff of all the UGC-funded institutions should be remunerated on the same basic terms in the context of its advice to the government on the revised expansion plan. The government accepted the UGC's recommendation and agreed to the implementation of common salary scales for academic and equivalent administrative staff primarily engaged in degree level work in July 1992. Meanwhile, the UGC itself had developed, and implemented for the assessment of recurrent grants for the 1991–92 single grant year and the 1992–95 triennium, a revised zero-based funding methodology which aimed to assess the institutions' recurrent grants on the same basis for students at the same level in the same discipline.

In respect of (b) above, the UGC promulgated in October 1992 a policy statement which described the agreed roles and missions of the seven UGC-funded institutions. This statement, reproduced at

Appendix 8.1, was drawn up following consultations with all the institutions on its terms. The statements of each institution's role and mission as contained in the policy statement were not intended to be exhaustive, nor were they to be cast in concrete, but they did represent the UGC's perception of the role of each institution for planning and funding purposes for the foreseeable future. Acceptance of, or at least aquiescence in, these statements was an important consideration for the UGC in agreeing to proceed with the institutions' requests for university status/ title.

Finally, as regards (c) above, the UGC agreed that the institutions' applications for institutional accreditation should be considered simultaneously in the context of Institutional Reviews of the three institutions in January 1993.

Accordingly, in January 1993, the UGC conducted Institutional Reviews of three UGC-funded institutions, namely the former two polytechnics and the former HKBC, to consider their applications for institutional accreditation and university status/title. The reports and recommendations of these Institutional Reviews were considered by the committee at its meeting in April 1993 and, subsequently, the committee recommended to the government to grant self-accreditation status to the three institutions. In July 1993 the Executive Council approved that the former polytechnics and HKBC should assume responsibility for accrediting their own degree courses, subject to periodic external reviews of their quality assurance and quality improvement processes by the UGC. This decision paved the way for the institutions to seek changes in their titles to become 'universities'.

Following the granting by the government of self-accrediting status to the institutions in July 1993, they were invited by the UGC to submit their proposals for new titles and associated legislative changes. The institutions' proposals were submitted in October 1993 and, following consideration by the UGC and the Administration, they were endorsed in principle by the government in May 1994. The necessary amendment bills to give legal effect to the institutions' proposed new university titles, namely The City University of Hong Kong, Hong Kong Baptist University and The Hong Kong Polytechnic University, and to changes in their internal governance structures, were subsequently passed by the Legislative Council on 16 November 1994.

At the same time, incidentally, the UGC reverted to its original title, dropping the reference to 'polytechnic' which had been introduced in 1972 with the entry of the Hong Kong Polytechnic in the UGC's ambit.

Conclusion

The seven years from July 1988 to June 1995 saw extraordinary developments in higher education in Hong Kong. Some of these developments, as described earlier, had their origins beforehand, but they all came to fruition during this period. The expansion of opportunity for higher education was the logical extension of expanding opportunity for secondary education in the 1970s and 1980s, which had seen enrolments in upper-secondary and sixth-form education more than double in ten years (EMB 1994), and the rising expectations of an increasingly affluent community (Hong Kong's GDP per capita has grown by an average of about 5% per annum for the past thirty years[5]). It was, however, given added impetus by events both inside and outside Hong Kong.

In the early 1980s, during the negotiations between the governments of Britain and China on the future of Hong Kong after 1997 (when the nineteenth century lease on 90% of the territory's land area expired), there had been considerable uncertainty in Hong Kong about what the future might hold and a significant increase in emigration. Even after the signing of the Joint Declaration in 1984, the 'brain drain' had continued. The government concluded that increased opportunities for higher education locally could help replace some of the talent being lost to emigration. At the same time, Hong Kong's economy, historically founded on large-scale low-end manufacturing of textiles and plastics, was rapidly moving up-market towards higher value-added manufacturing and service industries, with a concomitant increased requirement for a better educated, more highly trained workforce.

These internal pressures combined with the aftermath following the events in Tienanmen Square during June 1989 to convince the Hong Kong Government in that year to go further and invest even more heavily in higher education.

It still may be too soon to tell for sure, but most of the objectives of the expansion of Hong Kong's higher education system appear to have been achieved. As the UGC Chairman succinctly put it when submitting the committee's report on its Review of the Development of Higher Education in Hong Kong:

---

5   Source: Census and Statistics Department, Hong Kong Government.

The achievements in developing the Hong Kong tertiary education over the past few years are astonishing, perhaps unique in history. The number of places for students entering degree courses has been almost doubled and at a pace of increase never before achieved anywhere in the world. A high standard of teaching and learning has been maintained. Over the same period research, which was not a prominent feature of Hong Kong tertiary education in its early days, has expanded rapidly in both quantity and quality. Any one of these achievements, alone, would have been noteworthy but to have managed all of them simultaneously is extraordinary.

These achievements reflect great credit on all concerned. On the universities and colleges that have shown a remarkable ability to initiate new courses and expand existing ones despite the very limited scope for local recruitment of academic staff. On the students, many of whose parents education ended at primary school, in working so hard to achieve high educational standards. Not least on the government and people of Hong Kong for providing the funds through their taxes to make it possible. As we enter a period of consolidation all can be proud of what has been done over the past decade, often at break neck speed. (UGC 1996a)

Against this background, and in order to achieve the ambitious targets set for the expansion, Hong Kong's existing higher education institutions developed, increased in size and complexity, and broadened their horizons. New institutions were also founded. Among the existing institutions, three reached the stage of academic maturity to be recognised as self-accrediting universities. They were also accorded public and legal recognition of this by the change in their titles to universities. In this they were following a general trend to broaden the definition of what constitutes a university and a trend elsewhere in the Commonwealth to abolish the 'binary line' between universities and polytechnics.

Acknowledgements

The author wishes to acknowledge the help and advice received in the preparation of this chapter from Professor David Teather, Dean of the Faculty of Social Sciences at HKBU, as well as the assistance with the research given by Miss Mary Tsang and Ms Katrina Lai of the UGC Secretariat.

Appendix 8.1

Policy Statement of the University and Polytechnic Grants Committee of Hong Kong, entitled 'Higher Education in Hong Kong', October 1992

With effect from 1991–92, there are seven higher education institutions (HEIs) which are funded through the University and Polytechnic Grants Committee (UPGC). These institutions, listed alphabetically, are as follows:

(a)   City Polytechnic of Hong Kong

(b)   Hong Kong Baptist College

(c)   Hong Kong Polytechnic

(d)   Lingnan College

(e)   The Chinese University of Hong Kong

(f)   The Hong Kong University of Science and Technology

(g)   The University of Hong Kong

Each of these institutions is and will continue to be an autonomous corporation, with its own Ordinance and Governing Council. They have freedom to manage their internal affairs within the restraints of the Laws of Hong Kong. Because all are largely supported by public funds, and because of the social, cultural, and economic importance of higher education, the Government and the community at large have a legitimate interest in the operation of the institutions to ensure they are providing high standards of education in the most cost-effective manner. The UPGC advises the Government on the development of these institutions and on their financial needs.

The HEIs are diverse in character and in the differing contributions they make to the educational, cultural and economic development of Hong Kong. The differentiated roles of the institutions reflect their varying origins and the way they have responded to the complex and evolving needs of Hong Kong. At present the universities concentrate on first and higher degree work, emphasizing scholarship and research; the polytechnics offer a range of programmes including diplomas and postgraduate courses, with a strong emphasis on professional and vocational education; and the colleges are developing as predominantly degree-awarding institutions, aiming at providing a broad general education rather than a specialised professional training.

The distinctive and complementary roles of the institutions suit the community interest, making the best use of available resources. The UPGC views the system of higher education as a whole and, as far as possible, seeks to reconcile the aspirations of individual institutions with the needs of the territory. The aim is to develop a system of higher education that has an appropriate balance between programmes at different levels and in different areas and in which the institutions make contributions to the community through the provision of trained manpower, research collaboration, consultancy and other means. The

UPGC is conscious that a degree of co-ordination is necessary to avoid over-provision and under-provision at particular levels and in certain areas. It may not be practicable to meet all the aspirations of all institutions. Nevertheless, the Committee recognises that teaching is the common denominator of the HEIs. It also fully appreciates that research and scholarly activities are essential to academic health.

The Government decided in 1989 to implement an expansion plan for the UPGC-funded sector during 1991–95, with a view to increasing the present provision of first-year first-degree places to 14,500 in 1994–95, thereby providing education for about 18% of the mean of the relevant age group. This is an ambitious expansion plan which allows the whole UPGC-funded sector to increase substantially the provision of degree places, at both first-degree and postgraduate level. It meant that not only were there more students and new courses to be taught, but many more academic staff have been required to teach to degree level. Furthermore, postgraduate studies, taught and research, are being pursued in places where they had not been present previously, or where they had previously been present at a low level they have been significantly expanded.

In such a situation the maintenance of academic standards in general and teaching standards in particular, is a major challenge, the more so in an environment of budgetary constraint. The UPGC intends to place particular emphasis on effective procedures for monitoring teaching quality and cost-effectiveness. It recognizes that different methods of quality assurance may be appropriate in different situations and does not seek to prescribe any particular method as being of general application; however, it will expect to see the full involvement of external advisors, assessors or examiners in such a way that they can have an effective influence on the system.

This major expansion of the system of higher education will not have been fully effective unless there is proper scope for intellectual and professional development of academic staff to meet the new teaching challenges. For different individuals in different fields in different institutions professional development is achieved in different ways that include consultancy work, involvement in professional associations, advanced scholarship, editorial work, research and publication. The balance between these activities varies between institutions, between fields and between individuals.

The Committee believes that its view on the role and importance of research should be clearly understood, and that the role of research in the newly evolving system of Hong Kong higher education should be neither exaggerated nor underplayed. The UPGC has four main objectives in supporting research in Hong Kong HEIs:

(a)   to contribute to the economic, cultural and social well-being of Hong Kong;

(b)   to promote staff development and to train future academic staff;

(c)   as an essential part of the training of research students; and

(d)   to add to the sum of human knowledge.

In many cases a particular activity will meet several or even all of these criteria. As one aspect of staff development and as one of the means by which individual staff members may maintain currency in their subjects, it is anticipated that some research will be done in all UPGC-funded institutions.

The largest single commitment of UPGC resources to the support of research is staff time. All academic staff should have some available for career development and the pursuit of scholarship. However, the continued justification of the relatively favourable staff:student ratios that the UPGC has allowed, particularly in the existing universities, will depend upon their performance in research.

For some kinds of research further resources are needed beyond the time of the staff concerned. These may include specialist library facilities, laboratories, computers or costly instrumentation. By various means the UPGC makes provision for these too. But whereas provision is made for all to have time for research, if an individual or institution needs further resources it is necessary to compete for these and to convince others that the proposed activity is worthwhile. Funds may be available from a researcher's own institution, from the Research Grants Council (RGC), from other public bodies, from industry or from private foundations. The RGC has been established to make grants mainly in response to competitive bids from staff members in any of the HEIs in Hong Kong and it makes its decisions after a process of peer review involving both domestic and international referees. All institutions will be expected to demonstrate fairness and discrimination in their internal procedures for allocation of research resources, channelling them to those individuals and those departments that will put them to best use.

One likely consequence of budgetary constraint is the need to rationalise the provision and use of expensive facilities. It is to be expected over time that more than one institution will legitimately wish to carry out work requiring costly facilities of a particular kind. The UPGC/RGC may, as a condition of their support, require institutions to share facilities of this kind subject to reasonable safeguards both for the institutions that house the facilities concerned and for the users.

Although the UPGC does not exclude the possibility of research activity of any particular kind in any of the institutions for which it is responsible, it expects that at any rate for the foreseeable future the principal responsibility for the training of research students will fall to the universities and they will receive appropriate funding for this purpose. The UPGC will keep its policies for the allocation of research support under review and will respond to changing circumstances within the institutions and outside them.

Against the above background, the roles of the seven HEIs, as currently seen by the UPGC in broad terms, are described in sub-paragraphs (a)–(g) below. This description is intended to be illustrative, rather than exhaustive, and will serve as the basis for the Committee's assessment of academic plans and cost estimates from the institutions.

(a)   City Polytechnic of Hong Kong

      (i)   offers a range of courses leading to the award of Diplomas, Higher Certificates, Higher Diplomas and First Degrees;

      (ii)   offers a relatively small number of higher degrees and has research programmes in some subject areas;

      (iii)   emphasises the application of knowledge and vocational training; and

      (iv)   maintains strong links with industry and employers.

(b)   Hong Kong Baptist College

      (i)   provides predominantly courses at first degree level in Arts, Business, Communication Studies, Science and Social Science;

      (ii)   offers a small number of higher degrees and has research programmes in some subject areas;

      (iii)   emphasises a broad general education, to prepare students for entry to careers which require a wide intellectual background;

      (iv)   runs courses which provide suitable preparation for a career in teaching at primary and secondary schools; and

      (v)   maintains strong links with the community.

(c) Hong Kong Polytechnic

      (i)   offers a range of courses leading to the award of Certificates, Diplomas, Higher Certificates, Higher Diplomas, Professional Diplomas and First Degrees;

      (ii)   offers a relatively small number of higher degrees and has research programmes in some subject areas;

      (iii)   emphasises the application of knowledge and vocational training; and

      (iv)   maintains strong links with industry and employers.

(d) Lingnan College

      (i)   will offer first-degree courses in Arts, Business, and Social Sciences;

      (ii)   provides a General Education Programme which seeks to offer all students a broad educational perspective;

      (iii)   may run a small number of higher degree programmes and has research work in some subject areas; and

      (iv)   maintains strong links with the community.

(e) The Chinese University of Hong Kong

      (i)   offers a range of programmes leading to the award of First Degrees and postgraduate qualifications;

      (ii)   covers a range of subjects including Arts, Science, Social Science, and Business Administration;

    (iii) incorporates professional schools, such as Medicine, Architecture, Engineering and Education;

    (iv) offers research programmes for a significant number of students in every subject area; and

    (v) provides scope for academic staff to undertake consultancy and collaborative projects with industry in areas where they have special expertise.

(f) The Hong Kong University of Science and Technology

    (i) provides a range of programmes leading to the award of First Degrees and postgraduate qualifications;

    (ii) includes professional schools, particularly in the fields of Science, Technology, Engineering and Business;

    (iii) offers courses in Humanities and Social Science only at a level sufficient to provide intellectual breadth, contextual background and communication skills to an otherwise scientific or technological curriculum, and limited postgraduate work;

    (iv) offers research programmes for a significant number of students in every subject area; and

    (v) provides scope for academic staff to undertake consultancy and collaborative projects with industry in areas where they have special expertise.

(g) The University of Hong Kong

    (i) offers a range of programmes leading to the award of First Degrees and postgraduate qualifications;

    (ii) covers a range of subjects including Arts, Science, Social Sciences, and Business Administration;

    (iii) incorporates professional schools, eg. Medicine, Dentistry, Architecture, Education, Engineering and Law;

    (iv) offers research programmes for a significant number of students in every subject area; and

    (v) provides scope for academic staff to undertake consultancy and collaborative projects with industry in areas where they have special expertise.

Chapter 9

Hong Kong Baptist University

Daniel C. W. Tse

The history

The Hong Kong Baptist University (HKBU) began as a private, church-related college in 1956. Several factors prompted the decision of the local Baptist church leaders to establish the college as a four-year post-secondary institution after the North American tradition.

The closure of the door to higher education in Mainland China in the early 1950s

Before that time most of the aspiring young people graduating from Chinese secondary schools in Hong Kong, would go to China for their higher education. Besides the public universities, there were, altogether, thirteen well-known Christian universities[1] which were primarily established by the joint efforts of the missionary societies in the West, and they were popular in attracting many Hong Kong young people because of the Western-style education being offered there. Even the students graduating from the Anglo-Chinese schools (schools using English as the chief medium of instruction) would apply because there was only one university in Hong Kong and its primary mission was to provide training for a small number of professional people and an even smaller number of civil servants to staff the colonial government of the time. But the door to higher education in Mainland China was closed to students from Hong Kong in the early 1950s due to political conditions within the PRC, leaving a large number of secondary school leavers in a quandary with no place to go for further education. Unlike the present

---

1 These Christian universities were: St. John's University, Yenching University, Lingnan University, University of Nanking, Soochow University, Shantung University, Hangchow University, University of Shanghai, Ginling Women's College, Fukien Christian University, Hwa Nan Women's College, West China Union University and Huachung University.

day, going overseas for higher education was a real luxury which only a rich few could afford at that time.

The availability of Chinese intellectuals from Christian as well as public universities who left Mainland China to seek refuge in Hong Kong

After the establishment of the PRC in 1949, the thirteen Christian universities were forced to close down on account of their foreign connections. As a result, many teaching and administrative staff and students of these universities came to Hong Kong. At that time the economy of Hong Kong was nowhere near what it is today. For these highly capable intellectuals the most productive way to use their time and talent was to continue their original profession of teaching. In particular, those who had been teaching in Christian universities in China were eager to see a Christian institution established so that they could continue the mission to which they were committed.

The availability of resources from the mission societies or foreign education foundations which had withdrawn from China

Although these organisations were not rich by present-day standards, they were, nevertheless, the most significant sources of support to education and welfare in the early 1950s when Hong Kong was flooded with huge numbers of refugees from China (Lauby 1996).

The Baptist desire to build a Christian university in South China

Even before 1949, the Baptist churches in South China had already had the idea of building a Christian university for the southern part of China as a natural extension of their very successful enterprise in secondary education. In fact, a campus site had already been identified in a suburb of Guangzhou and a task force appointed to look into the logistics of setting up such a university. Only the change of government in 1949 interrupted the planning process.

HKBC: The loner

The Hong Kong Baptist College (HKBC), which was established in 1956, was neither the first nor the only institution that was established in Hong Kong during this period. There were the New Asia College, established in 1949 and which was mainly staffed by a group of Mainland scholars in Chinese philosophy, history and literature, and the Chung Chi College, which was established in 1951 with significant help from staff of the former Lingnan University of Guangzhou and financial support from the United Board for Christian Higher Education in China.[2] There were also several smaller institutions which were operating independently but decided to join together to form the United College in 1956. These three institutions later became the constituent colleges of the Chinese University of Hong Kong (CUHK).

The establishment of the CUHK was as much a political issue as it was an educational necessity. Yielding to the political pressures of the day, the government enacted a Post-secondary College Ordinance in 1959 and established a Joint Council of Post-secondary Colleges to bring New Asia, Chung Chi and United under a subvention scheme, and four years later (1963) the Chinese University of Hong Kong was established with the three colleges serving as its foundation. This move broke the convention of one university (British style) for each colony.

The question of why HKBC did not join the others to become a publicly funded institution under the umbrella of CUHK had been raised many times, but the answers remained speculative until very recently when documents from government archives shed more authoritative light on the issue. Letters and documents showed that the Hong Kong government at that time was extremely reluctant to expand tertiary education in any significant way and was content to keep the new university to be created as small as possible. Therefore, despite the fact that HKBC did apply to become a part of the Joint Council in 1959, the application was declined. But to be fair to the government, HKBC did not show an active interest in joining at the beginning because there was a strong element within the church which wanted to keep a clear separation between the church and the government. Besides, HKBC did enjoy some strong financial support from overseas, which could be withdrawn if the college chose to join the public sector.

Whatever the reason might have been, the end result was that HKBC had to go alone in the subsequent twenty some years without any government support and with very little government recognition, while overseas support remained at a fairly low level. The only factor which worked in the college's favor was that the great demand for higher education was still un-met until 1972 and the college was able to recruit as many students as it could take in. The establishment of the Hong

2   The Board had supported the 13 Chinese Christian universities and colleges before the withdrawal; its name was subsequently changed to United Board for Christian Higher Education in Asia.

Kong Polytechnic (HKP) in 1972 was a severe blow to HKBC because the competition for students was in favor of the new institution, which had the blessing and strong support of the government. In order to continue its improvement, the college had to step up its efforts to secure community support while knocking at the government door for some financial assistance and better recognition.

Installation of the new President

The passing away of the founding President, the late Dr Lam Chi-fung, in 1971 was another severe blow to the College. Dr Lam was succeeded by a young physicist who was at that time heading the Physics Department, and the succession was not without difficulties – mainly because of his age and his lack of administrative experience. In retrospect, people now say that the choice was wise. But for that person who survived all the internal power struggles and external prejudice, the initial period was a traumatic experience which he would rather forget.

The fight for public funding and recognition

From 1971 to 1977 the college went through a series of dramatic events. On the plus side the college began its campus expansion program in 1972, which continued for ten years with increased private donations. On the down side the college ran into recurrent financial difficulties and tried numerous attempts in vain to obtain financial support from the government. Finally, in 1977, a big storm hit the college when the government published its consultative Green Paper on the Development of Senior Secondary and Post Secondary Education. Included in that paper was a proposal to permanently leave HKBC out of the formal education system, thereby shutting the door on any direct financial assistance or proper recognition. Fortunately for the college, the consultation paper was written in such an arrogant and ungrateful manner, painting the college as if it were a nuisance rather than a contribution to education, that the whole community of Hong Kong felt offended. Encouraged by the community, the college rose to fight against the Green Paper with a series of public demonstrations and protests. The end result was that the proposal was defeated and in its place was a scheme of subsidy to HKBC in 1979, which, although meager and restrictive, was, nevertheless, the camel's nose into the tent, which finally resulted in the college being included under the ambit of the funding agent of the government for tertiary education – the University and Polytechnic Grants Committee (UPGC).

As a condition, the college was required to go through a formal assessment by the Council for National Academic Awards (CNAA) of the United Kingdom after the subsidy scheme was implemented. The institutional and course assessments took place in 1981 and the team summed up its report to the government by saying that if expansion of degree-level tertiary education was needed, HKBC would be the ready answer (CNAA 1981). The timing of the report was excellent because the government had just appointed a committee chaired by the then Director of Education, Mr Kenneth Topley, to review the need for higher education. After careful debates, the government took the unprecedented step of inviting HKBC to join UPGC, and public funding began in November 1983 when a new HKBC Ordinance was enacted.

Long march towards university status

1984 was the year when the long march towards university status began, albeit with great uncertainty. The college was given the green light in that year to develop some degree programs, but no promise whatsoever for it to develop into a fully-fledged university. In spite of this uncertainty, the college was determined to pursue the lofty goal. Thanks to the fact that the college had all along been aiming at the degree level in its design of courses, it was able to introduce its first two degree courses in 1986 and by 1989 all of the college honors diploma courses were converted to degree status with the help of CNAA, which acted as the validating body. Thereafter, the college began to develop MPhil programs in almost every field and, at the same time, planned taught master's degree courses in selected areas. In 1991 the college went through a formal institutional review conducted by the newly established Hong Kong Council for Academic Accreditation (HKCAA). It received a 'clean bill of health' report from the assessors and was declared an institution capable of providing education at both undergraduate and postgraduate levels (HKCAA 1991). It was only by that time that the intention was made clear that the college would be given university status in due course. In 1992 the college succeeded in introducing its first PhD program, and in 1993 achieved the status of self-accreditation. Full university status was given to the college on 16 November 1994 when a new university ordinance for the institution was approved by the Legislature. The long march towards university status had taken exactly eleven years to complete.

Challenges and strategies: pre-university days

In retrospect, the institution could justifiably be proud to say that it succeeded in pursuing its goals. But along the way there were indeed very rough rides which required carefully mapped out strategies for survival and for sudden changes of circumstances.

Fundraising for the 'odd year' out

When the government yielded to public pressure and introduced a subsidy scheme for HKBC in 1979, it also took the opportunity to force the college to restructure its courses in order to provide two years of Advanced Level (A-Level or Form 6 and Form 7) and two years of post A-Level education. This splitting of the four-year curriculum had the implicit effect of keeping the institution at a sub-degree level, one year short of the degree. The college foresaw the problem. Although unable to resist the government demand, it nevertheless successfully preserved a topping-up one-year course, albeit without subsidy, for those who wanted a university level education. The college took that decision in order to maintain the possibility for future degree level development. But it also meant that it had to step up its efforts of fundraising to support that final year's expenditure. Painful as it was, that decision and the fundraising efforts paid off handsomely. In 1981, when the college was celebrating its Silver Anniversary, it succeeded in getting 35 donors, each making a donation of HK$1 million or more to the college. The phenomenal success prompted a CNAA member who was present to witness the celebration to remark: 'No one would pay that kind of money to buy a dead horse. There must be something worthwhile at the Baptist College to attract this kind of donation'. Sure enough, at the end of the 1981 assessments the CNAA found that the splitting of the college program into 2+2+1 was unsound educationally and recommended that the two-year A-Level program be dropped so that the college could concentrate on developing an integrated post A-level three-year program, which became the forerunner of the degree courses. The college has since learned a great lesson: that keeping its goal alive with private and community support is very important and allows the institution to continue until the goal is reached.

Re-structuring

When the college was ready to develop its degree courses in 1984, it gave the whole institution and its entire curriculum a thorough review before adopting two strategies. The first strategy was to change the department-based structure to a faculty/school-based structure. It was a significant move because it reduced the cost centers from 28 to 5 in one stroke, thereby simplifying the management structure and achieving savings. The move also allowed the college to delegate responsibilities to the five deans who served as full-time academic officers to help co-ordinate the uphill drive, instead of leaving it to 28 heads of departments during this crucial period of development. The second strategy was to go for inter- and multi-disciplinary degrees as much as possible. The college recognised that real-life phenomena and problems were mostly multi-disciplinary and that the world trend was for multi-disciplinary collaboration rather than for isolation. Besides, this strategy enabled the college to develop only a small number of degree courses to cover all of the existing disciplines. For example, one of the first multi-disciplinary degree courses offered in 1986 was in combined sciences, which covered all of the five science disciplines. The strategy also paid off handsomely because it put the college in the forefront in promoting inter- and multi-disciplinary co-operation, breaking down the departmental walls of the more traditional universities. Within three years of the first introduction of degree courses the college became a 100 per cent degree-granting institution.

Dedication to 'whole person education'

When UPGC took over the funding responsibilities, the first item on its agenda was to discuss with the college its academic direction. During the 1977 Green Paper debate, the college was ridiculed by government officials for following the North American tradition of liberal arts education. These critics did not hide their disdain for that kind of education because they considered it lacking in practical value. But, in fact, the college never claimed that it resembled an American liberal arts college, it only claimed that it provided 'whole person education' after its Christian tradition. When confronted by UPGC on the meaning of 'whole person education', the college realized that it needed to clear its own mind as to what the claim meant in concrete terms. Consequently, a lengthy paper was produced by the college giving detailed explanation of the concept as well as how the concept could be realized in the education process (HKBC 1982). Although, apparently, no one at that time from the UPGC believed that the concept was realistic or practicable, in the end UPGC decided to coin the phrase 'liberal education with a vocational emphasis' as a general guideline for the future course development of the college. In response, the college counter-proposed that a complementary phrase 'vocational education with a liberal emphasis' be added to the guiding principle. The counter-proposal had proven to be significant because, together, the two complementary phrases not only described the existing academic profile more accurately, but also allowed the development of more professionally-oriented courses, while keeping the educational approach liberal. The experience taught the college that the clearing of the mind on its educational philosophy was very important for the institution, it helped focus the direction of its development to achieve the intended goals.

Staff development

For obvious reasons, there was little research strength which the college could brag about prior to the UPGC funding in 1983. But as the drive towards the university status intensified, and resources became more adequately available, it was equally obvious that research activities and strength of the staff would have to build up quickly. For the new recruits there was basically no problem. With an improved salary scale and reputation, the college was able to attract academic staff of the right calibre who were competent in both teaching and research. But for the long-serving staff who had no doubt done an excellent teaching job (as testified by the CNAA assessments), how to help them make a quick and successful shift to research was by no means an easy task. Fortunately for the college, since it had all along been aiming at the university level in its courses, its staff appointments were also pitched at that level (although not always successful in all departments) and the college was able to adopt a soft approach of positive encouragement and staff development to achieve its goal. Within a span of five years practically all of those who could benefit from a period of study leave (and most of them could) were given the opportunity either to pursue a terminal degree in the field or for research attachment in a reputable university. Appropriate salary increments were awarded to those who completed their development plans and less stringent research requirements were applied to them when promotion was considered. These deliberate measures had a very positive effect on the long-serving staff. As a result, although the pressures of higher research quality and output were on, most staff took on the challenge with cheerful spirits. In this way the college succeeded in preserving its humane ethos of a caring academic community.

Building a research culture

Right from the beginning it was clear that UPGC had no intention of creating a research institution out of the college, neither did the college aspire to become one on account of its historical commitment to education. But this did not mean that the college was not serious about research and scholarly activities. On the contrary, it was committed to building a research culture which had student participation at both the postgraduate and the undergraduate level. To carry out this commitment the college took the strategic decision to require honors projects for graduation in every field of study at the first-degree level. Though this strategy had great manpower implications, the college was willing to invest its resources in this manner. It succeeded in fulfilling the institutional goal of striking a good balance between teaching and research, and in having the two activities reinforcing each other.

Challenges and strategies: the transition

'Throwing a stone to find the way forward'

Although the college had successfully converted all of its courses to degree level in 1989, there was still no sign that UPGC would begin to consider the issue of university status. Meanwhile, the institution continued to suffer from the poor public image which the word 'college' projected. In Hong Kong the term 'college' could mean a secondary school or it could be a residential hall of a university (e.g. the Sir Robert Black College of the University of Hong Kong). In fact, the poor public image was not just a perceived or imaginary one, it was so real that the college regularly received letters from local and overseas institutions proposing to recruit 'school leavers' from it. Worse yet, a poll among its own students showed that a large number of them still had difficulty accepting the fact that the degree courses they were taking had already been properly validated at the international standards of university education.

In order to fight this image problem and to break the impasse of UPGC's silence on the university status issue, the college adopted a tactic known in Chinese as 'throwing a stone to find the way forward' (投石問路). The college submitted a proposal to UPGC in February 1989 formally suggesting that the status of the college be changed to that of a university in July 1994, which would have been more than ten years after the college became a publicly-funded institution (HKBC 1989). But in order to solve the immediate public image problem, the college also proposed that it be permitted to use the title 'University College' to clarify its newly achieved academic status (100% degree program). As expected, the proposal did draw the attention of UPGC to the problem the college was facing and, also as expected, the formal reply was 'No'. But the fact that UPGC had to formally discuss the issue in its meeting was significant because the college found out later that behind the formal negative reply there was actually a positive element. Simply put, UPGC did not agree that there should be an intermediate step in the development of the institution from a college to university. In saying so, the implication was that university status was indeed what UPGC had in mind as the next step for the college. When that implication was later confirmed informally by the UPGC Chairman as well as the Chief Secretary of the Government, the administration was elated because it finally saw a dim light at the end of the tunnel. Although the college could not publicise that informal confirmation, the latter was nonetheless a tremendous boost of morale to those who were responsible for the drive towards university status.

The first formal step

When UPGC announced that it would like to commission a comprehensive institutional review of the college in 1991, using the services and expertise of the newly-formed (June 1990) Hong Kong Council for Academic Accreditation, the college knew that the time had come for UPGC to take the first step to formalise the university status granting process. Immediately, it went into action and treated the exercise with utmost seriousness.

In spite of the fact that the Chairman and several members of the review panel were former members of the CNAA who were familiar with the development since 1981, the college decided to submit a document with full details of the path it had gone through in its ten years of academic development. The one-hundred-page report (54 pages of text and 46 pages of appendices; HKBC 1990), also covered the full range of topics normally required in a full-scale accreditation exercise of

North American institutions. In particular, the college gave prominent position to the mission statement in the report, singling out the concept of 'whole person education' as the guiding concept of the institution's development. The college chose to do so because it knew that the old CNAA team had a lot of reservations about the college claim on 'whole person education'. Instead of avoiding the issue, the strategy was to face it 'head on' – and it worked. In the end, not only did the college receive a 'clean bill of health' report from the Review Panel, the latter also went out of its way to confess that there had been initial doubts about 'whole person education' but the result of the review visit had dispelled them. The report said, in part:

> The Panel noted that the College regards the objective of 'whole person education' as a matter of high priority, ... The Panel was initially doubtful about the realization of this laudable aim, but by the end of the visit these doubts had largely been dispelled; ... Indeed, some students commented they were particularly attracted to the College because of the breadth and ethos of its whole person education approach. (HKCAA 1991, p.7)

Interestingly enough, when UPGC took the final step to verify the college's readiness for the university title in 1993, the step was also taken in the form of an institutional review, but this time it was the UPGC members and not the HKCAA members who formed the review panel. Again the college took the same approach of coming clean with its 'whole person education' philosophy, and the panel's finding was remarkably similar. In part, the panel said: 'The students met during the visit were impressive and appeared to be evidence for the success of the "whole person education" concepts of the College.' (UPGC 1993a, Annex B, Point ii)

Role differentiation

Between the two institutional reviews in 1991 and 1993, UPGC also took a formal step to discuss with all funded institutions their missions and roles. In particular, HKP, CPHK and HKBC were told that their roles had to be decided before they were given university status. This was considered a very crucial step because there was fear that without agreement on their respective roles, the three institutions might all aspire to become similar to one or another of the three existing universities (namely HKU, CUHK and HKUST), which would be undesirable.

In the role differentiation exercise, for obvious historical and practical reasons, both HKU and CUHK were formally declared as the comprehensive universities for the territory and HKUST became the specialist university. Agreement was also obtained from the two polytechnics to retain substantially their polytechnic nature by emphasising the technical and vocational nature of their degree and sub-degree programs. In addition, because of the newly emerging need to develop research in the tertiary institutions, HKU, CUHK and HKUST were designated to become research universities. The two polytechnics were asked to continue their efforts in research and consultancy activities that were closely linked to industry and would, therefore, play a smaller role in basic research. This pattern of role differentiation left a natural niche for the Hong Kong Baptist College. It found itself right in the middle of the spectrum. It became an institution with a primary objective of producing people at the first-degree level with wide intellectual background and not so much job specific training. It would also have a smaller role to play in postgraduate education and research.

HKBC had no difficulty accepting this role but it wanted to make sure that the roles did not define a pecking order, nor would they be set in concrete. It sought and obtained UPGC's clarification that the role statement only set out 'in broad terms the roles of the institutions in the foreseeable future ... The description of the roles is illustrative rather than exhaustive.'[3]

The clarification on this point was important to the later development of the institution. As was mentioned earlier, UPGC used 'liberal education with a vocational emphasis' as a guideline for the academic development of the college in the early 1980s, and the college argued that the emphasis should be on the word 'liberal' and the guideline should be interpreted as more about the educational approach than the content so that the college would not be barred from offering more professionally oriented courses.

In its reply to UPGC's letter about its role assignment the college also made use of its 'trademark' concept, 'whole person education', to state its position on teaching and research. It pointed out that in line with the concept of 'whole person education', excellence in teaching was naturally a very important objective to pursue and the institution would

---

3   UPGC letter to HKBC on Higher Education in Hong Kong, 16 October 1992.

gladly devote its efforts to set a high standard in this most important academic function. But, on the other hand, again following the concept of 'whole person education', no teaching could become excellent unless the teachers themselves were role models of eager learners through research and scholarly activities. Therefore, the institution must keep an equal balance on teaching and research and would strive to seek as much integration and co-ordination between teaching and research as possible. Thus the concept of 'whole person education' had helped rationalise the institution's acceptance of its role as agreed with UPGC and explained why it did not aspire to become a 'research' university *per se.*

Getting ready

After the successful overall institutional review of 1991, the role statement agreement of 1992 and the special institutional review for self-accreditation in 1993, the university status of the college was virtually assured. From that point on, the college was able to put its total efforts into building up the institution as a university according to its own mission and vision (Appendix 9.1). It started to review and strengthen the existing teaching programs and introduce innovative programs for the new era. Besides, internationalisation of the institution started to gain momentum and, on the physical and practical sides, the institution stepped up its plan on campus expansion as well as on building of an endowment fund for its future development. But, before all that, there were some administrative and legal issues which had to be dealt with and were rather time-consuming. Of these, the major ones were the conversion of staff titles and salaries to those of the existing universities and the revision of the College Ordinance on the governance to conform to the university structure.

Re-titling academic staff

On the staff retitling issue, the college decided to do away with the archaic British titles of lecturer, senior lecturer and reader in favor of the more common titles of assistant professor, associate professor and professor, while keeping the title of assistant lecturer as a probationary grade for promising young staff who were on their way to completing their terminal degrees. The new titling system turned out to be advantageous because it was more rational and flexible and was compatible with the Asian, Australian and North American systems with which the college had increasing contacts and interactions.

Revision of governance

The issue of revision of governance was also a sensitive one. When the college became a publicly funded institution in November 1983, the government took some measures to reduce the dominance of the Baptist constituency in the governance structure but still allowed a very substantial number of seats in the governing bodies to be filled by nominees of the Hong Kong Baptist Convention. However, for an institution with proper university status, the government was much more serious in making sure that the university was not dominated by any one constituency, let alone a religious one. The college accepted the general principle behind the government argument but felt strongly that for historical and moral reasons there must be permanent arrangements in the governance to recognise the contributions of the founding body. To achieve this goal the college adopted the approach of arguing for what it termed the 'meaningful but not controlling presence' of the Baptist constituency in the new university governance. The argument was accepted by both the government and the Hong Kong Baptist Convention and the college managed to increase the number of seats in the council from one (as proposed by government) to three and for the court membership from three to eight. Once again, the approach of realism with proper regard to history proved to be of great value in moving the institution forward over difficult hurdles.

Review of existing teaching programs

Apart from re-titling the academic staff and revising its governance structure, the university also reviewed its existing programs in order to identify areas for improvement, if necessary. In the end it was found that the existing structure of having five faculties/schools (namely Faculty of Arts, School of Business, School of Communication, Faculty of Science and Faculty of Social Sciences) was operating in a satisfactory fashion and it was not the right time to introduce any sweeping changes. The overall strategy, however, was to fortify 'whole person education' in the curriculum and delivery of all the courses. And as the university had all along been putting strong emphasis on teaching the students 'to learn how to learn' or to be equipped with self-learning ability, the Center for Educational Development (CED) and the Library were of particular importance to achieving the goal. With the opening of the new Shaw Campus, CED and the Library were able to have more space in which to operate. With its size almost doubled, the Library enjoys a more spacious area with fully-automated systems and first-rate facilities. The new office of CED also houses state-of-the-art facilities to help students as well as faculty members to enhance their learning and academic pursuits.

Innovative programs for the new era

HKBU acquired its university title at the time when Hong Kong was undergoing a most interesting period of transition. Politically, it was changing from a British colony to a Special Administrative Region of the PRC under the concept of 'one country, two systems'. Economically, the territory was also rapidly changing its emphasis from manufacturing to service industry. Local manufacturing activities had been drastically reduced while factories were being moved north of the border into South China, where labor and land costs were low. Hong Kong was more and more becoming a financial centre of the Asia Pacific Region, serving the huge and ever growing China trade. The modernisation drive of China and the opening up of its market to the world had created many new opportunities and possibilities for Hong Kong which could not have been imagined or predicted even ten years before. Against such an exciting background a question naturally arose: what should HKBU do in order to meet the challenges of the day and be ready for the twenty-first century?

To answer this question, the university has spent numerous hours to find the most appropriate answers that are in line with its mission and are within its own capabilities. In this regard, the university is pleased to say that it has initiated several programs which have either proven to be very successful and innovative or are showing promise of success.

As Hong Kong was going through the transition, the university was also aware of the rapid change of the job market for its students. The university foresaw that the time would come when the job market for graduates would not be confined to Hong Kong, nor would the Hong Kong job market be exclusively for graduates from the local institutions. Instead, Hong Kong graduates would have a market which extended to the China mainland and possibly overseas. It was clear to everyone that China would become one of the major expanding markets of the world and Hong Kong graduates would stand to benefit if they had a broad international perspective, good language facilities and an in-depth knowledge about China. It was based on this conviction that the university introduced an undergraduate course in China Studies in 1990. The students in the China Studies program spend five weeks in

Beijing during the summer prior to their final year. In order to facilitate their stay in Beijing, and to ensure that they have the best contact with top-level scholars and government officials, the university has signed a perpetual agreement with Tsinghua University (commonly recognised as the top university in PRC) to co-ordinate its summer program and has jointly built a residential facility on the Tsinghua campus to house the students. These arrangements have proven to be most successful and Baptist University has scored a big 'first' in this venture.

Following the success of the China Studies program, the university began to introduce another area studies course, the degree in European Studies, in 1994. To make sure that the graduates have high-level language proficiency and in-depth understanding of the European countries they are specialising in, the students are required to spend one year in France or Germany. They study in a French or German university for a period of time and are then placed in designated firms (arranged by the respective host universities in France and Germany) for real-life working experience for the rest of the year abroad. All of the students who are currently abroad (1996–97) have their internships sponsored by German and French firms which have offices in Hong Kong. Although the first cohort is yet to graduate, the signs are that they will be most sought-after by the German and French firms, who are eager to do business with China. Again, the program is another 'first' in the territory.

Internationalisation

Whilst the above-mentioned area studies programs benefit the students enrolled in them, the university feels strongly that the entire HKBU community should share the kind of international perspectives promoted in the area studies courses. One way to achieve the goal is to create a university-wide infrastructure which will encourage international dialogue and co-operation. The creation of the David C Lam Institute for East-West Studies (LEWI) is just the answer. Since its establishment in 1993, it has already proved to be of enormous value to the university. With the generous financial support of the former Lieutenant Governor of British Columbia, the Hon David C Lam, and his friends (mostly in Hong Kong), a privately funded building has been erected on the new Shaw Campus which offers ample space for the many international academic and research activities.

Basically, the new facility has enabled the university to do two important things. First, it provides the incentive for staff in the social sciences and humanities to have a more focused area of research. The university realises that as a smaller institution it cannot afford to spread its research strength too thinly without losing its impact. The East-West studies theme under LEWI is just the proper umbrella and Hong Kong, being a city where East meets West, is an ideal place to pursue research under such a theme. Second, it allows the university to attract overseas universities to join the LEWI international consortium by offering each member institution a permanent office plus conference facilities and administrative support within the new Shaw building. The university realises that many overseas universities would like to extend their activities in the Asia-Pacific Region in general, and in Mainland China in particular. Therefore, in designing the membership of the LEWI international consortium, the university has brought in 15 key universities from China and south-east Asia as associate members. These universities, although not required to contribute the US$100,000 to become full members of LEWI, are nevertheless very important contributors because of the opportunities and services they are able to offer to the other members in academic exchange and co-operation. As to the full members, a deliberate attempt has been made to spread the limited memberships (15 in total) on the basis of wide geographical distribution. At the time of writing, LEWI has four full members from North America, two from Australia, two from Continental Europe, two from the United Kingdom and one from Mainland China, with HKBU playing host as a full member (Appendix 9.2).

At the time the LEWI concept was being developed, the university was also conscious of the fact that Hong Kong was extremely well-placed for the development of international business studies. Merely offering a course in this subject area would have little impact because practically all tertiary institutions already run such courses. If a program was to have any significance, it must be innovative, and an international consortium after the LEWI pattern could be the answer. It was based on this conviction, and with the generous support of the Wing Lung Bank of Hong Kong, that the university went ahead to establish the Wing Lung Bank International Institute for Business Development (IIBD).

In addition to inviting the full members of LEWI to join the IIBD, the university also extended invitation to several universities in Mainland China and in south-east Asia, which are specially known for their strengths in business studies (Appendix 9.3). Again, the decision was based on the university's considered view that one of the main centres for international development in the next century will be the Asia-Pacific Region, including China, and a consortium based in this region would therefore, be very attractive to the international academic community. That view proved to be correct, and the responses from overseas as well as from the region were overwhelmingly positive. At the first Board of Directors Meeting of IIBD in 1995, members quickly endorsed a plan to organise the first IIBD Summer Institute in July 1997 in Hong Kong, taking advantage of the attraction of the historic event of sovereignty transfer. The curriculum of the one-month Summer Institute is planned jointly by four participating universities, each of which commits itself to send faculty members, to recruit students to the institute and to recognise the academic credits earned by the students at the institute. At the time of writing (January 1997) the planning of the Summer Institute has been completed. Signs are that the joint venture, being the first of its kind in Hong Kong, will turn out to be a great success.

Campus expansion

When the college was brought into the public system the first benefit was funding provision to re-design the existing campus facilities to bring them up to modern standards of tertiary education for 3000 students. Even then the college realised that the campus site was too restrictive and small for an urban university. Therefore, the college had been on the look-out to find space for campus expansion. The first opportunity arose when a nearby site which was occupied by the Government Supplies Department for storage purposes was vacated in 1986. Since it was also the time when the renovation and new building construction on the existing campus began, the college successfully argued that it needed some 'decanting' space to house some students whose studies were seriously affected by the noise and vibrations of the construction works, and took over the vacated government site. That move turned out to be most significant because it succeeded in reserving a most ideal site for its campus expansion when the government, in 1989, decided to quickly expand provision of higher education in Hong Kong. The construction of the new Shaw Campus began in 1993 and was completed in 1995, just in time to allow the newly retitled Hong Kong Baptist University to have a new look and the necessary facilities to release its full potential as a fully-fledged institution of higher education.

Some people might say that the institution was lucky, but the college would like to attribute its success to long-term projection of needs and perseverance in pursuing its goal. One good example is that when a nearby site was identified as suitable for the construction of a sports hall, it took the college ten years to persuade the Lands Office of the government to grant it the site and another seven years to complete the construction. Although the cost had gone up more than eight times in the meantime and the correspondence between the Lands Office and the college concerning the site had grown to one-foot thick, the college was still happy that its perseverance did pay off.

In fact, the college adopted the same approach concerning its future campus development. Even before the construction of the Shaw Campus began, the college had initiated a discussion with UPGC and the Lands Office concerning its long-term development needs. It argued that since the institution was now well established in the Kowloon Tong area, the prospect of moving to another greenfield site for new development was most unlikely. That being the case, UPGC and the government should reserve all the available sites in the vicinity for the new university so that when the expansion needs arose, there would be space available. At the time the discussion was initiated, the government had already started to allocate the sites south of Shaw Campus to various departments (including the Fire Services Department) for their development plans. Notwithstanding that, the college persevered in its argument until all but the Fire Services Department gave in. As it turned out, the government has just announced a new policy on student housing (January 1997) to support student hostel provision for urban universities such as HKBU. Having a residential campus has been a long-time dream of the institution, and the new policy is the result of the concerted efforts of many. If the college had not planned and pursued its goal into the unknown future, it would have had no land on which to build the new student hostels when the new policy was announced. This reminds me of the motto I wrote on the eve of the 25th Anniversary of the college: 'Work, as if we were going to die today, and Plan, as if we were going to live forever'.

Building the university foundation fund

Fundraising was not a new experience for the college. Before it became publicly funded, it had to rely on fundraising for all of its capital development from the day it was founded. However, fundraising for non-capital needs was a different matter. Although there had been small and infrequent attempts in the past, the concept of building an endowment fund of any substantial size did not cross the mind of the college until it began to see the light of gaining university status. In fact, the university status, or the promise of it, was the biggest contributing factor to the success of the college's endowment fundraising efforts. The college knew this from its past experience. Some years ago, when a potential donor was approached for a sizable donation, the polite reply was that the request would not be entertained until the college achieved university status.[4] Therefore, as soon as it was disclosed that the result of the self-accreditation assessment of 1993 was positive and that the university title was assured, the college lost no time in exploiting the news as a great fundraising opportunity.

At the foundation stone laying ceremony for the Shaw Campus in May 1993 the college publicly announced its intention to build an endowment fund (to be called the University Foundation Fund) of HK$100 million in order to enhance the development of the new university. Being cautious by nature, the college at first gave itself until March 1996 to achieve the goal, the date being the 40th anniversary date of the institution. However, the response from the Hong Kong community was so enthusiastic that the goal was reached before 1993 was over. Indeed, the mood was so euphoric among the alumni and well-wishing friends that the administration decided to double its fundraising goal to HK$200 million and announced the decision on the Founders' Day of 1994. The new goal was exceeded again before the end of 1995 and by the time the university celebrated its 40th Anniversary in March 1996 the University Foundation Fund had grown to over HK$250 million. The moral is, be bold, don't let an opportunity slip through your fingers.

Challenges and strategies: the way forward

Strategies in mass higher education

In the old days of university élitism the students were more self-motivated and had more uniform academic preparation and more favorable family and social backgrounds. The universities then would need only to provide an adequate learning environment and some

---

4   The donor did make a donation of HK$15 million to the college when the university title was granted.

guidance; the students would take over from there and with enthusiasm and hard work achieve reasonable standards at graduation. Therefore, under the élitist system the task of teaching was comparatively easier. The situation is quite different now. The average entry grades of the students are lower than before, but the graduation requirements are higher. This, when added to the fact that the students' backgrounds are more diverse educationally and socially, makes the educational objective of getting the students to graduate on time and with a proper level of academic achievement much more difficult, and the task of teaching much heavier. With the increase of research funding which places a welcome but heavy demand on faculty time, there is little wonder that faculty of the universities are all feeling the pinch.

Given the fact that higher education in Hong Kong is no longer as élitist as before, HKBU has spent much effort in revising its curriculum and teaching methods in order to cope with the situation. The following are some of the strategies adopted by the university to meet the needs arising from the new situation brought about by mass higher education.

Mentoring system

The university recognised the fact that new and enhanced teaching methodology as well as technology would need to be developed to assist the students who were no longer necessarily the top students of their class. In order to make sure that new students were able to get used to the university style of learning quickly, the university, after a year-long study and planning, introduced a workshop series program in 1996 for the first-year students before their formal academic course began. Students were given intensive training in the use of the automated library system and in computer hardware and software that would be needed in their studies, as well as the advanced multimedia technologies which are available on campus. In addition, a mentoring system was set up with one faculty member serving as mentor for five or six students. The mentors meet their groups about six times per semester to see that no students are left behind in their studies. The format of the meetings is deliberately informal and the mentors are literally provided with some 'tea money' so that discussions and exchange of views can take place over a cup of tea or coffee. Preliminary findings on the new program have been very encouraging and a proposal has been made to enable the mentors to share the experiences among themselves, again, over a cup of tea.

Quality assurance

With the increase in the number of universities in Hong Kong, tertiary education has become a formidable sector attracting a lot of public funds as well as public attention. As a funding body, it is natural that UGC (the 'P' of UPGC has been dropped because there are no longer polytechnics) is concerned that quality education is, and is seen to be, provided in the institutions which it funds. Also, since more research funding has become available on a competitive basis, there has been a dramatic increase of research activities and perceived pressure to do research on the university campuses – so much so that when, recently, the language abilities of the university students became a topic of concern in the community, some people began to blame the so called 'over-emphasis' on research for the 'decline' of university education. Although the perception is wrong, UGC still finds it necessary to openly remind the institutions that in spite of the importance of research, teaching is still the primary function of a university.

To drive home this point, UGC has initiated a series of reviews of the teaching and learning quality processes of the institutions it funds (Massy and French 1997). The Teaching and Learning Quality Process Review (TLQPR) exercises have caused some concern from some academics who consider them a typical UGC nuisance. HKBU, however, takes a different view because it has always regarded teaching as a 'sacred' duty. In that sense, the review exercises are welcome external help to focus staffs' attention to the institution's commitment. The university's strategy is to make the best of these exercises to truly improve the teaching and learning activities on campus and as a formal way of showing its teaching strengths among its peers. To this end, the university has created the Academic Quality Support Section for quality assurance in the Academic Registry, and the Academic and Professional Standards Committee under the chair of the Academic Vice President. The result of the last TLQPR exercise conducted in the spring of 1996 seems to have shown that the university had done rather well.

Striving for areas of excellence

The general academic profile of the university is not very different from that of CUHK or HKU, except that the university does not have heavy professional programs such as medical school or engineering faculty. In most other areas which the university has in common with others the funding differentials (not so much in unit cost as in the economy of scale) do put the university in a disadvantaged position for competition, let alone the perceived pecking order which UGC claimed to have tried to erase but never succeeded.

In the face of these realities, the university has to be extremely innovative if it hopes to establish some areas of excellence. Currently, the university is contemplating two approaches: one general, one specific.

On the general side, the university would like to make special efforts to fully implement the concept of 'whole person education' to such an extent that high-quality teaching and learning will become the hallmark of the university. The university has already had some success in this regard in the past, despite the fact that the campus facilities were less than ideal. Now, with the TLQPR in force, the new Shaw Campus in place and the hostels and university community centre construction in sight, the university should be able to achieve a higher standard of excellence in the overall student life and learning experience in the next five years.

On the specific side, the university does have several academic areas which have better potentials of becoming centres of excellence. The obvious one which comes to mind is the School of Communication. The school was started as a department in 1967, the same year in which television was introduced to Hong Kong. Because of the foresight of the institution in the development of this new field in a timely fashion, the school now enjoys a very high profile and good reputation in the community on account of the success of its graduates in the mass media industry. Currently, the school is reasonably well-equipped in terms of hardware facilities and the strength of the faculty is being consciously built up. However, due to the fact that the school originated as a small department, the departmental building is no longer adequate in meeting the needs of the school. As a result, it is now being housed in eight different locations on the Ho Sin Hang Campus, making student and staff interaction very difficult. The university has tried to persuade UGC to provide a purpose-built facility for the school and will continue to try through whatever means to provide a proper physical environment to make the school a centre of excellence.

Another area under consideration is physical education and recreational studies. This is a relatively new area but is rapidly developing to become a leader in the field because of its staff strength and the fine facilities for research and teaching. Thanks to the location of the Joint Sports Center which is adjacent to the Shaw Campus, the university enjoys some of the best sports facilities in the territory. The recently established Center for Physical Recreation and Wellness also has state-of-the-art equipment to put the program soundly on academic ground. The center received a boost when it attracted an endowment donation of HK$8 million in December 1996 to support its ongoing research and seminar activities. The department now has the highest number of PhD degree-holding staff in the field of physical education in Hong Kong and is already the strongest among its peers. Nevertheless, the university would like to make it a centre of excellence in the Asia-Pacific region and to develop larger scale co-operation with appropriate universities and official bodies in China.

As pointed out earlier, the university has taken a pioneering role in the development of inter- and multi-disciplinary studies at the undergraduate level. Its China Studies and European Studies programs remain the only programs of that nature being offered in Hong Kong. Although both courses are resource intensive because they involve student and staff travelling to the respective countries, the university considers it worthwhile to further develop them as unique programs for Hong Kong. Once the campus residential facilities are in place, the programs will have an added dimension of student exchange, strengthening the university's efforts of internationalisation. Since the programs have the participation of several departments and faculties/schools, this is an excellent way of involving a large number of staff in striving for excellence.

It is obvious that the university would not be able to become uniquely the leader in too many areas. Suffice it to say that with the serious implementation of the concept of 'whole person education', all staff will have a full role to play in contributing to the standard of excellence at Hong Kong Baptist University.

Strengthening focused research

When the university accepted its mission as stated under the section on 'Role Differentiation', it knew that it would not play the role of a major research university. On the other hand, the university is convinced that each and every one of its faculty members must be active in research and scholarly endeavors in order to stay fit as excellent teachers. To that extent, every academic unit has been encouraged and given the necessary resources to build up its research infrastructure so all can stay active in their respective fields. By and large, the university is pleased with the level of research activities for an institution of its size and mission. But, at the same time, the university is keen to see some excellent strengths developed so as to justify its research post-graduate degree programs. In this regard, it is proud to see small teams of staff from different academic units coming to the fore with impressive research results and publications. Except in the areas of scholarly writings, which are mainly individual efforts, all the research teams now have their focused areas identified. For example, for the physics people it is laser physics and quantum optics; for chemistry it is surface science. The biologists are actively engaged in the waste management aspect of the environment, the mathematicians in statistics. In the social sciences the establishment of LEWI has provided a good theme of East-West comparative studies under which various research topics are being pursued. In the arts applied ethics is showing its strength and translation has made its way into high-quality translated classics publications. The economists have concentrated their research efforts in Mainland China and the decision scientists are making contributions to the new field of financial derivatives.

In addition to the faculty/school or department-based research units, the university currently has four university-wide research centres in applied ethics, child development, translation and East-West studies. Support to these centres will be performance based and their operations will be reviewed periodically to make sure that their existence has enhanced focused research activities which might not have happened otherwise.

An even higher level, but very much focused, research unit is now being planned which will involve regional and international co-operation with HKBU playing host. When this has materialised, HKBU will become a regional centre of excellence in research and consultancy in this speciality area.

As much as we emphasise the building up of our research strength, we are also mindful of the fact that the staff who are strong in research tend to neglect their teaching duties and move towards research because that is where reward is usually given. In the light of that, the university has established a reward system which positively rewards research without compromising teaching. This is a strategy the university consciously adopts with a view to striking a balance between research and teaching and ensuring that both excellent research and outstanding teaching are duly rewarded.

New student recruitment yardstick

The university understands that with mass higher education it has to be more careful in recruiting the right calibre of students. Since the university is now being hampered by the fact that it is not being considered as the top or one of the top universities in town, it is not possible for it to sit tight and wait for the students with top grades to come in. On the contrary, the university must go out to recruit not just the academically best-qualified students but also those who have the potential to become leaders, who are academically competent, who have a positive attitude and outlook on life, who are serious about their career prospects and, therefore, about their studies and who have the proper attitude towards the institution. The university may have to settle for not the students with top examination grades but only the upper 25 per cent. Notwithstanding that, the selection from that group of students is very important and, therefore, personal interview before admission should become an essential practice for the future recruitment process of the institution.

Forging ahead towards internationalisation

The university had a good start in this area when it hosted the founding conference of LEWI in co-operation with the Organization for Economic Cooperation and Development (OECD) in 1995. The conference was such a great success that the university was requested by OECD to hold a second one in 1996. The University of Amsterdam was so impressed and attracted by the concept of LEWI and its performance that it immediately applied to join as a full member (the one-off membership fee is US$100,000). The internationalisation effort received another boost when two groups of European studies students were sent to Germany and France for their one-year internship in 1996. One of the hosting universities (University of Paris XII) has requested that their postgraduate students be admitted to the HKBU MBA course for one semester as an exchange for their hosting the HKBU students. The request is very much welcome by HKBU since student exchange is one of the major means of internationalising its campus. In fact, plans are already in place for extensive overseas student exchange once the campus residential facilities are available.

Another major project of internationalisation was launched by the IIBD in June/July 1997. The university took advantage of the historic event when the sovereignty of Hong Kong reverted to China to organise this month-long summer institute. Since it is a truly international co-operative program from planning to implementation, the university has high hopes that this annual activity will have a long and prosperous life in the years to come.

To celebrate its emergence as a newly-titled university, the institution announced the establishment of six university fellowships in 1995. Scholars from overseas and from China Mainland are invited to come for a period of three to five months, with all expenses paid plus a modest (US$3,500) monthly stipend. The fellows are expected to participate in research and seminar activities in order to provide fresh academic stimulation and insight to the university community. At the same time, six fellowships were also established (three for research and three for teaching) to send HKBU faculty members to overseas universities of their choice for research or teaching attachments. The university hopes that through these efforts (made possible through private endowment incomes) the staff will have better opportunities of exposure in the high-quality international academic circle.

Transformation into residential campus

In searching for ways to distinguish the university among its peers, the university found that building on the success of its 'whole person education' philosophy, as attested by both the HKCAA review panel of 1991 and the UGC review panel of 1993, was indeed one of the promising possibilities. In order to make a real difference in this area, a residential environment in which students could experience a live-in campus life is necessary. But, with the previous government policy of supporting hostel provision only at remotely-located universities, a residential campus for an urban institution like HKBU could only remain as a dream. Dream as it may be, the university decided that it should work out a master plan when it learnt that the government was willing to reserve the sites south of its Shaw Campus for future development. When the master site plan was disclosed in early 1995, it sounded so far-fetched and dream-like that some students even ridiculed the President in their student paper by saying that it was too early for him to 'sleep', let alone to 'dream'. The plan was to build four hostel towers, each of which would house 350 students, so that each student would have one year of live-in campus life experience during his or her three-year studies. For the rest of the commuting students, a university community centre was to be constructed with large lounges so as to make it possible for them to stay long hours on campus and with a place to rest and relax.

Two years after the plan was released, the university is pleased to note that the government has now decided to support hostel construction for HKBU and the number of places will increase to 1629, making it possible for the university to recruit a small number of overseas and China Mainland students to live in with the Hong Kong students, thereby further enriching their university campus life. The university is also fortunate to have received a grant of HK$55 million from the Charitable Foundation of the Hong Kong Jockey Club to construct the university community centre as planned.

Building the financial framework

At present, about 80 per cent of the university's recurrent expenditure is covered by the triennial UGC grant. This is indeed a very fortunate situation. However, the university is keen to have more financial freedom if it is to develop according to its own educational ideals. Assuming that the current funding provisions and student fees structure remain unchanged in the foreseeable future, the university would like to gain another private income equal to 10 per cent of its annual budget from endowment investment and annual donations. Ideally, the endowment should be big enough to generate half of it; the other half would come mainly from the annual giving plans of alumni and friends. To achieve this goal the size of the endowment should be as large as the yearly expenditure and the annual giving plan will have to be well-developed, particularly among the alumni.

The concept of alumni annual giving is well practised in North America but not quite developed yet in Hong Kong. The university would like to see a large number of alumni, each giving a small but regular sum annually to support his or her alma mater. In order to achieve the goal, cultivation of alumni loyalty is of crucial importance and the best time to start doing it is while they are students on campus. As to the existing alumni, the university has already set up an alumni affairs office to build a world-wide alumni network. It is a long-term investment and the result might not be seen for ten or fifteen years.

Catching the opportunity as it flies

Because of the mission and nature of the university, there is hardly an existing course in its curriculum that could be 'earth shattering' or attracting the attention of the world, no matter how well it is run. Although the university is happy with its mission and role, there has always been a desire to find something which, if done well, would put the university on the map for the world to see. That opportunity finally came in 1995 when the Hong Kong government decided to push for the development of Chinese medicine as a proper profession.

In recent years there has been a heightened interest in alternative medicine in general and Chinese medicine in particular around the world, partly because there is increasing evidence that Chinese medicine is effective in health care and partly because of the escalating costs of Western medicine. For Hong Kong, the promotion of Chinese medicine also has a political dimension because of the change of sovereignty on 1 July 1997. Adding to these favorable factors is the determination on the part of China to introduce Chinese medicinal products in the world market. The university, after following these trends for two years, decided that the time was right to formally propose to offer a degree course in Chinese medicine in the triennium of 1998–2001. When the proposal was submitted to UGC for consideration in the summer of 1996, the university was already aware that even if UGC agreed to the proposal, it would not attract additional funding through an increase of student number quota. But the university was so convinced that the development was very significant for Hong Kong, and would have a world-wide impact if it were done right, that it was willing to redistribute its student numbers to have a modest start of 30 students for a four-year course. The university is pleased to learn that UGC has endorsed the proposal.

By sheer coincidence, a team of experts from the Massachusetts Institute of Technology was commissioned jointly by the Hong Kong government and private industry in 1995 to study the future of Hong Kong industry. After more than a year of investigation and assessment, the team announced its findings in January 1997, in the same week when the HKBU proposal was endorsed by UGC. Among other things, the team identified Chinese medicinal products as a top priority development for Hong Kong's industry. The coincidence has given the university a tremendous boost of spirit, knowing that it has made the right decision at the right time. The university is convinced that it has the potential to develop a world-class program in Chinese medicine on a modern scientific basis for the following reasons:

- it has an active and committed team of scientists who are well trained, not only in modern science but also in Chinese medicinal plant research
- it has the backing of, and alliance with, the best-known universities in China in Chinese medicine and medical research
- it has world-wide contact with researchers and educationalists who are involved in the same field – an international network can be easily built up on the existing connections
- it will be the only university in Hong Kong which is fully committed to the task and is likely to receive strong support from the Hong Kong community
- it has the proper management and quality control mechanisms in place, which are most important in establishing credibility for the discipline.

The university plans to start a research program in Chinese medicine as soon as possible, while doing the preparatory work for the full-time degree course. For practical reasons it would like to see the legislation for the protection and governing of the Chinese medical profession in place before starting the student recruitment, because only a course which leads to a publicly recognised professional qualification can attract good students. The course will be supported initially by its science faculty but a separate School of Chinese Medicine will eventually be established at HKBU.

Conclusion

Although the main direction and the general program are now set for the next five years, there is still no room for complacency for this university which seems to have had more than its fair share of difficulties. In fact, just at the time the university had built up its momentum for smoother running, the UGC announced that there would be a 3 per cent reduction of the grants to the institutions for each year of the next triennium beginning 1998 and the numbers of students admitted would be frozen for the time being. Consequently, the university has urgently to consider how to minimise the impact of such a decision. Specifically, because of the lack of economy of scale, the impact of the cut could be severe to the university. It must find better-than-average ways to cope with the situation in order to stay competitive. At present, all of the existing courses are, by comparison, relatively small and there is very little trimming that can be done to make room for new development. Furthermore, most of the courses have only been running for a short time and are developing healthily and steadily, thus the university is not ready to consider closing down some in order to develop others.

In view of this, the administration feels that it should adopt a more pro-active approach and that the regular channels and forums through which regular developmental plans are evolved are no longer sufficient. Consequently, it has decided that a one-day brainstorming session on strategic planning involving all of the major academic and administrative planners should be held on 25 January 1997, just one day after the completion of this writing.

A lot of background information has been provided to the participants and a format to guide the order of discussions has been worked out (Appendix 9.4). It is expected that the brainstorming session will generate more insight into what the university must do in order to stay on top of the circumstances and continue its drive towards excellence in selected areas in the twenty-first century.

Appendix 9.1
Hong Kong Baptist University at a glance

Mission: Hong Kong Baptist University, as a community of scholars, is committed to a distinctive mission of higher education that incorporates teaching, research and service, and which inculcates in all who participate a sense of value that extends beyond the mere acquisition of knowledge. The university seeks to achieve and to foster excellence, intellectual freedom, the highest ethical standards and a firm commitment to the provision of an environment which develops and sustains the whole person in all these endeavours.

Role: In the context of higher education in the Hong Kong community, the university provides opportunities for both undergraduate and postgraduate studies in arts, business, communication, science and social sciences, including teacher education. In keeping with the commitments to the education of the whole person, the university offers programs with characteristics which aim to provide a liberal and intellectually broad education. These programs include emphases on the integration of knowledge from various disciplines and the relevance of that knowledge in its international perspective.

Staff and students: Expressed in terms of 'full-time equivalents', there were, in the academic year 1996–97, 974 staff, 313 academic staff members and 661 general staff members. In the same year there were 4755 students (headcount), equivalent to 4429 FTE. In FTE 4074 were undergraduates (almost all full-time), 236 were enrolled in postgraduate coursework awards (all part-time) and 119 were enrolled in MPhil and PhD postgraduate research awards (two-thirds of whom were full-time). There were more women students than men (in the ratio of three women to two men). In the case of staff, there were more men than women (in the ratio of five men to four women).

In addition to the above staff and students, involved in work funded by the government and by student fees, the School of Continuing Education operated a fully self-funded program. In this, in the academic year 1996–97, 2392 students were enrolled part-time in degree programs of HKBU itself and 1990 were enrolled part-time in degree programs leading to the awards of overseas universities. In addition, some 37,655 semester enrolments were recorded in non-degree studies offered by the School of Continuing Education.

Departments and faculties/schools: There are 25 academic departments, organised in five faculties/schools – that is, Faculty of Arts, School of Business, School of Communications, Faculty of Science and Faculty of Social Sciences. Except for the School of Communication (which became a separate school as recently as 1991), the four remaining faculties and schools are approximately of equal size.

Beside the David C. Lam Institute for East-West Studies, the university has research centres in applied ethics, child development and translation. A number of other research centres are located in the faculties and schools.

Estates: The university occupies two adjacent campuses in Kowloon Tong: the Ho Sin Hang campus, with 24,000 m^2 of land and 48,000m^2 of buildings and the newer Shaw campus, with 27,000m^2 of land and 43,000 m^2 of buildings. The Joint Sports Centre, adjoining the Ho Sin Hang campus, comprises 34,000 m^2 and is used by Baptist University, City University and Hong Kong Polytechnic University.

Expenditure: Expenditure in the financial year 1996–97 was HK$764 million, of which 50 per cent went to teaching and research, 12 per cent to academic support services, 13 per cent to buildings and grounds, 9 per cent to administration and 15 per cent to staff accommodation, student services and other operating expenses.

Appendix 9.2
Member institutions of the David C. Lam Institute for East-West Studies (LEWI)

Asia:	Ateneo De Manila University
	Hong Kong Baptist University
	Keimyung University
	Tunghai University
Australia:	University of Western Sydney, Hawkesbury
	Swinburne University of Technology

Continental Europe:	University of Amsterdam
	Lund University
Mainland China:	Fudan University
	Jilin University
	Lanzhou University
	Nanjing University
	Peking University
	Shanghai University
	Sichuan Union University
	Tsinghua University
	Wuhan University
	Xiamen University
	Xi'an Jiaotong University
	Yunnan University
	Zhongshan University
North America:	Baylor University
	Mercer University
	Ohio University
	Simon Fraser University
United Kingdom:	University of Leeds
	University of Strathclyde

Appendix 9.3

Member institutions of the Wing Lung Bank International Institute for Business Development (IIBD)

Assumption University
Ateneo De Manila University
Hong Kong Baptist University
Baylor University
Mercer University
Ohio University
Simon Fraser University
Lund University
Stockholm University
University of Leeds
University of Strathclyde
Swinburne University of Technology
University of Western Sydney, Hawkesbury
Shanghai Jiaotong University
Tsinghua University
Zhongshan University

Appendix 9.4

Programme for HKBU strategic planning retreat, January 1997

1. Strategic Assessment: The Present Position

- External Perceptions
    the UGC
    the Hong Kong community
    Hong Kong schools and potential students
    the international academic community
    the major universities in China
- Internal Perceptions
    student views
    alumni views
    staff views
- In what ways is the University different from the 'competition'?

2. Strategic Vision: Where We Wish To Be

- Statement of Educational Values
- The University's Mission Revisited
- Are There Conflicts Between the Mission and the Role Statements?
- Positioning for Distinct Recognition:
    Academic Programmes
    Teaching Commitments
    Research and Other Scholarly Activities
    Service and Administration
- The International Dimension

3. Strategic Planning: A Framework For The Future

- Organisational/Structural Issues
- The Financial Framework
- Criteria for New Course Development
- Criteria for Discontinuance of Courses
- Criteria for Areas of Excellence
- Staff-related Issues
    the Distribution of Duties (Teaching/Research/Administration)
    the Reward System Based on Performance in Various Areas
- Student-related Issues
    the Quality of Students Admitted
    Language Matters

4. Strategic Action: A Road Map To Our Destination

- What Priorities are to be Assigned to New Developments?
- What are the Appropriate Next Steps?

Chapter 10

City University of Hong Kong

David Mole and Enoch C.M. Young

Under British administration, the Hong Kong government's educational policy has closely followed policy developments in England, both in substance and in timing. When the government accepted the desirability of expanding the capacity of the higher education sector to deliver 'high-end' vocational training, it created two large British-style polytechnics to do the job – Hong Kong Polytechnic in 1972 and City Polytechnic of Hong Kong in 1984. As the polytechnic era came to an end in Britain in the 1990s, Hong Kong followed suit and, since 1994, has been steadily converting its 'polytechnics' and 'colleges' into 'universities'.

Expansion of higher education and the decline of the binary system

This chapter is built around the experience of the rise and decline of the 'binary, polytechnic-university system' seen from the viewpoint of City Polytechnic, later City University of Hong Kong. City Polytechnic of Hong Kong (CPHK), which became City University of Hong Kong in January 1995, eleven years after its foundation, had been expected to develop a portfolio of programmes and a research mission consistent with the 'polytechnic philosophy' – professional and vocational education, mostly 'sub-degree'; strong links with local business, employers and the community; and an emphasis on applied work and consultancy. In fact, the binary division did not prevent CPHK from becoming a large, degree-granting institution that undertook functions not very different from those of the established universities.

Only a few years after its foundation, CPHK began to build up its undergraduate degree programmes and developed a range of taught postgraduate degrees. By the time its status was adjusted, it had already graduated students with PhDs, formed five Research Centres in 1993, appointed staff to Professor and Reader ranks and, in 1994, created a School of Graduate Studies, all of which clearly signalled an intention to take up a fully rounded role as an institution of higher education.

The government, through the University Grants Committee (UGC), its arms-length, funding agency, accepted, even encouraged, these ambitions to accommodate plans to expand the tertiary sector. This expansion, in true Hong Kong style, was accomplished at break-neck speed. Government, UGC and institutional attention was focused on the immediate problems and issues that expansion raised. Since undergraduate degree places were the heart of the increase in numbers, 'sub-degree' work was marginalised. Also, recruitment of good staff by the polytechnics meant providing terms of service and academic conditions of work that matched those of universities.

The shift to university status when it came for CPHK did not, therefore, require any fundamental change in its operations. Formally speaking, conversion to university status meant only two things: the alignment of salary scales with those of teachers in the local universities and a grant of authority to validate degrees (hitherto, external validation and revalidation by CNAA, subsequently by Hong Kong Council for Academic Accreditation, had been required). Indeed, the university has been able to argue quite credibly that the grant of university title was no more than an acknowledgement of existing circumstances – CPHK had been a 'university' for a number of years before it was able to call itself a university.

Nevertheless, although it may have had a loose fit in the period of its development, the binary system in Hong Kong shows some of the remarkable capacity for life-after-death familiar elsewhere. There are both external and internal reasons for the persistence of binary systems. The external reasons in the Hong Kong case are quite straightforward. Neither the government, through the UGC, nor the public have fully accepted that a unified system is now in place.

The University Grants Committee and the binary divide

The UGC's view of the situation was made clear at the outset when, as one of the conditions on which university title was granted to the former polytechnics, it insisted on their agreement to statements of purpose. These statements, which would read narrowly for a technical school, let alone a university, were designed to provide the UGC with the leverage necessary to prevent the former polytechnics deviating too far from their existing role. The official view of the situation has recently been consolidated in 'Higher Education in Hong Kong', the October 1996 report of the UGC. This document defines the missions of the local institutions in terms already set out in 1993, before the unification of the system was attempted.

The mission statement reads, in part, 'City University and Hong Kong Polytechnic University, which were until recently polytechnics, place emphasis on the application of knowledge and vocational training', a description that makes deliberate use of the term 'vocational' rather than 'professional' education. The report also describes Hong Kong University of Science and Technology (HKUST), but not the two former polytechnics, as housing 'major' professional schools, notwithstanding the fact that HKUST's portfolio of programmes is virtually identical to that at City University and despite the fact that City University has a law school and professional programmes in social work while HKUST does not. The mission statements also restrict the research of the former polytechnics to so-called 'selected areas', while the two older universities and HKUST are invited to undertake research across the full range of disciplines.

In drafting and attempting to maintain restrictive statements of purpose for the former polytechnics, UGC does not appear to have taken into account the existence of the non-UGC sector of higher education in Hong Kong – notably, the institutions under the Vocational Training Council and the Open University of Hong Kong. If Hong Kong higher education is to be regulated through a set of mission statements, this will need to be done across the entire system. Current UGC thinking seems to reflect a desire to cover off the whole range of post-secondary functions within the university sector.

The official position goes beyond verbal definitions. As a publicly funded organisation (and universities in Hong Kong are unusually reliant on public funds), student intake-allocations by level (undergraduate, postgraduate, etc) must be negotiated with the UGC. With the deliberate aim of concentrating 'research' at only three universities, research student numbers are sharply constrained for the new universities. At the same time, the UGC continues to fund a large number of Higher Diplomas through the two former polytechnics. While, in some jurisdictions, 'sub-degree' programmes are smoothly articulated to undergraduate degrees, providing a useful extension of university work, this is not possible in Hong Kong where the government, through the UGC, insists on differentiating the 'vocational' purposes of Higher Diplomas from degrees and discouraging entry to degree programmes from Higher Diplomas.

UGC's effort to maintain a differentiation in the role of the various local universities would be less discouraging if it were not for current funding arrangements. Under the funding formula, the only funds that are performance-based are granted for research, with research performance measured by quite narrow academic criteria. Applied work, and much other scholarly work of local and commercial interest, does not attract funds. Meanwhile, student numbers, but not teaching performance, attract funds to support teaching and learning. Thus only the universities with a UGC-approved mission to undertake a traditional research role can increase their level of support by improving performance in the role assigned to them. Other universities must either drift away from their official mission or resign themselves to lower levels of support.

Through these policies the essentials of the binary system have been enshrined, despite the ending of its formal basis. Having allowed City University to stretch the terms of the 'polytechnic' mission to facilitate rapid expansion, now that the exigencies of the expansion are behind us, UGC is attempting to enforce a return to a narrow reading of the university's mission.

UGC has adopted this stance for the usual mix of opportunist and principled reasons. The desire not to rock the boat, in particular at the time of writing (mid-1997), is quite understandable. Once the question of institutional missions becomes open, how will it ever be closed? At the same time, UGC argues that a system of undifferentiated, comprehensive universities does not make sense for a small self-contained system of higher education, while the notion that most of the research should be concentrated in a few universities, where economies of scale and synergies will be available, has a superficial plausibility. Given this, does it not follow that the former polytechnics, now universities, should retain their firm commitment to vocational education and close links to industry?

Public attitudes

If the UGC, with all its direct access to information about tertiary education, has been reluctant to accept that a new era has begun, it is not surprising that the essentially similar quality of local universities has not yet become clear to the local community. Objective criteria such as they are – the understandings of insiders that this or that department is better (or worse) than cognate departments in other universities, the number of academics with an international reputation, innovative and well-marketed programmes – all have remarkably little impact on the public mind. We continue to live with a stratification of local universities in which the 'oldest' appears at the top and 'newest' at the bottom.

The consequences of this established 'pecking order' are significant. Hong Kong's main instrument for allocating entry-level students to universities and programmes is designed to ensure that the 'best' students get the best chance to enter the programme of their choice. Universities that enjoy the most established reputation get virtually all of the best qualified students, while less well-prepared and motivated students cascade in strict succession down the pecking order. The new universities find themselves, year after year, with the hardest educational job to do and without the high fliers who will carry their alma mater's claims into the wider society.

This problem is then compounded in two ways. Achievement in primary and secondary schooling, in Hong Kong as elsewhere, is linked to social privilege. The band of students achieving entry to City University is, generally speaking, struggling with economic and related problems as well as having an academic mountain to climb. Second, many of our students begin their career with us with a sense of having failed. Any experienced educator will recognise this as a difficult starting point for students and teachers.

At first sight, therefore, the new universities face a very formidable obstacle to their development and integration into a unified system. However, there are important features of the situation of the new universities in Hong Kong that make it probable that the current situation is temporary, not permanent.

The impact of growing student numbers

The most obvious feature is the continuing impact of the very rapid expansion of student intakes over the last ten years. As this impact widens and deepens, it is unlikely that the current structure of higher education can survive. This will be especially the case if a new round of expansion is attempted to bring participation rates in Hong Kong up to international norms.[1] Although the former polytechnics and colleges were important vehicles for this expansion, the two established universities and the newly-formed HKUST have also experienced an enormous escalation in student numbers. This has meant that, despite the privileged selection of students that universities with higher public reputations have enjoyed, all the universities find themselves in much the same boat when it comes to dealing with this much enlarged intake.

This 'levelling' of the various institutions is the more obvious because the real differences among students with apparently sharply different performance as school leavers are, perhaps, not so great as all that. Many of those who have raised themselves to the minimum standard required for university entrance have needed to work from a lower base than those who scored higher. Also, while most of our students at City University are the first in their family to reach university, this is now true of university students across Hong Kong. No university in Hong Kong is any longer in the business of providing higher education to the children of a stable élite.

The mere expansion of student numbers is only an aspect of a broader change in the character and purpose of higher education in Hong Kong. This change has been the result of the rapid development of the regional economy and the related shift in the city's economic base from basic, labour-intensive manufacturing to the provision of sophisticated international services. While academics in other countries are contending with similar social trends, the speed, scale and depth of the adjustment in Asia generally, and in Hong Kong in particular, are startling. It need hardly be added that these social changes are accompanied in Hong Kong by substantial and challenging political changes.

Rapid growth and rapid change introduce two elements into the situation that are relevant when considering the future of the binary divide, and beyond that to the future generally for Hong Kong's system of higher education.

---

1   *Editor's note*: By September 1994 sufficient places were available in the first year of first-degree courses in Hong Kong universities and colleges for 18 per cent of the school leaving-age cohort. But, in addition, at least 10 per cent of the relevant age group gained entry to first-degree courses in overseas universities – mainly in Australia, Britain, Canada and USA. (Morris, McClelland and Yeung 1994)

Vocational training and professional education

The first element is that the frontier between so-called vocational training and professional education is becoming more permeable and unstable. This distinction has never been easy to make. What distinction can there be in the level of intellectual difficulty, or the epistemological basis, of 'civil engineering' relative to 'building and construction', or 'bio-chemistry' relative to 'environmental science'? Moreover, any relevant modern education is 'T-shaped', a mix of technical, specialist depth and generalist breadth. A useful vocational education is no less T-shaped than a useful professional education.

It would, of course, be naïve not to recognise that the vocational-professional distinction being deployed here is code for a kind of class distinction. But it is exactly this core of the divide that is threatened by modern social development. In Asia the growing middle class is unusually open and dynamic. As the occupational base of this new middle class spreads, who is to say where vocations leave off and professions begin? A binary divide built on this foundation cannot endure for long.

Accountability

The second consequence of expansion, and the enormous increase in funding related to the expansion, is that the circle of stakeholders in the system is becoming more diverse, stretching beyond the familiar world of government insiders, employers and professional bodies to include more numerous, and more vocal, taxpayers, legislators, students, parents and alumni. This has resulted in an increased demand for accountability, quality and efficiency.

UGC has responded to these demands by launching a system of assessment reviews. Assessments of research performance have been followed by a searching Teaching and Learning Quality Process Review (TLQPR) (Massy and French 1997), and the TLQPR is now to be complemented by a review of management performance and value-for-money. Through these reviews the UGC has signalled its perception of community demands and is attempting to enforce its view of how these demands should be met.

Meanwhile, the reviews have exerted an important influence on the management of the universities. The core assumption of the TLQPR is that 'quality' can be, and should be, managed. Where quality is to be managed, the quality of teaching and learning cease to be a private matter between teachers and their students, becoming the collective concern of the institution as a whole. The upcoming review of university 'management processes' will have a similar effect on business operations as 'benchmarking', value-for-money audit, performance indicators and performance pledges become a normal part of our routines. External review is both increasing the demand on university managers for proactive control of the operation and adding to the tool kit available to them to do the job.

This is important in the present context because, in undertaking these reviews, it has been necessary to treat all the universities on a level playing field. In the recent past the distinction between non-universities (subject to substantial external control) and universities (allowed a decent degree of autonomy) was built into the system. 'Accountability' has now become a requirement that all institutions must be prepared to satisfy equally, without regard to status, while the management style that is linked to accountability will inevitably become a standard template into which all the funded institutions must fit.

The above review of the external conditions under which the new universities in Hong Kong operate suggests that while the immediate situation is unpromising, the future is more open. UGC and public perceptions that the system of higher education is really two systems, whatever the institutions may be called, is founded on a distinction between levels of professional education and institutional roles that cannot be sustained intellectually or socially.

Internal responses to a continuing binary divide

The main issue for the new universities, certainly for City University, has been, and remains, how to ensure that the best use is made of opportunities as they open up. To accomplish this the university has undertaken two important, ongoing projects: first, the clear definition of strategic goals and the means to achieve them and, second, the establishment of a system of governance and quality management consistent with greater institutional and professional autonomy.

The first step in the process of defining goals was to develop a 'mission statement'. After prolonged and open consultation, this statement was presented on the occasion of the university's change in status. The then Vice-Chancellor, Professor Y.C. Cheng, noted that while 'no university funded by public money has the absolute freedom to take up whatever role in society it chooses', the university has 'a duty to look beyond the day-to-day work of performing a task we have been set...the wider community we serve relies on us to make plans for the future. How else can we assist in shaping that future?'

The University Vision that opens the statement – 'to be internationally recognised as a leading university in the Asia-Pacific region' – nicely captures the university's ambition and its sense that it is misunderstood. The Mission Statement proper manages to straddle most of the functions expected of a fully-developed university making explicit reference to the 'advancement of knowledge', 'professional education' and 'applied research'.

As is usual with this kind of exercise, the process by which the statement was derived was more important than the actual outcome. This process required that tensions in the organisation be brought to the surface and, if not finally resolved, at least clarified. In a number of important ways these tensions reflect the university's history.

First, the largest units at City University are in engineering and business. There are smaller law and social work programmes and a number of other interesting programmes, such as translation and in the sciences. But the work-a-day professional orientation of the university is an important influence on its tone and technically-oriented programmes will continue to dominate the institution for some time to come.

At the same time, a large proportion of our students continue to study in Higher Diploma programmes. At City University this government-mandated differentiation has been institutionalised in the organisation by the creation of a College of Higher Vocational Studies. The college now undertakes all the university's sub-degree work. Students of the college can enter after form five – rather than form seven for degree programmes – and follow explicitly vocational programmes. The college represents about one-third of the university's under-graduate teaching and, therefore, exerts a major influence on the entire operation.

Finally, we have faced the problem of creating the right balance between the research and teaching roles of the university, and within the research role the balance of 'academic' and 'applied' work. These difficulties are too widespread in modern higher education to require special explanations here but it is certainly true that the polytechnic legacy of staff interests and training have made the search for solutions more troubled.

It should be said at once that there is nothing in this legacy of the 'polytechnic' in curriculum, sub-degree studies and research that is evidently inconsistent with status as a 'university'. It is easy to imagine a modern university being content with a mission as an educator of professionals in business and engineering, with a research programme strongly driven by the desire to apply results to local needs and with a range of awards from higher diplomas to postgraduate degrees. Indeed, many staff continue to believe that there is real merit in educating students for clear professional roles and supporting this education with strong on-going links with professional bodies, employers and local enterprises. Nevertheless, there is an equally strong feeling that a university needs to lift its gaze a little higher than this.

A university strategic plan

Further clarification and consolidation of the university's goals has, therefore, been essential and the development of a mission statement became the precursor to a full-scale exercise to produce the university's first strategic plan. The production of the plan began with intensive meetings among senior managers to frame 'strategic directions' and 'key success indicators'. These meetings were followed up by the formation of seven broadly-based task groups covering the major issues. The task groups then reported to a day-long planning forum.

Up until this point, most key issues remained open. What was now required was a draft plan that set out some clear choices. This difficult step was made easier by the arrival of a new University President, Professor H.K. Chang, who took responsibility for creating this draft. This long, careful process has resulted in a five-year plan under the title *Towards a New Era of Excellence*, covering the period from 1997–2002. The plan is a comprehensive effort to define goals across the university's entire operation. In the present context, however, two issues are of principal importance: the reform of our curriculum and the role of research in the institution.

One of the main features of the plan is the intention to greatly broaden the scope of the university's undergraduate education. The plan argues that a modern professional education, geared to the needs of Hong Kong and its region, requires that graduates have more than technical skills. They need to be proficient communicators, able to straddle more than one discipline and to have the confidence to enter a culturally diverse workplace. To achieve this will require supplementing the current complement of objective-oriented, vertically-integrated programmes with cross-disciplinary courses and courses that introduce students to a wider world of scholarship.

To make it possible to open up the curriculum, the university is shifting to a credit unit system, with requirements for out-of-discipline studies and cultural studies specified as a set of distributional requirements. Core programmes will be retained but it is expected that these will ultimately take up only two-thirds of a student's curriculum. After some resistance to the extent and speed of the changes being proposed, staff have come to embrace the new approach to the curriculum. This is good evidence that the university is moving in step with quite general trends.

The role of research

When university status was first in prospect, the effort to enhance the organisation's research profile moved high on the agenda. This was encouraged by a bias in UGC funding arrangements. Because UGC's research funding is performance based, being geared to the number of identified 'active researchers', while funding for teaching is based on student numbers, not teaching performance, it is not surprising that Heads and Deans, if not senior managers, began to emphasise research performance among their staff. In the short term the emphasis on research seemed to be consistent with the general desire to move closer to some perceived model of the 'university' and to be closely linked to the goal of advancing the university's regional and international reputation.

However, the strategic plan represents an attempt to strike a more productive balance between teaching and research and accepts that there are limits on the development of the university's research role, not, however, for the reasons articulated by UGC. While UGC argues that not every university in Hong Kong should try to become a research-led operation on the international model, City University's plan argues that no university in Hong Kong is likely to succeed with such a strategy. Pre-eminence in science and engineering research depends on major government research funding, funding levels that are well beyond anything to be contemplated in this region. Pre-eminence in social sciences and humanities also depends on solid funding and on a critical mass of scholars, something that is difficult to organise in Hong Kong.

To match the big American schools in research is a challenge for even the oldest and greatest of European and Japanese schools. While much excellent research is being done in Hong Kong universities (not least City University) and, in some areas, local departments are world leaders (including some at City University), no university in Hong Kong has yet made a credible show achieving a broad international research reputation.

The strategic plan proposes two goals that are relevant in this environment. First, there will be an attempt to focus resources selectively. Second, the plan makes it clear that the university will support and reward only high-quality research. The value of teaching as a core activity, and of applied work and consultancy, are reasserted. Staff are urged not to sacrifice either students or the community in the struggle for publications in academic journals.

Implementing this part of the plan and finding the right approach to research for the university are not likely to be easy. Selection of research areas must involve more losers than winners, and the career interests and incentives of staff are not obviously in harmony with those of the university. Nevertheless, the university is now committed to early action to define a productive research role.

Governance and quality assurance

The effort to agree a strategic plan should be seen in the context of general developments in governance and management that have followed university status. In the run up to its new status, the university embarked on substantial adjustments to its system of governance. The changes were designed to turn what had been characterised as an 'administration-led' organisation into an 'academic-led' organisation.

Senior academic appointments, including Vice-Presidents, Deanships and Headships, have been made 'concurrent' with teaching posts to make it easier for rotation through these offices to take place. Both Deans and Heads also go through an open selection process designed to provide academic staff with a substantial say in the outcome. At the same time, the Senate committee through which curriculum decisions had been processed, was disbanded in favour of faculty-based committees, leaving central university committees with only an academic planning role.

These formal changes are, perhaps, not so important as the cultural change that has accompanied them. A greater assertiveness and readiness to accept delegated responsibility has begun to emerge, making it possible to turn over important areas of management to collective deliberation and consensus building. This new style has, of course, brought its own problems, problems mostly expressed in grumbles about 'too many committees'. Nevertheless, there has been a decisive and useful break with the past.

The attempt to nourish a more open and a more collegial style of management has been particularly important in the development of a devolved, staff-based system of quality assurance. External validation had inevitably led to document-heavy, event-centred processes. Moreover, there had been a tendency for the central agencies that were ultimately responsible to external validation bodies to exert undue control over academic decisions.

Once external validation of programmes was no longer required and the university came to reinvent its own quality process, it took the view that effective quality management in an institution of higher education is characterised by five features: it is supported by a quality culture, it is capable of covering the entire student experience, the processes facilitate continuous improvement, control of the quality process is delegated as far as possible to responsible staff and the process provides credible guarantees to stakeholders. In this approach there is an emphasis on self-regulation and reliance on professional expertise that the university feels is consistent with an appropriate degree of academic autonomy and academic freedom.

The arrangements now in place include: a consistent set of Senate 'guidelines' that are chiefly concerned with processes, a more open set of documents supplied by the Senate's Quality Assurance Committee providing examples of 'best-practice' and a rigorous system of quality-process audits. These internal audits are modelled on the external quality-process audits familiar in Britain, New Zealand and elsewhere. They are designed to allow for the maximum delegation of responsibility for quality consistent with the university's need to remain accountable to stakeholders.

Towards a post-binary system of higher education

The development of a broader curriculum at City University, a better focus on its core role in teaching and learning and a shift to a more mature corporate culture are all designed to position the university to make the maximum contribution to its community as it takes on a broader role and shakes off the more restrictive features of the polytechnic legacy. The key question is whether this effort will be supported, or thwarted, by the policy makers. This question is not of only local importance. The policy environment has become a critical determinant of systems of higher education in more and more jurisdictions. The interface in Hong Kong between universities and the government is unusually direct and simple, given the small size of the system and the relative lack of differences in the relation of the universities to the funding agency – all rely absolutely on public funding. The issues being posed for Hong Kong educators may, therefore, provide insights for others dealing with the same questions in more varied and complex systems. There are two main aspects of the general question.

First, is it wise for government to distribute, by fiat, different educational roles among institutions? It is, of course, true that not all universities should, or could, provide for all specialisms. Governments therefore have a legitimate role to play in ensuring that the needed range of programmes is provided efficiently across the higher education system. But this does not imply that enforcing broad differences among universities is necessary or helpful. Certainly, the distinction between vocational and professional education must frustrate the emergence of a proper balance in the curriculum between breadth and depth and force students into premature choices. If policy makers do wish to nurture differences in the 'character' of universities, a more subtle distinction than this will be needed. Moreover, in determining the roles of the UGC-funded institutions it would be wise to think through the structure of the entire higher education sector.

A more subtle distinction will certainly be called for in Hong Kong as local institutions begin to develop their own versions of credit unit systems. Hong Kong's second and third universities – Chinese University of Hong Kong and the new Hong Kong University of Science and Technology – have both been organised with American models in mind and have always used credit unit regulations. Now even Hong Kong University, venerable by Asian standards, is converting to credit units with the explicit objective of opening up its own programmes. The narrow, specialised, three-year degree, under threat in Britain for several years past, is now equally threatened in Hong

Kong. UGC will need to understand the fall-out from this process for their attempt to define institutional missions.

Second, is it helpful to foster academic research and teaching by concentrating research resources in a few universities and encouraging a greater teaching commitment among the others? This is a policy that makes sense only if there are, in fact, organisational reasons to expect that: (1) deliberately preventing a university from developing its research potential is good for its commitment to teaching and (2) deliberately favouring the development of an institution into a 'comprehensive' university produces better research performance. Both of these propositions are doubtful. No university can hope to be a successful agency for teaching unless its academic staff, to a greater or lesser extent, are involved in research. Careerist research ambitions, unchecked by a vigilant management, can have an adverse impact on student education, but this does not imply that research should be stopped! Nor is it true that economies of scale, or synergies, in research can be captured by having all kinds of research going on in one place. Research is a discipline-specific, internationalised project. The crudeness of the distinction between a 'research-led' university and 'teaching-led' university is damaging and unhelpful in the search for a balance between teaching and research that advances educational goals.

Unfortunately, as noted above, current funding arrangements reinforce the impact of bad policies. Because the only performance-related funding goes to academic research, teaching and applied work are undervalued and underfunded. It is these funding arrangements that reveal most clearly the UGC's failure to accept the former colleges and polytechnics into the university system.

The way forward, in this context as in many others, is not to over-regulate. This is not primarily a matter of institutional autonomy and academic freedom, valuable as these are. A more open assignment of roles must encourage healthy competition and an effort to measure performance and take it into account when allocating funds. Programmes should go to the university demonstrably best able to handle them. Support for research should go to those demonstrably able to make productive use of funds. Entrenching the privileges of the comprehensive universities can only lead to complacency among the winners and the demobilisation of the losers.

City University has worked hard to establish a system of governance that is open to change and allows central bodies to be agents of change. Respect for professional expertise and for professional autonomy is critical to the success of such systems. It is to be hoped that the government, through UGC, will also attempt to be an agent of change across the entire system of higher education. If it wishes to be such an agent of change, it will also have to recognise the value of autonomy and the right of institutions to make the best of their own circumstances. Ending the rigidities of the binary system was a step in the right direction.It would be a pity if an era of universities-misnamed-polytechnics was to be followed by an era of polytechnics-misnamed-universities.

Appendix 10
City University of Hong Kong at a glance

Vision: City University of Hong Kong aspires to be internationally recognised as a leading university in the Asia-Pacific region.

The university is on the fringe of the main urban area of Kowloon at a key transit hub. It occupies a large, integrated, low-rise building with restricted space but good facilities for sports and the best Chinese restaurant among the local universities.

Admission of students to City Polytechnic of Hong Kong began in 1984. By 1990 more than 10,000 students were registered. By 1995, when CPHK became City University of Hong Kong, this had risen to 16,000. Student numbers have now stabilised with approximately 3000 postgraduates (most part-timers in taught master's programmes), 8500 studying for three-year undergraduate degrees (one-quarter part-time) and 6500 for higher diplomas (one-third part-time). Almost all of our students are from Hong Kong but an increasingly successful effort has been made to recruit exchange students and non-local students.

The School for Continuing and Professional Education (SCOPE) is large and growing, with 5500 participants in 1996.

The university offers approximately 100 programmes leading to awards (about 30 in business, 40 in science and engineering). Currently, programmes tend to be vertically integrated and objective oriented, but this pattern is now beginning to change. Also, while past expansion has been effected by increasing the range of programmes, greater consolidation is now taking place.

The university's commitment to research has been growing rapidly. Research work at the university attracts in excess of HK$250 million per year and is supported by 12 Research Centres.

The total annual recurrent income of the university is about HK$1900 million, with a recurrent cost per full-time equivalent student of about HK$130,000 per year.

Part V

Conclusions

Chapter 11

Prospects for the Future of Higher Education

David C.B. Teather

In this final chapter it is appropriate to address future prospects for higher education in each of the three jurisdictions that are the focus of this book. It is notable that the repositioning of the binary line was accompanied by very rapid growth in student numbers. While it is clear from the accounts in preceding chapters that the contexts of growth in student numbers were significantly different in each of the three jurisdictions, it is important to assess to what extent future growth is likely. This will lead to discussion of the purposes of higher education for different groups of students, the impact of information and communications technologies on teaching and learning in universities, and the movement of students across jurisdictional boundaries. But factors other than student numbers affect the size and complexity of universities, notably their research and service functions. These dimensions of university work will also be touched on in this chapter.

University expansion in historical perspective

It is commonly supposed in Britain that the considerable increase in student numbers in higher education that occurred in the 1960s resulted from government policies of the time, including the adoption of the recommendations of the Robbins Report (DES 1963). A rather different explanation was put forward in 1982 by E.G. Edwards, the foundation Vice-Chancellor of the University of Bradford, in a profound and powerfully-argued volume entitled *Higher Education for Everyone.*

Edwards observed that the expansion of student numbers that is usually attributed to Robbins actually began seven years before, in 1956. From an historical analysis of student numbers in higher education, not only in Britain but also in France, Germany, Italy, Belgium and the Netherlands and extending from the early years of the nineteenth century, Edwards concluded that growth in student numbers in these countries had essentially been demand driven. In fact, the number of students in higher education had increased at a very regular but exponential rate with a doubling time of 25 years from about 1860 to the late 1950s. Then expansion at a new exponential rate began, with the much shorter doubling time of nine years.

The regularity of this process of exponential growth, only temporarily disturbed by world wars and major recessions, led Edwards to conclude that the mechanism of expansion had a high degree of internal momentum. He concluded that demand for entry to higher education was essentially from the offspring of the managerial and professional classes, a section of the population that was itself expanding at a similar, exponential rate throughout this period. His analysis of entrants to higher education by social class and gender showed, even after the 'Robbins' expansion had run its course, that access to higher education in Britain was still highly correlated with these factors. In the year 1976, for example, 85 per cent of sons and 56 per cent of daughters of fathers in professional occupations entered higher education, while only 2 per cent of the sons and 1 per cent of the daughters of fathers in unskilled work did so.

Edwards (1982) concluded: 'that something like the Robbins principle has, in fact, prevailed throughout most of the modern expansion [of higher education in Britain since the 1860s] that, in the main, the provision of places has corresponded to the effective demand, that numbers of students have risen in proportion to those both able and willing to enrol' (p.67). And while one might assume that ability, in the narrow sense of innate intelligence, is evenly distributed across the population as a whole, willingness or motivation to enrol in higher education is, in Britain and the other European countries studied, highly class-specific. For the great majority of the offspring of the working classes throughout the period under consideration, the idea of enrolling at university did not enter consciousness as a serious life option – it would have seemed as remote as flying to the moon!

Among the growing managerial and professional classes, however, Edwards suggested that there was, from the 1860s onwards, 'a new consciousness of the potential value' of higher education which was 'a response not to any particular pull from employment or any particular provision by universities, it was rather a product of the whole new climate of social, cultural, scientific, economic and industrial winds of change' (p.47). He postulated a similar awakening in the 1950s to account for the 'extraordinary explosion in University and higher education expansion, common to all the countries of the advanced world' (p.52), which began in the mid-1950s and continued into the 1970s. Whereas before the mid-1950s 'higher education had been merely one of several ways of conserving (and for a minority of gaining) social and economic status, at this stage in the 20th Century it was becoming a virtual necessity for many of the roles played by the upper and middle, professional and managerial classes' (p.57).

What kind of higher education was provided for the sons and daughters of these professional and managerial people? The ideal model in England, and this was also reflected in the thinking and practices of the earliest universities in Australia and in the University of Hong Kong, was one that provided for the total development of young people. This included the fulfilment, integration and economic functions discussed in Chapter 1 through, respectively, the development of personal talents, the further enhancement of a sense of social and civic responsibility and education and training for entry to a career. Formal instruction in the universities was complemented by residence in a college or hall. This provided a more adult version of the formula for education adopted in the nineteenth century by the English public (i.e. private) schools.

As Roger Scott pointed out in Chapter 2, the provision of scholarships widened access to this form of higher education for a few bright scholars from the working classes. In Australia, which had, before the First World War, one university in each of its state capitals, many students commuted each day to their classes from their homes; and many more, particularly in faculties of commerce, combined part-time study with full-time work. The distances involved in travelling interstate precluded the development of a national catchment for higher education, such as that which developed in the UK. From 1911 onwards, beginning at the University of Queensland, some provision was also made through correspondence study for those who could not attend classes face-to-face.

There are, however, no good reasons to believe that the influence of gender and socioeconomic background on entry to higher education in Australia has been markedly different from that reported above in the case of Britain. British immigrants to Australia reproduced there the cultural and social patterns and institutions of 'home' and, although it can be argued that the new country offered somewhat greater opportunities for social mobility, the difference was one of degree. As indicated in Chapter 1, Australia has experienced several waves of immigration, since the Second World War successively from Britain, Southern Europe, the Middle East and Asia. It is notable, as Scott pointed out in Chapter 2, that the sons and daughters of more recent immigrants are more likely to enter higher education than are the sons and daughters of Australians of British descent whose forebears emigrated to Australia in earlier times. Few indigenous Australians were enrolled in higher education until the 1980s, but their numbers are now increasing.

To what extent would the explanation proposed by Edwards for the pattern of growth of higher education enrolments in countries of Western Europe make sense in Hong Kong? As in the case of Australia, the present-day population of Hong Kong – with the exception of the villagers of the New Territories and their descendants – is comprised largely of immigrants, and of the descendants of immigrants, who arrived in the jurisdiction after it became a British colony. Indeed, the population has increased rapidly from 1.5 million in the early 1950s to 6.5 million today. While the predominant spoken language is Cantonese, significant numbers of Hong Kongers trace their origins to other parts of China (Skeldon 1994).

Traditional Chinese culture places enormous importance on education. The civil service examinations, based on knowledge of the Confucian classics, had their origins two thousand years ago in the Han dynasty and were discontinued only in the closing years of the Qing, in the first decade of the twentieth century. Success in these examinations was the passport to employment, power and status in the Imperial administration. These benefits reflected not only on the individual himself but on his whole extended family. Preparing bright youths for these examinations often required the resources of the whole clan. And although families in Hong Kong, as in mainland China, are now smaller and organised more along the lines of the typical Western nuclear model, consciousness of the importance of a good education and a willingness of family members to pool resources to provide for it remains.[1] Rutanen (1996) points out that in the numerous theories about the success of today's dynamic Asian economies: 'there is one element that is common to every one of them: an emphasis on education' (p.191).

During the first half of this century the number of students admitted to the only university in Hong Kong was quite small. Moreover, the brief of the University of Hong Kong was not limited to providing education for the people of Hong Kong alone. The emphasis was on providing access to Western knowledge through the medium of English, and students were admitted from throughout mainland China as well as from Hong Kong itself.[2] Meanwhile, as Daniel Tse pointed out in Chapter 9, many students from Hong Kong chose to study in mainland China, particularly at the Christian universities. After the communist victory of 1949 this was no longer possible. The migration from mainland China to Hong Kong in the early 1950s both increased the need to provide more education and, because the inflow included scholars from Chinese universities, provided the means to meet that need. Private initiatives were eventually complemented by government action when, as Nigel French describes in Chapter 8, several of the private colleges established in the 1950s were brought together with government funding in 1963 to form the Chinese University of Hong Kong.

The kind of industrial development witnessed in Britain over the last 150 years was telescoped in Hong Kong into the last 50. Labour-intensive manufacturing grew to make Hong Kong Britain's first industrialised colony. Then the 'open door' policy of mainland China saw, from 1978, the relocation of this industry into China, where wages were lower and land cheaper. Hong Kong rapidly developed a metropolitan service economy comparable with those of other major world cities. Public education provision was first built at primary, then at secondary levels, and then with a vocational emphasis to equip students to fill lower-level jobs in the civil service. Top jobs were reserved, until recent times, for expatriates, most of whom had obtained their education in Britain. While in the seven years preceding the return of Hong Kong to Chinese sovereignty the public provision of higher

---

1 A personal anecdote is illustrative here. Talking with a porter at a block of apartments in Hong Kong, I learned that she regularly put aside part of her wages to provide for the education of her cousin's daughter, who was then studying at a university in Queensland.

2 See footnote 5, Chapter 1, p.19.

education increased rapidly, the number of places available in many disciplines was still linked closely to 'manpower planning' projections which took little regard of the wider purposes of higher education.

It has always been the practice, however, for the sons and daughters of the rich in Hong Kong to obtain a higher education in the West – in Britain, North America, Continental Europe and, sometimes, Australia. As Hong Kong became more affluent, more families could afford to send their children overseas for upper secondary schooling and for university. Since the number of university places in Hong Kong grew only slowly until the 1990s, many families chose to do so. Morris, McClelland and Yeung (1994) conservatively estimate the proportion of Hong Kong students going overseas each year since 1985 to be 10 per cent of the age cohort, mainly to Australia, Britain, Canada and USA.

The Hong Kong government has made much of the fact that sufficient places are now available at first-degree level in publicly-funded institutions in Hong Kong for 18 per cent of the relevant age cohort. And it is notable that, even though fees payable by full-time undergraduate students have been raised to HK$43,100 (US$5500) per annum, four-fifths of the cost of running these institutions is met by the government through the University Grants Committee. Students who cannot afford to pay the fees have access to grants and loans, for the fees themselves and for living expenses. But for every two Hong Kong students who are undertaking higher education in Hong Kong with this quite generous level of public support, one is studying overseas with no government support whatever. Such a policy has pros and cons, but it is set to continue into the future, since, under the terms of the Basic Law of the Hong Kong Special Administrative Region, Hong Kong citizens will continue to have the right to study overseas if they wish to do so.

The recent rapid expansion of higher education in Hong Kong, from a total of 63,000 students in 1987 to 89,000 in 1994 and with a much higher proportion at the later date enrolled in higher level courses, had in common with the expansion of higher education in Britain in the Robbins era of the 1960s the fact that massive public resources were invested. The universities at the end of the period of rapid expansion were better housed, better equipped and better staffed than they were at the beginning. By contrast, in Britain in more recent times, when total numbers of students rose from 940,000 in 1989 to 1,422,000 in 1993, investment was not of the same order. Public funding per student fell in real terms from £6300 in 1990 to £5200 in 1993 and is projected to fall further to £4300 by 1998 (see Appendix 5.6, p.109).

real terms from £6300 in 1990 to £5200 in 1993 and is projected to fall further to £4300 by 1998 (see Appendix 5.6, p.109).

One often speaks of the size of a university in terms of student numbers, with the notion that these will roughly correlate with other measures of size – particularly with the size of the community of academic staff. However, as James Murray points out in Chapter 7, in the unified higher education system of the United Kingdom 'the FTE student numbers in two institutions across the former binary line may be similar but the total income of the institutions may vary by a factor of two or three'. Murray made this observation in the light of large differences in income generated from research, to which we will return below; here it is worthwhile observing that there is nothing sacrosanct about particular staff-student ratios. As Scott observed in Chapter 2, these have varied considerably in Australian universities during the last 50 years and are likely to adjust further in that country in the immediate future under government pressure for unit cost reduction. As can be seen from the data presented in the appendices to several of the chapters in this book, overall staff-student ratios for the newly-designated universities considered here vary from 1:14 to 1:21.

For the present, let us return to the theme of prospects for the future expansion of student numbers in the higher education systems of the three jurisdictions considered in this book. Edwards (1982), in his review of the expansion of higher education in Britain and several other countries of Western Europe from 1800 onwards, claimed: '...higher education has served continuously as the preparation for responsibility at the top. It may be defined as the level of education associated with policy-making, with managing, with setting the goals and overseeing the standard of economic, social and cultural development.' (p.11). In the knowledge society of the future, Edwards argues, international economic leadership will go to those countries with the most highly educated populations, and that democracy itself will only be effective in proportion to the extension of higher education among the majority of the population.

We have seen that in the fifteen years since the publication of *Higher Education for Everyone*, all three jurisdictions considered in this book have witnessed increased demand for entry to higher education and have taken a variety of initiatives to meet that demand. The exceptionally rapid rise in age participation rates in British higher education, from 19 per cent in 1989 to 30 per cent in 1993, can be seen as a partial catching up after age participation rates in Britain increased less rapidly than those in other countries of Western Europe in the

1970s and 1980s. The participation rate in higher education in Australia is already substantially ahead of that in Britain, while in Hong Kong an age participation rate of the same order as that in Britain is achieved because the provision of higher education in Hong Kong itself is effectively supplemented as thousands of young people from Hong Kong enrol every year in universities overseas.

If Edwards' thesis is correct, if, with comparatively minor hiccups from year to year, demand for entry to higher education continues to increase, it remains to been seen how each jurisdiction will square the circle of mobilising the resources necessary to satisfy the demand. Australia, in 1988, introduced an innovative system of deferred payment (discussed by Scott in Chapter 2), recouping the students' contributions to the cost of providing university education by means of an additional tax on personal income payable after the graduates' income reached a threshold level. Hong Kong has increased substantially the level of fees payable and, at the time of writing, proposals under consideration in Britain may alter long-standing arrangements for student financial support. But if the link postulated by Edwards (1982) and others between levels of education in the population and economic performance are real, it makes sense for governments to invest adequately in education – otherwise, the inevitable outcome will be the need down the track to spend much more on social welfare benefits and other costs associated with economic and social dislocation. The links also postulated by Edwards between levels of education in the population and the effectiveness of democratic forms of government are no less important.

Teaching methods and new technology

Of course, more of the same provided in the same way is not always what is required. Earlier in this chapter we described the dominant model of residential higher education organised to meet the total developmental needs of the sons and daughters of managerial and professional people. But in England in the nineteenth century the introduction of external degrees by the University of London, complemented by the work of private colleges that provided tuition by correspondence, opened the possibility of study at university level to thousands whose circumstances precluded attendance on campus. Most histories of higher education pay scant attention to such provisions. But external studies, in both

Britain and Australia, grew, even despite traditional skepticism. In 1951, for example, the Professorial Board of the University of Sydney made its views clear by resolving: 'External studies are necessarily greatly inferior to internal studies'; and may 'give the illusion of a university education without the reality' (Smith 1979, p.2).

This resolution reflected the dominant model of university education for school leavers. What is debatable, of course, is whether the students who sought enrolment in courses by correspondence at the University of Sydney and elsewhere really required the same kind of university education that had traditionally been provided for school leavers. Typically, these external students were older and had usually already taken on work and family responsibilities. Many in the 1950s were practising teachers in the employ of the State Department of Education, seeking to improve their own educational qualifications better to serve their pupils in the remote, farming communities of country New South Wales. Arguably, they had already developed their sense of social and civic responsibility and did not need the developmental possibilities provided by the social milieu of a college or hall of residence.

Clearly, it is important for higher education systems to respond to the diversity of needs which exists in the population at large. Some older students embark on university study for the first time, but bring to their studies considerably more experience of life than do the school leavers who may be enrolled in the same course. Skilful teaching may, of course, stimulate a sharing of experiences for mutual benefit, but alternative approaches are also possible. For example, in the mid-1980s Griffith University in Queensland launched an innovative, interdisciplinary BA degree especially for older students, with the specific aim of capitalising upon their interests and experience.

For some, embarking upon university study for the first time later in life can awaken awareness of a new world – as was excellently portrayed some years ago in the cinefilm *Educating Rita*, which featured a mature-aged student at the UK Open University. For others, who return to university study in mid-career, experience of further study is of value because it serves narrower, career-specific goals. A rather different range of purposes again is served by university education in retirement, as the University of the Third Age has demonstrated.

Important in this connection are developments in information and communications technology. Education by correspondence was made possible by the advent of efficient postal services. Since that time the mass media (newspapers, radio, film and television) and the interactive courses. Two of the jurisdictions considered in this book, Britain and Hong Kong, have established Open Universities, while Australia has a consortium arrangement for the provision of university courses employing public broadcast media. Daniel (1996), in a book which explores the potential of developments in information and communications technologies for universities throughout the world, maintains that the Open Universities 'provide a powerful response to the crisis [in higher education] of access and cost. Each accounts for a substantial proportion of the university students in its country and teaches them at a fraction of the cost of the other universities' (p.8). In Hong Kong the HKOU charges student fees at approximately the same level as do the universities funded through the UGC; but whereas these student fees are sufficient to cover the whole of the operating costs of the HKOU, they contribute only about one-fifth of the cost of the other public universities (Dhanarajan *et al.* 1994).

In the post-industrial societies, including Britain and Hong Kong, the Open Universities have contributed primarily to providing cost-effective higher education to mature-aged students rather than to school leavers. They are providing a 'second chance' for access to higher education to those who, for whatever reason, did not gain entry as school leavers with other members of their age group. The OUs thus help to redress the intergenerational inequities associated with rapidly-expanding higher education provision for school leavers. Also, the OUs provide opportunities for the continuing education of those who already have a higher education qualification but whose professional or life interests lead to the need for additional educational input in the form of structured courses or supervision of research.

In Australia no national Open University has been created as such, although the possibility was seriously debated and was the subject of a report to the Commonwealth Government in the 1970s (Karmel 1975). It was argued that many of the existing higher education institutions were, at that time, providing education at a distance through correspondence, often augmented by the use of other media. Today, as the new information and communications technologies reduce the scale of operation necessary to sustain viable and competitive distance education courses, many more universities in Australia, Britain and elsewhere are offering distance education courses.

People with access to the new technology – and, increasingly, universities are either providing such access and/or are requiring their

People with access to the new technology – and, increasingly, universities are either providing such access and/or are requiring their students to purchase their own PCs – gain advantages whether they study on-campus or off-campus. Indeed, today we see a merging of teaching methods which dissolve many of the former differences between on-campus and off-campus study. Access to virtual libraries on the world wide web, coupled with rapid two-way communication between student and teacher, and between students themselves, on the internet, hold the promise of radical transformation of teaching methods. As Gould (1997) points out, the lecturer is freed from the necessity to provide basic information since students can access this for themselves. What the university can then uniquely provide are 'tutorial services', a virtual replication of the Oxbridge model of tutorial teaching.

The new information and communications technologies also reduce drastically the differentials of distance in cost and access to higher education. A personal anecdote is in order here. Fifteen years ago I was based in an Australian university and teaching a course on educational administration by correspondence, and a few of my students were located overseas – one in South America. Delays in the postal services and the exorbitant cost of telephone calls added a heavy burden of frustration to that student's experience. Today, as Smith (1996) points out, about 10 per cent of the 57,000 overseas students enrolled in Australian higher education institutions are undertaking their courses while living in other countries.

Overseas students and international education

It is now appropriate to turn our attention to students who undertake higher education in jurisdictions other than their home. As mentioned above, quite large numbers of students from Hong Kong go overseas for undergraduate study, while Australia and Britain both enrol large numbers of students from overseas in their universities. Indeed, in the case of Australia the higher education system is currently about 10 per cent larger than it otherwise would be because of the presence of students from overseas.

The situation of Australian universities in relation to students from overseas changed radically with the reform of 1988. Previously, most students from overseas had come to Australian universities on government scholarships. Since that time, the universities have been permitted, indeed are required by government, to charge fees to students from overseas which represent the full economic cost of the students' enrolment. Many universities embarked upon a major marketing effort to attract full-fee students from overseas, and numbers – the majority from countries of east and south-east Asia – have risen steadily each year. IDP Education Australia in 1995 (quoted in Smith 1996) provided the following estimates of the numbers of international students for the world as a whole (and the numbers from Asia) to the year 2025, though it is predicted that a sizeable proportion of these 'international' students will not leave their home country to study:

1995	1.5 million worldwide (0.68m Asia)
2000	1.8 million worldwide (0.84m Asia)
2005	2.3 million worldwide (1.1m Asia)
2010	2.8 million worldwide (1.5m Asia)
2015	3.4 million worldwide (1.8m Asia)
2025	4.9 million worldwide (2.9m Asia)

Australian universities, in common with those in Britain, Anglophone Canada, New Zealand and USA, use the English language as the medium of instruction and this, together with the use of English in everyday life, is doubtless perceived as an advantage by many of the students from Asia who choose to study in these countries. The relative proximity of Australia to east and south Asia, the similarity of time zones and the climate are advantages specific to Australia.

The major reason for successive Australian governments since 1988 to encourage Australian universities to enrol more students from overseas has been financial and, at a time of tightening funding from other sources, this has also been the major reason for the universities actively to seek students from overseas. An arrangement which is financially advantageous for Australia and Australian universities, and for Britain and British universities, is, however, not so for the students' home countries. A number of countries from which the students come are taking steps to build up their own higher education systems and, in some cases, the exodus to study abroad may be short-lived.

The presence of students from Asia on Australian or British campuses enriches campus life and gives the home students some opportunity to learn from the overseas students about foreign cultures. Useful though this experience of mixing with visitors from abroad is, it falls a long way short of the experience of actually living and working in a foreign culture. Few Australian students take the opportunity to study overseas, and while the number of Britons who study abroad is larger, few of them study in Asia. Thus, while many students from Asian countries gain a good, first-hand knowledge of Australia or of Britain by living and studying there, few Australian or British students of the current generation have a similar opportunity to gain first-hand knowledge of an Asian society. There is an urgent need for greater reciprocity in these arrangements.

While a proportion of the students from Hong Kong who go overseas for their higher education subsequently make their careers overseas, many return to Hong Kong. Even those who stay overseas typically retain strong family links with Hong Kong and, as the experience of Taiwanese in the USA has shown, many return in mid-career bringing their skills and experience to enrich their home communities. Assessing the economics of profit and loss on such international migrations, for study and other purposes, is a complex and long-term matter.

While most of the faculty members of universities in Hong Kong have studied in either Britain or North America (Teather, Tsang and Chan 1997), the undergraduate student population in Hong Kong universities is very homogenous – almost all are from Hong Kong. At the time of writing (mid-1997) this may be about to change since there is the prospect of admitting, for the first time since 1949, small numbers of undergraduate students from mainland China to Hong Kong universities. This prospect is attractive to many Hong Kong academics since the perception is fairly widespread that the recent expansion of student numbers in Hong Kong universities has led to a decline in the quality of students admitted. Students from mainland China would, however, be high fliers since less than two per cent of the school leaving age cohort is admitted to university on the mainland. At present, the Hong Kong government permits up to four per cent of the undergraduate student quota to be from outside Hong Kong.

In the case of postgraduate research students, the situation is very different. At the time of writing, up to 20 per cent of the quota of Hong Kong government-funded places can be filled by research students from outside Hong Kong, and this limit will soon be raised to 30 per cent. Most of the research students from outside Hong Kong currently enrolled in Hong Kong universities are from mainland China. They comprise both staff from mainland universities and recent graduates.

In 1994 Cheng pointed out that Hong Kong then had, compared with mainland China: 0.5 per cent of the total population, 2.5 per cent of all university students, 10 per cent of all postgraduate students and

Kong will become a place on the Chinese soil which is most productive in terms of higher level intellectuals.' (p.4).

Hong Kong has great potential to contribute to higher education in mainland China by using the considerable resources built up in its universities, which have come of age with the demand-driven resource-led expansion of recent years. This contribution could be made in ways which also benefit Hong Kong, both in the short term with the positive impact of highly motivated and competent students from the mainland in undergraduate classes and as research students and in the longer term as these graduates from Hong Kong universities return to the mainland and progress to positions of influence in mainland society. The matter is one for the Hong Kong government since it alone is responsible, under the terms of the Basic Law of the Hong Kong SAR, for educational policy in Hong Kong. But, clearly, it is a matter which should be handled with care since the resources necessary to fund the enrolment of students from the mainland in Hong Kong universities will come from the Hong Kong taxpayer. Denial of access to potential students from Hong Kong while admitting students from the mainland could become a contentious issue.

For universities in Hong Kong to be of maximum benefit to both Hong Kong and mainland China in the years to come, it will be essential not only for them to continue to broaden and deepen their interactions with mainland universities but also to do so with respect to universities in the West. My colleagues and I have argued this point elsewhere (Teather, Tsang and Chan 1997), but, briefly, a key aspect of Hong Kong's future role – as it has been in the past – will be to provide a window for China to the West and a window for the West to China. Nowhere is this more important that in the realm of ideas.

Research and service

In discussing future prospects for higher education we have, up to now in this chapter, been concerned with universities as teaching institutions. It is important also to consider the role of universities in research and the other services they perform in their communities. The perceived importance of research has increased in recent years and the notion of service to the community is also receiving greater attention. Both of these trends can be expected to continue as awareness grows of the implications of the knowledge society.

Both of these trends can be expected to continue as awareness grows of the implications of the knowledge society.

The case for the involvement of academic staff in research is two-fold. First, it is often claimed that research is essential for good teaching. Second, the outcome of the research itself may have intellectual and/or practical value. With regard to the first proposition, Barnett and Bjarnason observed, in Chapter 5, that there is, as yet, no real consensus: 'it just may be that teaching in the context of research is more likely to produce the enquiring minds which advanced capitalism requires than teaching conducted without that environment'. Certainly, however, it is possible to ask more specific questions about the relationships between teaching and research. To what extent is it feasible, desirable or necessary to involve today's undergraduate students in research projects? To what extent should students be involved in, or informed about, current research of academic staff members? If this is desirable, there is the obvious implication that the focus of the staff member's teaching and the focus of his or her research should be closely aligned. Or might it be sufficient that academic staff be kept generally intellectually active by involvement in research not necessarily directly connected with their teaching? Is it necessary for *all* academic staff to be currently undertaking research or will the active involvement of a few sufficiently stimulate the desired attitudes of enquiry in colleagues and students? Or might it be sufficient for all, or some, academic staff to have demonstrated research proficiency at some previous date, as evidenced by completion of a research degree? Some would argue that, in practice, unless the field of research of a staff member is closely connected to his or her teaching, the two activities are neither complementary nor synergistic but represent, instead, merely competing calls on the staff member's time.

Different universities take different stands on such matters. For example, at Hong Kong Baptist University all undergraduate students undertaking honours degrees (i.e. almost all the undergraduate students enrolled in the university) have to undertake an 'honours project' which is an individually-supervised research exercise. At that university over 70 per cent of academic staff have doctoral degrees, while at the more recently established Hong Kong University of Science and Technology it is a matter of policy that all staff appointed to the grades of Assistant Professor and above have doctoral degrees.

The value of the research undertaken by members of academic staff is a separate issue from the effect of research on teaching. The value of the research is assessed by peers, as, for example, when a research paper is submitted to a journal or when a research proposal is submitted for funding. In the case of applied or contractual research, the value is assessed by those who commission the research. There are, however, widely different traditions of what passes for research in different academic disciplines. Some areas of work, for example in the physical sciences, may be regarded as truly international – a carbon atom behaves as a carbon atom whether it is at the equator or the pole – and are susceptible to international peer review. Other areas, by contrast, may be meaningful only in their own cultural context. Some areas of work may be concerned with the elaboration of theory, others with practical application. Some research, for example in physics or astronomy, may require access to costly equipment; other research may require the resources of large-scale survey; while other projects may require access to rare library material. Yet other work may, however, be done with little by way of resources except the time of the researcher.

The term 'research' covers, therefore, a wide range of activities. Any judgement of the extent of research activity appropriate for a particular institution needs to take account of this complexity. And whatever the official policy espoused by government agency or institution, it is clear that the actual activities of members of academic staff will be affected by their professional socialisation, their self-concept and their perception of what is important for career advancement, both in the institution in which they currently work and in the institution(s) in which they might aspire to work in the future.

The extent and kind of service provided by a higher education institution to its community varies greatly with its context, though all universities today need to act as a bridge or conduit between their local communities and the wider world. Writing on this issue on a previous occasion (Teather 1982), I quoted the foundation Professor of Management at the University of Otago, a university located in the city of Dunedin (population 100,000) in the South Island (population 900,000) of New Zealand. Professor Rossell wrote:

> The case for careful examination by the University of its role in the community is related to our size. We dwarf all other organizations and institutions. Our position is in marked contrast with that of universities in large industrial societies where government departments, industries, and corporations contain a great deal of talent and may themselves be centres of excellence.

In the South Island of New Zealand, government departments and statutory boards are small, key staff are often over-worked, and therefore are often unable adequately to serve the region.

Frequently, it is the University and only the University to which organizations can turn for professional assistance, for research, and upon which the region relies for services and progress. In some cases, organizations are themselves so unaware of possibilities that the University may have to take the initiative.

A few years later, the University of Otago was operating, through its medical and dental faculties, School of Law and other departments, no less than nine separate clinics which offered services to the general public and also served the university's own interests in teaching and research. In each of the three jurisdictions which are the focus of this book, universities can gain greatly by tapping community resources to assist in the development of projects that serve both community and university purposes. Given good management, such projects diversify the university's resource base, strengthen its relationships with its communities and add value for both university and community.

Differentiation

Consideration of the likelihood of future growth in the higher education systems of Australia, Britain and Hong Kong tells us little, however, about the future composition and texture of these systems of higher education. Clearly, all the universities will remain in the business of teaching students, but different universities have different disciplinary profiles, different proportions of undergraduate and postgraduate students, different proportions of school leavers and older students and different proportions of students on and off campus. These patterns will continue to change not only in line with the long-term aims and aspirations of the individual institutions but also under the influence of government policies, market forces and technological developments.

The extent to which research and the training of future researchers will become, or will remain, an important part of the work of the new universities will depend also on government policies and other factors. Prior to the granting of university titles to the three recently-designated universities in Hong Kong there was agreement between the universities and the University Grants Committee on mission statements. Mole and Young, in Chapter 10, argue that the mission

government financial incentives at the margin have been dispro-
portionately influential on the policies of individual institutions.

In order to retain a degree of institutional autonomy, particularly in
times of uncertainty, institutions in all three jurisdictions have in recent
years sought to augment government funding with funding from other
sources. As mentioned above, this has been the prime motivation for
universities in Australia and in Britain to market their courses to
students from overseas. And in Hong Kong, as described in the case of
HKBU by Daniel Tse in Chapter 9, institutions have sought
endowment from foundations and individuals. In all three jurisdictions
there has been growth in the marketing of consulting and other services
by the universities, and this trend is likely to continue.

Don Aitkin observed in Chapter 3: 'In the life of all universities of any
age there are periods of transition from one shape to another. These are
periods, literally, of 're-form', in which the university's structure, or
purpose, or social location, or relationship to the state changes in a
powerful way'. He goes on to point out that the reform of Australian
higher education in the late 1980s resulted in a situation in which 'the
settled status hierarchy implicit in the binary system had gone forever',
presenting the newly-designated University of Canberra with 'a
splendid chance to decide what kind of a university it would set out to
be.'

In this connection, Aitkin observed:

> There is no single model of a university. Universities can teach
> many things, or few. They can do a great deal of research, or very
> little. They can be situated in city centres, or in green fields. They
> can be private bodies, statutory corporations, state instrumentali-
> ties, or combinations of these forms. They can have only under-
> graduate students, or only postgraduate students, or a mixture.
> They can be very wealthy, or very poor. They can be very big, or
> very small. They can be very old, or very new. Their essential char-
> acter is that they have students, and that the students have teachers.
> The other essential characteristic is that in some sense universities
> are knowledgeable about the present limits of knowledge.

We have seen through the case studies of the preceding chapters that the
six recently-designated universities described have indeed chosen to
respond in a variety of ways to the opportunities and challenges of their
contexts. All are proceeding generally along the routes charted at their
foundations, but changes in their external environments are resulting in
some adaptations – for example in UK the incorporation of research

respond in a variety of ways to the opportunities and challenges of their contexts. All are proceeding generally along the routes charted at their foundations, but changes in their external environments are resulting in some adaptations – for example in UK the incorporation of research briefs to a greater extent than had hitherto been anticipated. Perhaps the most striking apparent change of tack, however, is the case of the University of Humberside. At the time that Foster and King were writing Chapter 6, the university was operating on several sites in Hull and Grimsby. Since that time, the plans foreshadowed at the end of Chapter 6 have been brought to fruition – a new campus has been opened in the City of Lincoln and the university now goes under the title of the 'University of Lincolnshire and Humberside'. But this is not simply a matter of opening another campus and doing more of the same. The location of the new campus, the circumstances of its establishment (in partnership with a strong local initiative) and pressures from the changing national environment of higher education have led to the possibility of 'internal differentiation between the main sites [of the University], with the move to Lincoln establishing a more traditional, élitist approach and the campuses in Hull offering mass higher education'.

This is indeed a telling example of the general prognosis in Chapter 5 by Barnett and Bjarnason. They observed that within the common framework of the unified higher education system now established in Britain, and the government's policy objectives of (i) the continuing orientation of the universities to the world of work and (ii) the need for them to demonstrate effective and prudent use of public resources, diversity will be permitted. Barnett and Bjarnason suggest 'the next twenty years will be characterised by experimentation with the various forms of institutional life permitted by the framework'.

Limits to development

In none of these three jurisdictions is the ability to provide higher education limited in any absolute sense by lack of resources. Each of the societies has the wealth to provide, by public and private means, what is required. What may from time to time be lacking is the political will. In Britain in the 1970s, when the age participation rate in higher education fell significantly below those of other countries of Western Europe and far below those of USA and Japan, Edwards (1982) spoke of a 'failure of national confidence in the future of higher education' (p.159). This was in marked contrast with the political leadership shown in the establishment of the UK Open University a decade earlier.

In Hong Kong the Confucian legacy has left a high regard for education, so much so that the families of one in ten of the school leaving age cohort vote with their cheque books to purchase overseas the higher education that is not yet available in Hong Kong, despite the very rapid expansion of local provision in this decade. It is to be hoped that the new government of the Hong Kong SAR will have a broad vision of the purposes to be served by higher education and will translate this into action in due course.

In Australia and Britain what is needed, similarly, is a broader awareness of what is at stake, both economically and socially, in preparing for the global, knowledge society of tomorrow that is almost with us today. A greater realisation is needed of the likely consequences of failure properly to prepare a larger number of young people, and of older people through lifelong learning, for the challenges and opportunities of the knowledge society. A greater realisation is needed of the magnitude of the difference which could be made in these societies by the full educational empowerment of a much higher proportion of citizens and workers. Dividends would accrue for personal development, community life and social cohesion; for innovation, productivity and economic growth.

The case studies in this book amply demonstrate the vigour of the new generation of universities that has been created with the repositioning of the binary line in each of these three jurisdictions. The task now is to ensure that the new universities have the resources they need to fulfil their promise and their responsibilities.

Bibliography

Ainley, P. (1994) *Degrees of Difference: Higher Education in the 1990s.* London: Lawrence and Wishart.

Aitken, D. (1991) *Getting the Balance Right.* Address of the Vice-Chancellor to the Staff of the University. Canberra: University of Canberra, February 21st.

Armitage, C. (1996) *The Weekend Australian,* 24–25 August, p.6.

Ashenden, D. and Milligan, S. (1993) *Good Universities Guide to Australian Universities (annual).* Melbourne: Mandarin.

Australian Universities Commission (1964/5) *Report of the Committee on the Future of Tertiary Education in Australia.* Martin Report. 3 vols. Canberra: Government Printer.

Barnett, R. (1994) *Limits of Competence.* Buckingham: Open University Press and Society for Research into Higher Education.

Bastin, N.A. (1992) 'Further and Higher Education Act 1992 – The end of the binary line.' In *Education and the Law.* Glasgow: Longman.

Birrell, R. and Khoo, S. (1995) *The Second Generation in Australia: Educational and Occupational Characteristics.* Canberra: Australian Government Publishing Service.

Bradley, D. (1993) 'Illusion or reality? Diversity in the Unified National System.' *Journal of Tertiary Education Administration 15,* 2, 117–137.

Brown, H. and Sommerlad, E. (1992) 'Staff development in higher education – towards the learning organisation.' *Higher Education Quarterly 46,* 2, 179–190.

CBI (1994) *Thinking Ahead: Ensuring the Expansion of Higher Education into the 21st Century.* London: Confederation of British Industry.

Chapman, B. (1996) 'A return to inequity.' *The Australian,* 23 August, p.19.

Charlesworth, M. (1993) 'From Dawkins to Where?' *Journal of Tertiary Education Administration 15,* 1, 7–18.

Cheng, K.M. (1994) *Development of Higher Education: Hong Kong and China.* Key-note paper presented at the symposium on 'The Future Development of Higher Education in Hong Kong'. Hong Kong: Society of Hong Kong Scholars, February 26th.

CNAA (1981) *Report to the Director of Education, Hong Kong.* London: Council for National Academic Awards.

Coaldrake, P. (1996) 'Australian higher education management review.' *Association of Commonwealth Universities Bulletin of Current Documentation 123,* April, p.2.

Coalition (1996) *Higher Education: Quality, Diversity and Choice.* Canberra: Liberal/National Parties.

Crothall, D. (1994) 'The university's vision post-enterprise.' In M. Nobel (ed) *Achieving a New Learning Environment. Building on Enterprise.* University of Humberside Conference Proceedings.

CSUP (1992) *Teaching and Learning in an Expanding Higher Education System.* The MacFarlane Report. Edinburgh: Committee of Scottish University Principals.

Cumming, A. (1994) 'Education, amalgamation and development: The Faculty of Education at Queensland University of Technology.' In K.T. Kennedy (ed) *Reshaping Teacher Education: Faculty Renewal or Organisation Downsizing.* Australian Curriculum Studies Association.

CVCP (1985) *Report of the Steering Committee for Efficiency Studies in Universities.* The Jarratt Report. London: Committee of Vice-Chancellors and Principals of the Universities of the United Kingdom.

CVCP (1995a) *The Growth in Student Numbers in British Higher Education.* Briefing Note, February 1995. London: Committee of Vice-Chancellors and Principals of the Universities of the United Kingdom.

CVCP (1995b) *Funding Higher Education – Main Options for Extra Resources.* Briefing Note, September 1995. London: Committee of Vice-Chancellors and Principals of the Universities of the United Kingdom.

Daniel, J.S. (1996) *Mega-Universities and Knowledge Media: Technology Strategies for Higher Education.* London: Kogan Page.

Davies, S. (1989) *The Martin Committee and the Binary Policy of Higher Education in Australia.* Melbourne: Ashwood House.

Dawkins, J.S. (1988) *Higher Education: A Policy Statement.* Canberra: Australian Government Publishing Service.

de Wit, H. (ed) (1995) *Strategies for Internationalisation of Higher Education: A Comparative Study of Australia, Canada, Europe and the United States of America.* Amsterdam: European Association for International Education.

DEET (1993a) *National Report on Australia's Higher Education Sector.* Canberra: Australian Government Publishing Service.

DEET (1993b) *The Transition from Elite to Mass Higher Education: Conference Proceedings.* Canberra: Australian Government Publishing Service.

Department of Employment, Education, Training and Youth Affairs (1995) *Higher Education Management Review: Summary of Committee Report and Recommendations.* http://www.deetya.gov.au/pubs/hedmanrv.htm

Derham, Sir D. (1979) 'Mobility of students and staff internationally.' In T. Craig (ed) *Pressures and Priorities: Report of Proceedings of the 12th Congress of the Universities of the Commonwealth*. London: Association of Commonwealth Universities.

DES (1963) *Higher Education Report*. The Robbins Report. Cmnd. 2154. London: Her Majesty's Stationery Office.

DES (1985) *The Development of Higher Education into the 1990s*. Green Paper. Cmnd. 9524. London: Her Majesty's Stationery Office.

DES (1987) *Higher Education – Meeting the Challenge*. White Paper. Cmnd. 114. London: Her Majesty's Stationery Office.

DES (1991) *Higher Education: A New Framework*. White Paper. Cmnd. 1541. London: Her Majesty's Stationery Office.

DFE (1994) *Higher Education in the 1990s*. London: Department for Education.

Dhanarajan, G., Ip, P.K., Yuen, K.S. and Swales, C. (eds) (1994) *Economics of Distance Education: Recent Experience*. Hong Kong: Open Learning Institute Press.

Dixon, T. (1990) 'Reorganising a university.' *Australian Journal of Communication 17*, 3, 39–62.

Doyle, K. (1996) 'Strengthening strategic planning practices to improve management in higher education.' *Managing Higher Education in a Changing Environment Conference*, Sydney, 23/24 September.

Drucker, P.F. (1993) *Post-Capitalist Society*. New York: Harper Business.

EC (1986) *Education Commission Report No. 2*. Hong Kong: Education Commission of Hong Kong and Government Printer.

EC (1988) *The Structure of Tertiary Education and the Future of Private Schools*. Report No 3. Hong Kong: Education Commission of Hong Kong and Government Printer.

Education Yearbook 1995/96. London: Pitman Publishing.

Edwards, E.G. (1979) 'Towards a relevant university.' *International Journal of Institutional Management in Higher Education 3*, 2, 253–270.

Edwards, E.G. (1982) *Higher Education for Everyone*. Nottingham: Spokesman.

EHE (1989) *Key Features of the EHE Proposals 1988–89*. London: Department of Employment, Enterprise in Higher Education.

EMB (1994) *A Guide to Education and Training in Hong Kong*. Hong Kong: Education and Manpower Branch and Government Printer.

Encel, S. (1989) 'Higher education in Australia – centralization or industralization?' In C. Bridge (ed) *Higher Education in Australia after the White Paper*. London: University of London.

European Journal of Education 25, 2, 105–122.

Evans, B., Cook, A., Slee, R. and Bates, R. (1989) *Changing the culture of QUT.* Brisbane: Leadership Centre, Brisbane College of Advanced Education.

Gaskell, S.M. (1989) 'Education and culture: A perspective from higher education.' *Higher Education Quarterly 43*, 4, 318–332.

Gibbons, M., Limoges, C., Nowotny, H., Schwartzman, S., Scott, P. and Trow, M. (1994) *The New Production of Knowledge: The Dynamics of Science and Research in Contemporary Societies.* London: Sage Publications.

Gilbert, A. (1996) 'Unis need their public slice.' *The Australian,* 14 August, p.13.

Goodlad, S. and Hirst, B. (eds) (1989) *Peer Tutoring: A Guide to Learning by Teaching.* London: Kogan Page.

Gould, B. (1997) *Regional Universities and Development in New Zealand.* Keynote paper presented at the conference on 'The Response of Higher Education Institutions to Regional Needs'. Byron Bay, NSW: Southern Cross University, July 23–25.

Hague, Sir Douglas (1991) *Beyond Universities: A New Republic of the Intellect.* London: Institute of Economic Affairs.

Halsey, A.H. (1992) *Decline of Donnish Dominion: The British Academic Professions in the Twentieth Century.* Oxford: Oxford University Press.

HEFCE (1995) *Promoting Excellence – Annual Report 1994–95.* Bristol: Higher Education Funding Council for England.

HEQC (1996) *Quality Audit Report on the University of Humberside 1996.* London: Higher Education Quality Council.

HESA (1995) *Higher Education Statistics for the United Kingdom 1992/93.* Cheltenham: Higher Education Statistics Agency.

HESA (1996) *Students in Higher Education Institutions 1994/95.* Reference Volume. Cheltenham: Higher Education Statistics Agency.

Higher Education Management Review (1995) *Higher Education Management Review: Report of the Committee of Inquiry.* Canberra: Australian Government Publishing Service.

HK Government (1977) *The Development of Senior Secondary and Post Secondary Education.* Green Paper. Hong Kong: Government Printer.

HKBC (1982) *A Position Paper on Educational Philosophy and Academic Outlook at Hong Kong Baptist College.* Hong Kong: Hong Kong Baptist College.

HKBC (1989) *HKBC – University Status and Title*. Hong Kong: Hong Kong Baptist College.

HKBC (1990) *Report to Hong Kong Council for Academic Accreditation for Institutional Review*. Hong Kong: Hong Kong Baptist College.

HKCAA (1991) *Institutional Review Report: Hong Kong Baptist College*. Hong Kong: Hong Kong Council for Academic Accreditation.

Howlett, B. (ed) (1997) *Hong Kong 1997*. Hong Kong: Government Printer.

Huntington, S.P. (1993) 'The clash of civilizations?' *Foreign Affairs 72*, 3, 22–49.

Huntington, S.P. (1996) *The Clash of Civilisations and the Remaking of World Order*. New York: Simon and Schuster.

Jackson, N. (1995) 'The road to universal modularity.' In *HEQC Update no. 8*, December 1995. London: Higher Education Quality Council.

Jones, P. (1996) 'Just what does good management of universities entail?' *Campus Review*, 3–9 July, p.8.

Juddery, B. (1996a) 'Dawkins's vision splendid fading.' *Canberra Times*, 3 July, p.14.

Juddery, B. (1996b) 'TAFE upgrade "challenges universities".' *Campus Review*, 2–8 Oct., p.3.

Karmel, P. (1990) *Reflections on a Revolution: Australian Higher Education in 1989*. AVCC Papers No. 1. Canberra: Australian Vice-Chancellors Committee.

Karmel Report (1975) *Open Tertiary Education in Australia: Final Report of the Committee on Open University*. Canberra: Australian Government Publishing Service.

Knight, J. and de Wit, H. (eds) (1997) *Internationalisation of Higher Education: Asian Pacific Countries*. Amsterdam: European Association for International Education.

Kogan, M. (1993) 'The end of the dual system?' In C. Gellert (ed) *Higher Education in Europe p.53*. London.

Lauby, P.T. (1996) *Sailing on Winds of Change*. New York: United Board for Christian Higher Education in Asia.

Lingard, B. (1994) 'Equity and diversity in mass higher education: some policy issues.' *The Australian Universities Review 37*, 2, 20–33.

Lowe, I. (1990) 'The dying of the light.' *Australian Universities Review 1 & 2*.

Mackinnon, D. and Statham, J. (1995) *Education in the UK, Facts and Figures*. London: Hodder and Stoughton in association with the Open University.

Mahony, D. (1994a) 'A comparison of the Australian and British post binary higher education systems.' *Higher Education Research and Development 13*, 1, 71–84.

Mahony, D. (1994b) 'Counter Images of Australia's movement to an undifferentiated higher education system: an analysis.' *Higher Education 28*, 301–323.

Mahony, D. (1995) 'The rise of an Australian multi-sectoral university: Swinburne Institute of Technology.' *Higher Education Review 27*, 2, 29–49.

Marginson, S. (1993) *Education and Public Policy in Australia*. Cambridge: Cambridge University Press.

Martin, A. (1990) 'R.G. Menzies and the Murray Committee.' In F. Smith and P. Crighton (eds) *Ideas for Histories of Universities*. Canberra: Australian National University.

Massey, W.F. and French, N.J. (1997) *Teaching and Learning Quality Process Review: A Review of the Hong Kong Programme.* http://www.ugc.edu.hk/documents/papers/wfm_njf5.html

McCollow, J. and Knight, J. (1993) 'Higher education in Australia: an historical overview.' In M. Bella, J. McCollow and J. Knight (eds) *Higher Education in Transition*. Brisbane: University of Queensland.

McNay, I. (1995) 'From the collegial academy to corporate enterprise: the changing cultures of universities.' In T. Schuller (ed) *The Changing University?* Buckingham: Open University Press and Society for Research into Higher Education.

Meek, V.L. and Harrold, R. (ed) (1989) *TAFE and the Reconstruction of Higher Education*. Armidale, NSW: University of New England.

Mellor, B. (1980) *The University of Hong Kong: An Informal History.* (2 vols). Hong Kong: Hong Kong University Press.

Mellor, B. (1992) *Lugard in Hong Kong*. Hong Kong: Hong Kong University Press.

Moodie, G. (1996) 'The cost of inefficient cutting.' *The Australian*, 11 September, p.30.

Morris, P., McClelland, J.A.G. and Yeung, Y.H. (1994) 'Higher education in Hong Kong: the context and the rationale for rapid expansion.' *Higher Education 27*, 125–140.

Neave, G. (1990) 'On preparing for markets: trends in higher education in Western Europe.' *European Journal of Education 25*, 2, 105–122.

New Zealand Treasury (1987) *Government Management: Brief to the Incoming Government. Volume II: Education Issues.* Wellington: The Treasury.

Ngok, L. and Lam, A. (1994) *Professional and Continuing Education in Hong Kong.* Hong Kong: Hong Kong University Press.

Nichols, J. (1995) 'The possum turns on rosy memories.' *Campus Review,* 25–31 May.

Ohmae, K. (1991) *The Borderless World: Power and Strategy in the Interlinked Economy.* London: Fontana.

Penington, D. (1990) 'Can real universities survive the Unified National System?' In J. Anwyl (ed) *1989 Spring Lectures on Higher Education.* Melbourne: University of Melbourne.

Postiglione, G.A. (ed) (1992) *Education and Society in Hong Kong: Toward One Country and Two Systems.* Hong Kong: Hong Kong University Press.

Prickett, S. (1994) 'Enterprise in higher education: nice work or ivory tower versus exchange and mart.' *Higher Education Quarterly 48,* 3, 169–181.

QUT (1991) *QUT 1996.* Brisbane: Queensland University of Technology.

Robertson, D. (1994) *Choosing to Change.* London: Higher Education Quality Council.

Robinson, E.E. (1968) *The New Polytechnics.* London: Cornmarket.

Rutanen, P. (1996) 'Learning societies and GII/GIS (Global Information Infrastructure/Global Information Society).' In D.C.B. Teather and W. Chan (eds) *Institutional Strategies for Internalisation of Higher Education.* Hong Kong: Hong Kong Baptist University.

Salter, B. and Tapper, T. (1994) *The State and Higher Education.* London: Woburn Press.

Schön, D. (1987) *Educating the Reflective Practitioner.* London: Jossey-Bass.

Scott, P. (1995) *The Meanings of Mass Higher Education.* Buckingham: Open University Press and Society for Research into Higher Education.

Scott, R.D. (1988) 'The amalgamation of James Cook University with the Townsville CAE.' In G. Harman and V. Meek (eds) *Institutional Amalgamations in Higher Education: Process and Outcomes in Five Countries.* Armidale, NSW: University of New England.

Scott, R.D. (1995a) *Theories and Practices: Contrasts Between Strategic Management in Tertiary Institutions and Government Departments: Working Paper no. 37.* Brisbane: Australian Centre in Strategic Management, Queensland University of Technology.

Scott, R.D. (1995b) 'Bureaucracy and academe: crossing the divide (Part 1).' *Campus Review,* 15–21 June, p.8.

Scott, R.D. (1995c) 'Bureaucracy and academe: crossing the divide (Part 2).' *Campus Review*, 22–28 June, p.8.

Scott, R.D. (1995d) 'Keynote address: Milestones of change in Australian higher education.' *Travelling Through Transition: The Inaugural Pacific Rim First Year Experience Conference*. Brisbane. July.

Segal Quince Wickstead Ltd. (1994) *Thematic Evaluation of EHEI, Research Series No.38*. London: Employment Department.

Shattock, M. (1994) *The UGC and the Management of British Universities*. Buckingham: Open University Press and Society for Research into Higher Education (GATE).

Skeldon, R. (ed) (1994) *Reluctant Exiles?* Hong Kong: Hong Kong University Press.

Smith, K.C. (ed) (1979) *External Studies at New England: A Silver Jubilee Review, 1955–1979*. Armidale NSW: Department of External Studies, University of New England.

Smith, R. (1996) 'The national higher education perspective.' In *Transnational Education and the Quality Imperative: London Conference Proceedings*. Washington DC: Global Alliance for Transnational Education (GATE).

Stephens, M.D. (1977) 'Some national trends.' In A.H. Thornton and M.D. Stephens (eds) *The University in its Region: The Extra-Mural Contribution*. Nottingham: Department of Adult Education, University of Nottingham.

Tasker, M. and Packham, D. (1994) 'Training minds for tomorrow: a shared responsibility.' *Higher Education Quarterly 48*, 3, 182–193.

Teather, D.C.B. (ed) (1982) *Towards the Community University: Case Studies of Innovation and Community Service*. London: Kogan Page.

Teather, D.C.B. (1990) 'The "reform" of Australian higher education and some implications for staff development.' In I. Moses (ed) *Higher Education in the late Twentieth Century: Reflections on a Changing System*. Sydney: Higher Education Research and Development Society of Australasia.

Teather, D.C.B. (1994) 'Teaching, teacher education, teacher education institutions and the learning society.' Keynote address in W. Driscoll and W. Halloway, *Building Bridges in Teacher Education*. Armidale, NSW: International Society for Teacher Education.

Teather, D.C.B. (1995) 'The changing roles of universities in national and regional development.' In D.C.B. Teather and W. Chan (eds) (1995) *Proceedings of the Inaugural Conference of the David C. Lam Institute for East-West Studies*. Hong Kong: Hong Kong Baptist University.

Teather, D.C.B., Tsang, H.H. and Chan, W.W.Y. (1997) 'International dimensions of higher education in Hong Kong: progress and prospects.' *Journal of Studies in International Education 1*, 1, 9–26.

THES (1991) *Directors Spurn 'poly' Name*. Times Higher Education Supplement, March 1.

THES (1991) *Scotland's Chance*. Times Higher Education Supplement, April 26.

THES (1991) *Post-Binary Politics*. Times Higher Education Supplement, May 24.

Training Agency (1989, 1990) *Enterprise in Higher Education*. Sheffield: Training Agency.

Treyvaud, E.R. and McLaren, J. (1976) *Equal but Cheaper: The Development of Australian Colleges of Advanced Education*. Melbourne: Melbourne University Press.

Trow, M. (1989) 'The Robbins trap: British attitudes and the limits of expansion.' *Higher Education Quarterly 43*, 1, 55–75.

Truscot, B. (1945) *Redbrick and These Vital Days*. London: Faber.

UGC (1996a) Extract from letter from Mr Antony K.C. Leung JP, Chairman of University Grants Committee to the Rt Hon Christopher Patten, Governor of Hong Kong, 25 October.

UGC (1996b) *Higher Education in Hong Kong: A Report by the University Grants Committee of Hong Kong*. Hong Kong: Government Printer.

UPGC (1976) *Special Report 1965–1976*. Hong Kong: University and Polytechnic Grants Committee of Hong Kong.

UPGC (1983) *Report January 1983 – December 1984*. Hong Kong: University and Polytechnic Grants Committee of Hong Kong.

UPGC (1984) *Advice on an Open University in Hong Kong*. Paper no. 1277. Hong Kong: University and Polytechnic Grants Committee of Hong Kong.

UPGC (1993a) *Report on Institutional Reviews of City Polytechnic of Hong Kong, Hong Kong Baptist College and Hong Kong Polytechnic*. Annex B. Hong Kong: University and Polytechnic Grants Committee of Hong Kong.

UPGC (1993b) *Higher Education 1991–2001: An Interim Report*. Hong Kong: University and Polytechnic Grants Committee of Hong Kong.

University Grants Committee/National Advisory Body Joint Statement (1984) *A Strategy for Higher Education into the 1990s*. London: Her Majesty's Stationery Office.

Vanstone, A. (1996a) *Keynote address: Policy perspectives on higher education financing.* Canberra: Centre for Economic Policy Research Symposium. http://www.deetya.gov.au/minwn/vanstone/vs25_6.htm

Vanstone, A. (1996b) 'A case of practice what you preach.' *The Age*, 2 July, p.13.

Walker, A. (1994) *Building the Future.* Hong Kong: Longman.

Wanna, J., O'Faircheallaigh, C. and Weller, P. (1992) *Public Sector Management in Australia.* Melbourne: Macmillan.

Williams, G. (1993) *Changing Patterns of Finance in Higher Education.* Buckingham: Open University Press and Society for Research into Higher Education.

Williams, G. and Fry, H. (1994) *Longer Term Prospects for British Higher Education, Report to the Committee of Vice-Chancellors and Principals.* London: Centre for Higher Education Studies, University of London Institute of Education.

Williams, G.L. (1995) *British Higher Education: Thirty Years of Decline in University Autonomy.* Unpublished Paper. London: Centre for Higher Education Studies, University of London Institute of Education.

Wong, Y.L. (1996) *A History of the Hong Kong Baptist University.* [In Chinese]. Hong Kong: Hong Kong Baptist University.

The Contributors

Professor Don Aitkin, historian and political scientist, is the Vice-Chancellor of the University of Canberra and was Vice-President of the Australian Vice-Chancellors' Committee 1994 and 1995. Since the mid-1980s he has played an influential role in the evolution of national policies for research and higher education in Australia, especially as the first Chairman of the Australian Research Council and a member of the Australian Science and Technology Council.

Professor Ronald Barnett is Professor of Higher Education and Dean of Professional Development at the Institute of Education, University of London. His books include *Higher Education: A Critical Business, The Idea of Higher Education* and *The Limits of Competence.* He is also the principal author of a report for the UK National Committee of Inquiry into Higher Education (the Dearing Committee) analysing the responses to the Committee's public consultation.

Svava Bjarnason is an independent research consultant in higher education. Amongst other projects, she is research officer on a two-year project with colleagues at the Institute of Education, University of London, examining the changing patterns of undergraduate curricula in Britain. She is a doctoral candidate at the Institute of Education with a particular interest in scholarship and teaching in higher education.

Professor Peter Coaldrake is Deputy Vice-Chancellor of the Queensland University of Technology. In 1995 he was a member of the Higher Education Management Review (Hoare Committee), which provided a report to the Australian Government on management practices and issues in Australian universities.

Dr David Foster studied history at the Universities of Sheffield and Lancaster, and Education at Manchester. After teaching History in schools and teacher education courses, he moved to Hull College of Higher Education in 1979 and witnessed, first hand, its progress to university status. Whilst there, he held a variety of posts at Head of Department level, both academic and administrative. He took early retirement in 1996 and currently works in Malaysia as an educational adviser.

Nigel French has been the Secretary-General of the University Grants Committee of Hong Kong since 1990, serving the Committee throughout the period of dramatic expansion in Hong Kong's higher education sector from 1991 to 1995. He joined the Hong Kong Government as an Administrative Officer in 1973 and, prior to his present position, held a range of appointments in different branches of the Hong Kong Civil Service.

Professor Roger King is the Vice-Chancellor of the University of Lincolnshire and Humberside. Prior to graduating from the Universities of London and Birmingham, he worked in the private sector and for the Civil Service. Subsequently, he lectured at Manchester Polytechnic and was appointed Head of Behavioural Sciences at Huddersfield Polytechnic. He is a well-known writer on political science, a regular contributor on higher education issues (including as a columnist for the *Times Higher Education Supplement* for three years), a member of the British Council's Committee for International Co-operation in Higher Education and a member of the Executive Committee of the Association of Commonwealth Universities.

Dr David Mole has lived in Hong Kong since 1989 where he is Senior Assistant Registrar at the City University of Hong Kong. His work in university administration followed a varied career chiefly in Canada as a journalist, government economist and academic. He holds a PhD in Political Economy from the University of Toronto and has held teaching positions with the University of Toronto, McMaster University and the University of Manitoba.

Professor James Murray joined Napier College in 1967 as Head of Department of Production Engineering after working as an Engineer with Ferranti and as lecturer at Heriot-Watt University. He has held a number of posts at Napier, including Dean of Technology and Dean of Professional Studies. In his time as Assistant Principal he was responsible for academic standards and played an important role in the transition from polytechnic to university before retiring in 1995 from the post of Vice-Principal.

Professor Roger Scott has been Dean of Arts at the Queensland University of Technology since 1994. Between 1990 and 1994 he was Director-General of the Education Department in the Queensland Government. He came to that position from the post of inaugural Vice-Chancellor of the University of Canberra. He has published extensively in the fields of public policy and educational administration and has served on federal government enquiries into management education (1980–82) and aboriginal education (1993–94).

Lawrence Stedman is Principal Policy Adviser to the Deputy Vice-Chancellor at Queensland University of Technology. Prior to joining QUT in 1995 he was involved in policy development and management of Australian Federal Government support for health research and, between 1993 and 1995, was Secretary to the Medical Research Grants Committee of the National Health and Medical Research Council.

Professor David Teather is Dean of the Faculty of Social Sciences, Hong Kong Baptist University. Previous posts include Professor and Dean at the University of New England, Deputy Principal of Armidale College of Advanced Education and foundation Academic Director of the Higher Education Development Centre, Otago University. A graduate of University College London, his books include *Staff Development in Higher Education* and *Towards the Community University.*

Dr Daniel C.W. Tse has been the President and Vice-Chancellor of the Hong Kong Baptist University (the former Hong Kong Baptist College) since 1971. He obtained his bachelor's and master's degrees at Baylor University and his PhD in Physics at the University of Pittsburgh in 1965. Among his many other public services, the committees he currently chairs include: Bilingual Laws Advisory Committee, Standing Committee on Language Education and Research, Preparatory Committee on Chinese Medicine and Board of Directors of World Vision Hong Kong.

Professor Enoch C.M. Young was Vice-President and Professor of Physics at the City University of Hong Kong until February 1998 when he became Director of the School of Professional and Continuing Education (SPACE) of the University of Hong Kong. He was appointed as Foundation Head of Department of Applied Science at City University in 1987. He also served as Dean of Science and Technology (1990–92), Academic Secretary (1993–94) and Director of the School of Graduate Studies (1994–96). Professor Young served as a member of the Hong Kong University Grants Committee from 1990 to 1993 and is now on its Panel on Teaching and Learning Quality Process Review. He is the author of about 160 publications in the areas of cosmic radiation, astrophysics, environmental radiation and quality assurance in higher education.

Subject Index

Name Index